Fernand Papillon, August Rodney Macdonough

Nature and Life

Facts and Doctrines relating to the Constitution of Matter, the new Dynamics, and

the Philosophy of Nature

Fernand Papillon, August Rodney Macdonough

Nature and Life

Facts and Doctrines relating to the Constitution of Matter, the new Dynamics, and the Philosophy of Nature

ISBN/EAN: 9783337069773

Printed in Europe, USA, Canada, Australia, Japan

Cover: Foto ©ninafisch / pixelio.de

More available books at **www.hansebooks.com**

NATURE AND LIFE.

FACTS AND DOCTRINES RELATING TO

*THE CONSTITUTION OF MATTER, THE NEW DYNAMICS,
AND THE PHILOSOPHY OF NATURE.*

BY

FERNAND PAPILLON.

TRANSLATED FROM THE SECOND FRENCH EDITION, BY
A. R. MACDONOUGH, Esq.

NEW YORK:
D. APPLETON AND COMPANY,
549 AND 551 BROADWAY.
1875.

ENTERED, according to Act of Congress, in the year 1875, by
D. APPLETON & COMPANY,
In the Office of the Librarian of Congress, at Washington.

PREFACE BY THE AUTHOR.

This volume contains a series of essays written and published at different times, some of a general character, and others more special, and all relating to the activity of natural forces, especially those of life. The mere bringing together of these fragments has presented an opportunity of completing a methodical and uniform whole, combining exactness in details with generality of doctrines, and distinctly tracing the precise aspect of each group of phenomena in the picture of the close and universal relations that bind the whole together. An exposition is thus offered under an elementary form, in language freed from technical dress, of the most essential truths established of late by physics, chemistry, and biology, regarding the mechanism of natural forces, and the arrangement and combination of the fundamental springs of being in the world, especially in the living world. I indulge the hope that such a work might meet a kindly welcome from minds, ever increasingly numerous, that regard science as the subject neither of idle curiosity nor of passing entertainment, but as the object of earnest sympathy and of serious examination. Such, at least, is the principal purpose of this book.

It has another, also. The evident disposition of the present day is to repose infinite hopes on the natural sciences, and to expect unlimited benefits from them. I certainly shall not view this inclination as an illusion, and this volume sufficiently attests the high value I set upon all that can encourage and foster such feelings. But precisely because I am not suspected of enmity to those sciences, it has seemed to me the more necessary to indicate a fatal mistake accompanying those commendable sentiments; I mean the mistake of those who, after loudly praising the excellence of science, denounce the weakness and deny the authority of metaphysics.

Now, my reader will come upon more than one page manifestly inspired by the conviction that science, properly so called, does not satiate the mind eager to know and to understand, and that therefore metaphysics holds a large and an authorized place in the activity of human thought. While I have retouched every thing in these essays which seemed to me, from an exclusively scientific point of view, susceptible of a higher degree of exactness and precision, I have, on the contrary, preserved with jealous care the literal tenor of all the passages expressly written under the influence of that conviction. And I have done so, not because of any peculiar value in those reflections, many of which are nothing more than a very imperfect representation of my way of-seeing, but because those reflections were then made for the first time, with absolute spontaneousness, and without the slightest system or premeditation. The reader will thus be able to see how general ideas naturally emerge from deep and close contemplation of a group of various details, how forcible their unsought impression is; in other words, how surely thought, following orderly and regular evolution, without studied intention as without dogmatic aim, arrives at the loftiest philosophic certainties.

The thinker who freely seeks for truth, continuously changes his position in his aspirations toward mind and the ideal. He deserts the regions of phenomena and concrete things, to rise to those of the absolute and eternal. The farther he withdraws from the former, which had at first absorbed all his attention, the more strikingly does the perspective in which he viewed them alter. At last, he discerns nothing else in them but spectres without substance, and delusive phantoms. And in the degree and extent of his drawing near to the eternal and the absolute, reality comes more surely within his ken, and he gains a more vivid feeling and a keener conception of it. He measures the distance he has traversed, and values the worth of his own contemplations by the fullness of lucid clearness which enlightens his faint view of the first principles of things, and by the depth of humble reverence with which he bows before the mysterious Power which created all!

CONCARNEAU (FINISTERRE), *May*, 1873.

CONTENTS.

	PAGE
The Constitution of Matter, and the New Dynamism..	1
The Philosophy of Nature, and Leibnitz's Ideas......	30
The General Constitution of Living Beings...........	62
Light and Life..	101
Heat and Life...	129
Electricity and Life...................................	155
Odors and Life..	179
Medicaments and Life..................................	204
Animal Grafts and Regenerations.....................	229
Ferments, Fermentations, and Life...................	255
Great Epidemics—Asiatic Cholera.....................	278
The Physiology of Death...............................	303
Heredity in Physiology, in Medicine, and in Psychology.	330

NATURE AND LIFE.

THE CONSTITUTION OF MATTER, AND THE NEW DYNAMISM.

WHATEVER empirics and utilitarians may say on the subject, there are certainties apart from the experimental method, and there is progress disconnected with brilliant or beneficent applications. The mind of man may put forth its power in laboring in harmony with reason, yet discover genuine truths in a sphere as far above that of laboratories and manufactures as their sphere is above the region of the coarsest arts. In a word, there is a temple of light that unfolds its portals to the soul neither through calculation nor through experiment, which the soul nevertheless enters with authority and confidence, so long as it holds the consciousness of its sovereign prerogatives. When will professed scientists, better informed of the close connection between metaphysics and science, whence our modern knowledge of Nature has sprung, better taught in the necessary laws that govern the conflict of reason with the vast unknown, confess that there are realities beyond those they attain? When will science, instead of the arrogant indifference it assumes in presence of philosophy, admit the fertility beyond estimate of the latter? It may be that the hour of this reconciliation, so much to be longed for, is less remote than many suppose; at least, every day brings us nearer to it. The spirit of Descartes cannot fail to arouse before long some genius mighty enough to revive among us a taste and respect for thought in all the departments of scientific activity. Deserted as high abstractions are for the moment, they are not, thank Heaven, so utterly abandoned as to deprive study of its ardor, and essays of their success, when these relate to the problem of the constitution of matter. In fact, this is a question which for several years past has occupied some among our own *savants* and thinkers, as completely as it has employed most of those of the rest of Europe, a question which bears witness with peculiar eloquence to this fact, that, if philosophers are forced to borrow largely from science, in its turn science can retain clearness, and elevation, and strength, only by drawing its inspiration from, and recognizing its inseparable connection with, the abstract consideration of hidden causes and of first principles.

I.

Matter is presented under a great variety of appearances. Let us consider it in its most complicated state, in the human body, for instance. In this, ordinary dissection distinguishes organs, which may be resolved into tissues. The disintegration of the latter yields anatomical elements from which direct analysis extracts a certain number of chemical principles. Here the anatomist's work ends. The chemist steps in, and recognizes in these principles definite kinds arising from the combination, in fixed and determinate proportions, of a certain number of principles that cannot be decomposed, substantially indestructible, to which he gives the name of simple bodies. Carbon, nitrogen, oxygen, hydrogen, sulphur, phosphorus, calcium, iron, which thus set a limit to experimental analysis of the most complex bodies, are simple substances, that is to say, they are the original and irresolvable radicals of the tissue of things.

We now know that matter is not indefinitely divisible, and that the smallest parts of the various simple substances existing in those that are naturally compound have not all the same dimensions, nor equal weights. Chemistry, by a course of analyses and measurements, has succeeded in determining the weights of atoms of the different elements, that is to say, taking as a unit an atom of the lightest element, hydrogen, in determining the weight of the atoms which are equivalent to this conventional unit in the various combinations. Though many *savants* continue to maintain that atomic weights are nothing but relations, and that the existence of atoms is a mere logical device, it seems more reasonable to admit, with the majority of those who have studied this difficult problem closely, that these atoms are actual realities, while it may be very far from easy to settle precisely their absolute dimensions. In any case, we may affirm that these dimensions are very much less than those presented by the particles of matter subjected to the most powerful and subtile methods of division, or decomposed by the imagination into its minutest elements. "Let man," says Pascal, "investigate the smallest things of all he knows; let this dot of an insect, for instance, exhibit to him in its diminutive body parts incomparably more diminutive, jointed limbs, veins in those limbs, blood in those veins, in that blood humors, and drops within those humors —let him, still subdividing these finest points, exhaust his power of conception, and let the minutest object his fancy can shape be that one of which we are now speaking—he may, perhaps, suppose that to be the extreme of minuteness in Nature. I will make him discover yet a new abyss within it. I will draw for him not merely the visible universe but all besides that his imagination can grasp, the immensity of Nature, within the confines of that imperceptible atom." In this Pascal displays a feeling as true as it is deep of the infinitely small, and it is interesting to observe how the amazing revelations of the microscopic world have justified his eloquence and foresight; and yet this microscopic world, whose minutest representatives, such as vibrios and bacteria, are hardly less than the ten-thousandth part of $\frac{1}{25}$ of an inch, how coarse it is compared with the particles thrown off by odorous bodies, and with the inconceivably minute quantities which chemistry, physics, and mechanics, now measure without seeing them, or make their existence plain without grasping them. We may mention some instances which can give us an idea of these.

According to Tyndall, when very minute solid particles, smaller than the luminous waves, are diffused in a medium traversed by light, the light is decomposed in such a way that the least waves, the blue ones, predominate in the reflected rays, and the largest ones, the red waves, in the transmitted rays. This ingenious physicist thus explains how the blue color of the sky depends and must depend on the existence of solid particles, excessively minute, diffused in infinite quantity through the atmosphere. Tyndall is not disinclined to the idea that these imperceptible atoms might very well be no other than those germs of microscopic organisms the presence of which in the atmosphere has been proved by the labors of Pasteur, as well as the part they take in the phenomena of putrefaction and fermentation. The ova of these beings, which are barely visible under the microscope after attaining full development, and of which the number, ascertained by the most decisive evidence, confounds the boldest imagination, these would be the elements of that vital ether, as we have termed it, that dust which gives its lovely blue tint to the vault of the sky. "There exist in the atmosphere," Tyndall says in closing, "particles of matter that elude the microscope and the scales, which do not disturb its clearness, and yet are present in it in so immense a multitude that the Hebrew hyperbole of the number of grains of sand on the sea-shore becomes comparatively unmeaning." And, to give an idea of the minuteness of these particles, Tyndall adds that they might be condensed till they would all go into a lady's traveling-bag. Manifestly these particles escape any kind of direct measurement and observation. Their objective reality can no more be demonstrated than that of the particles of ether can be made evident. Yet there are certain facts which aid us to form a clear conception of them. Let us dissolve a gramme of resin in a hundred times its weight of alcohol, then pour the clear solution into a large flask full of pure water, and shake it briskly. The resin is precipitated in the form of an impalpable and invisible powder, which does not perceptibly cloud the fluid. If, now, we place a black surface behind the flask, and let the light strike it either from above or in front, the liquid appears sky-blue. Yet, if this mixture of water and alcohol filled with resinous dust is examined with the strongest microscope, nothing is seen. The size of the grains of this dust is much less than the ten-thousandth part of $\frac{1}{25}$ of an inch. Morren makes another experiment, proving in a still more surprising way the extreme divisibility of matter: Sulphur and oxygen form a close combination, called by chemists sulphuric-acid gas. It is that colorless and suffocating vapor thrown off when a sulphur-match is burned. Morren confines a certain quantity of this gas in a receiver, places the whole in a dark medium, and sends a bright ray of light through it. At first nothing is visible. But very soon in the path of the luminous ray we perceive a delicate blue color. It is because the gas is decomposed by the luminous waves, and the invisible particles of sulphur set free decompose the light in turn. The blue of the vapor deepens, then it turns whitish, and at last a white cloud is produced. The particles composing this cloud are still each by itself invisible, even under strong microscopes, and yet they are infinitely more coarse than the primitive atoms that occasioned the sky-blue tint at first seen in the receiver. In this experiment we pass in steady progress from the free atom of sulphur parted from the oxygen-atom by the ether-waves to a mass apparent to the senses; but, if this mass is made up of free molecules which defy the strongest magnifiers, what must be the particles which have produced those very molecules!

A last instance of another kind will complete the proof as to the minuteness of the elements of matter. When a clear solution of sulphate of aluminum is poured into an equally clear solution of sulphate of potassa, the mixture at once grows turbid, and after a few seconds myriads of little crystals, sparkling like diamonds, make their appearance in the liquid, which are nothing else than crystals of alum. If we suppose the diameter of these crystals to be $\frac{1}{25}$ of an inch, it will follow from this experiment that in the lapse of a few seconds crystals had the power of producing themselves containing tens of millions of molecules, each composed of ninety-four atoms, grouped in admirable harmony. The motions of these chemical atoms take place under the influence of the same forces that guide the motions of those enormous agglomerations of atoms called stars. The revolution of one sun around another takes a thousand years, while these atoms in course of combination perform hundreds of millions of such revolutions in the millionth part of a second!

By varied and delicate calculations, Thomson has succeeded in establishing the fact that, in liquids and transparent or translucent solids, the mean distance between the centres of two contiguous atoms is comprised between the ten-millionth and the two-hundred-millionth part of $\frac{1}{25}$ of an inch. It is not easy to form an exact conception of dimensions so small, of which nothing, among the objects that affect our senses, can convey any idea. Thomson judges that the following comparison may aid us to appreciate them: If we imagine a sphere as large as a pea magnified, so as almost to equal the earth's volume, and the atoms of that sphere enlarged in the same proportion, they will then have a diameter greater than that of a shot, and less than that of an orange. In other words, an atom is to a globe the size of a pea what an apple is to the terrestrial globe. By arguments of quite another kind, drawn in part from the study of chemical molecules, in part from the phenomena of capillarity, Gaudin has ascertained, for the dimension of the smallest particles of matter, figures very nearly the same as Thomson's. The maximum distance apart of the chemical atoms in molecules is the ten-millionth part of $\frac{1}{25}$ of an inch. Gaudin follows Thomson in the attempt to give some sensible notion of the truly amazing minuteness of a dimension like this. He calculates, upon this estimate, the number of chemical atoms contained in about the size of a pin's-head, and he finds that the number requires for its expression the figure eight followed by twenty-one ciphers. So that, if we attempted to count the number of metallic atoms contained in a large pin's-head, separating each second ten millions of them, we should need to continue the operation for more than 250,000 years!

There are, then, atoms in matter, and atomism is a fact, whenever we rest in the affirmation of the existence of atoms. But these are not the real principles, the simple and irreducible elements of the world. After decomposing sensible matter into atoms, we must subject the latter to an analysis of the same kind. Let us, then, consider any two heterogeneous atoms whatever, an atom of iron and an atom of hydrogen, for instance, and examine in what respect they can really, essentially, differ from each other. What is it which at bottom truly distinguishes these two atoms, as atoms? It is not any peculiarity of form, solidity, fluidity, hardness, sonorousness, brightness, because these properties evidently depend on the mutual arrangement and disposition of atoms, that is, because they are not relative to the individuality of each atom, but to that of the whole which they form by being grouped together. Neither is it any caloric property, or optic, or electric, or magnetic one, because these properties result from the movements of the ether, within the more or less complex aggregate of the respective atoms of these two substances. Now, if these atoms, taken separately, differ from each other in virtue of none of the properties just enumerated, they can only be dissimilar as regards two attributes, dimension and weight; but difference in weight results from difference in dimension, and is not a qualitative difference, but simply a quantitative one.[1] Consequently, any two heterogeneous atoms whatever, compared together, as atoms, have scarcely any of the differential attributes peculiar to the groups which they make up by aggregation, and represent no more than two distinct functions, two different values of one and the same initial matter, of one and the same primitive quality or energy. This simple demonstration establishes the unity of substance, not as a more or less plausible physical hypothesis, but as a metaphysical certainty, alike underivable and necessary. If we add now, reserving the demonstration for a later period, that dimension, corporeal extension itself, as Leibnitz said and as Magy has lately proved, is only a resultant of force, it will become evident that matter, in the last analysis, is reduced to force.

Tyndall, in his biography of Faraday, tells us that one of the favorite experiments of this physicist gives a true image of what he was: "He loved to show how water, in crystallizing, eliminates all foreign substances, however intimately mingled they may be with it. Separated from all these impurities, the crystal becomes clear and limpid."

---

[1] We purposely take no notice of chemical forces, which can only be regarded as attractions, and must therefore be explained by forces acting outside of the atom itself.

This experiment is especially the true image of what Faraday was as a metaphysician. For him nothing had so great a charm as those serene transparent regions, in which science, cleared of impurities, appeared to his great mind in all the glory of its power and splendor. He yielded himself to it with absolute abandonment. He particularly loved to dwell upon the problem which is now engaging us: "What do we know of an atom apart from force?" he exclaims. "You conceive a nucleus which may be called a, and you surround it with forces which may be called m; to my mind your a or nucleus vanishes, and substance consists in the energy of m. In fact, what notion *can* we form of a nucleus independent of its energy?" As he holds, matter fills all space, and gravitation is nothing else than one of the essentially constitutive forces of matter, perhaps even the only one. An eminent chemist, Henry Saint-Claire Deville, lately declared that, when bodies deemed to be simple combine with one another, they vanish, they are individually annihilated. For instance, he maintains that in sulphate of copper there is neither sulphur, nor oxygen, nor copper. Sulphur, oxygen, and copper, are composed, each of them, by a distinct system of definite vibrations of one energy, one single substance. The compound, sulphate of copper, answers to a different system, in which the motions are confounded that would produce the respective individualities of its elements, sulphur, oxygen, and copper. Moreover, Berthelot long ago expressed himself in exactly the same manner. As long ago as 1864 that *savant* said that the atoms of simple bodies might be composed of one and the same matter, distinguished only by the nature of the motions set up in it. This decisive saying a great number of *savants* and philosophers in France and abroad have repeated and are still repeating, with good reason, as the expression of a solid truth.

If the smallest parts which we can imagine and distinguish in bodies differ from each other only by the nature of the motions to which they are subjected, if motion alone rules and determines the variety of different attributes which characterize these atoms, if, in a word, the unity of matter exists—and it must exist—what is this fundamental and primary matter whence all the rest proceed? How shall we represent it to our minds? Every thing leads to the belief that it is not essentially distinguished from the ether, and consists in atoms of ether more or less strongly held together. It is objected that the ether is imponderable; but that is an unfounded objection. Doubtless it cannot be weighed; to do that we must compare a space filled with ether to a space empty of ether; and we are evidently unable to isolate this subtile agent, whose particles counterpoise each other with perfect equilibrium throughout the universe. Yet many facts attest its prodigious elasticity. A flash of lightning is nothing more than a disturbance of equilibrium in the ether, yet no one will deny that lightning performs an immense work. However this may be, it is impossible to think of the energies that make up the atom otherwise than as of pure force, and the ether itself, whose existence is demonstrated by the whole of physics, can be no otherwise defined than by the attributes of force.[1] It follows from this that atoms, the last conclusion of chemistry, and ether, the last conclusion of physics, are substantially alike, although they form two distinct degrees, two unequal values, of the same original activity. All those physico-chemical energies, as well as the analogous energies of life, only show themselves to us, save in rare exceptions, clothed with that

---

[1] "Setting aside any theory, it would be hard to find in all these terms, dilatation, propagation, radiation, vibration, reflection, refraction, attraction, repulsion, polarization, etc., any thing else than phenomena of motion."—CHARLES DE RÉMUSAT, "Philosophical Essays," vol. ii., *On Matter*.

uniform we call matter. A single one of these energies shows forth, stripped of this dress, and bare. It rules all the others, because it knows them all without their knowing it. It is not power merely, but consciousness besides. It is the soul. How define it otherwise than as force in its purest essence, since we look upon it, as on the marble of the antique, in splendid nakedness, which is radiant beauty too?

Whether we consider coarser matter which can be weighed and felt, or that more subtile, lively, and active matter we call ether, or again the spiritual principle, which is energy simple, we have then always before us only harmonious collections of forces, symmetrical activities, ordered powers, more or less conscious of the part they play in the infinite concert whose glorious music the Creator composed. Let us set aside for a moment the variety of groupings which determine the succession and the manifold aspects of these forces, and there will remain, as constituent principles of the web of the universe, as irreducible and primordial ingredients of the world, nothing but dynamic points, nothing but monads.

The term of the rigorous analysis of phenomena is, definitely, the conception of an infinity of centres of similar and unextended forces, of energies without forms, simple and eternal. We ask what these forces are, and we assert in answer that it is impossible to distinguish them from motion. Force may be conceived, but not shaped to the fancy. The clearest and truest thing we can say of it is, that it is an energy analogous to that whose constant and undeniable presence we feel dwelling in our deepest selves. "The only force of which we have consciousness," says Henry Sainte-Claire Deville, "is will." Our soul, which gives us consciousness of force, is also the type of it, in this sense that, if we wish to pierce to the elementary mechanisms of the world, we are imperiously driven to compare its primal activities with the only activity of which we have direct knowledge and intuition, that is to say, with that admirable spring of will, so prompt and sure, which permits us every moment to create and also to guide motion.

Motion may serve to measure force, but not to explain it. It is as subordinate to the latter as speech is to thought. In truth, motion is nothing else than the series of successive positions of a body in different points of space. Force, on the other hand, is the tendency, the tension, which determines the body to pass continually from one to the other of these points; that is to say, the power by which this body, considered at any instant in its course, differs from the identical body at rest. Evidently this something which is in one of these two bodies and is not in the other, this something that mathematicians call the quantity of motion, which is transformed, on a sudden stoppage of motion, into a certain quantity of heat, this something is a reality, distinct from the trajectory itself; and yet nothing, absolutely nothing, outside of the inner revelation of our soul, gives us the means of understanding what this initial cause of the motive forces may be. The distinguished founder of the mechanical theory of heat, Robert Mayer, defines force to be "whatever may be converted into motion." There is no formula that so well expresses the fact of the independence and preëminence of force, or so completely includes the assertion of the essential reality of a cause preexisting motion. The idea of force is one of those elementary forms of thought from which we cannot escape, because it is the necessary conclusion, the fixed and undestroyable residue from the analysis of the world in the alembic of our minds. The soul does not find it out by discursive reasoning, nor prove it to itself by way of theorem or experiment; it knows it, it clings to it by natural and unconquerable affinity. We must say of force what

Pascal said of certain fundamental notions of the same order: "Urging investigation further and further, we necessarily arrive at primitive words which cannot be defined, or at principles so clear that we can find no others which are clearer." When we have reached these principles, nothing remains but to study one's self with profoundest meditation, not striving to give an image to those things whose essence is that they cannot be imagined. From the most general and abstract point of view, then, matter is at once form and force, that is, there is no essential difference between these two modes of substance. Form is simply force circumscribed, condensed. Force is simply form indefinite, diffused. Such is the net result of the methodical inquiries of modern science, and one which forces itself on our minds, apart from any systematic premeditation. It is of consequence to add that the merit of having formulated it very clearly and noted its importance belongs to French contemporary philosophers, particularly to Charles Lévèque and Paul Janet.

II.

If the web of things, the essence of matter, is one single substance, who was the Orpheus under whose spell these materials gathered, ranged, and diversified themselves into natures of so many kinds? And, first of all, how can the extension of bodies proceed from an assembling of unextended principles? The answer to this first question does not seem difficult to us. Extension exists prior to matter. They are two distinct things, without any relation of causality or finality. Matter no more proceeds from extension than extension proceeds from matter. This simple remark suffices to settle the difficulty of conceiving how the dimension of objects results from a group of dynamic points which have no dimension. Extension existing before every thing else, it is quite clear that, when certain primal energies come into union to give rise, through a thousand successive complications, to phenomena and to bodies, what they really produce is not the appearance of extension, which is the mere shadow of reality, but it is that collection of varied and diverse activities which enable us to describe and define phenomena and bodies.

It is no longer a subject of doubt, in the minds of *savants* who have got beyond experimentation, that extension is an image and a show rather than an essential constituent property of bodies. The extension of bodies is a phenomenon which takes its rise in the collision of force with our minds. Charles de Rémusat, so long ago as 1842, gave an original and remarkable demonstration of this. He maintains that force is the cause of extension, meaning by that that the sensation of extension is a modification of our sensibility, occasioned by forces analogous to those which produce sensations of a more complex kind. When you experience an electric shock, you are struck. Percussion is the sensation of contact, in other words, of impulsion by something that has extension. Now, in this instance, Rémusat says, the cause of percussion, electricity, has no extension. Therefore, he adds, either electricity is nothing, or else it is a force which affects us in a way that may be compared to the effect of extension. So that a force, wanting the usual appearances of extension, may produce the same effects on us that a solid body in motion does. Within a few years a profound metaphysician, Magy, has pointed out by new arguments that corporeal extension is merely a show which springs from the internal reaction of the soul against the impression made on the sensorium, and which the soul translates to outward bodies, by a law analogous to that which makes it localize in the separate organs of sense the impression which it has nevertheless perceived only in the brain. Each sensation of taste, smell, light, or sound, is a phenomenon of psychological reaction which occurs in the soul when it is teased with a certain degree of energy by nerve-action, which in its turn depends on an outward action; but there is no relation of resemblance between the latter and the sensation it provokes. The ether, which, by its vibrations in unison with the elements of our retina, produces sensations of light in us, has in itself no luminosity. The proof of this is, that two rays of light meeting under certain conditions may annul each other, and produce darkness. Now, Magy maintains that the subjectivity of extension is of the same order with that of light. Extension in general is explained by purely dynamic reasons, as readily as that particular extension is which serves as a kind of support for luminous phenomena, which evidently result from vibrations of the unextended principles. Helmholtz, in his latest writings, fully adopts this doctrine of corporeal extension.

We thus see that there is no difficulty in reconciling extension with unextended forces, and the phenomena of extension with principles of action; but this is only the first part of the problem, and it becomes necessary now to ascend from these unextended forces and active principles to those more or less complex manifestations which make up the infinite universe, adorning space with imperishable variety. Let us imagine this universe filled with the greatest conceivable number of active principles, all identical, diffused uniformly throughout immensity, and consequently in a state of perfect equilibrium. All will be torpid in absolute repose, in which form without shape and force without spring will be as though they were not. Between a homogeneous, motionless substance, identical with itself throughout space at all points, and nihility, reason perceives no difference. In such a system, nothing has weight, for there is no attracting centre; heat is no more possible for it than light, since these two forms of energy are bound up with the existence of systems of unequal vibrations, of diversified media, and varying molecular arrangements. *A fortiori*, the phenomena of life will be incompatible with this universal unity of substance, this unchanging identity of force.

The objective existence of things, the coming into reality of phenomena, can only be conceived, therefore, as the work of a certain number of differentiations taking place in the deep of that universal energy of primal matter, which is the last result of our analysis of the world. Motion, of itself alone, is enough to explain a first attribute of that energy, namely, resistance, and its consequence, impenetrability; but this is only on the condition that this motion shall take place in various directions.[1] Two forces urged in opposite directions, and coming to a meeting, manifestly resist each other. It is probably by collisions of this sort that those variable condensations of matter, and those heterogeneous groupings of which the world presents the spectacle, have been determined. A rotary movement, communicated to a mass without weight, can only engender concentric spheres, which gravitate toward each other in consequence of pressure by the interposing ether. The famous experiments of Plateau are decisive in this respect. That accomplished physicist introduces oil into a mixture of water and alcohol, having exactly equal density with the oil itself. He inserts a metallic strip into the midst of this mass of oil, which is free

---

[1] "Any relation of action implies at least *twofoldness*. We have then at once dissimilarity, and it would be more correct to say, action takes place only between dissimilars. Between like things, action requires at least a difference of place, yet even with that difference like things act but slightly on each other. The production of such a phenomenon requires opposition in forces between them. In chemistry, only dissimilars act on each other. All Nature witnesses that a certain degree of difference between bodies is needed for their mutual action."—CHARLES DE RÉMUSAT.

from the action of any force, and turns it about. The oil takes the form of a sphere, and, as soon as the rotation grows very rapid, breaks up, and parts into a number of smaller spheres. The celestial spheres were probably formed in the same way, and an exactly similar mechanical action produces those clear dew-drops, glittering like diamonds, on the leaves of plants.

All physical phenomena, whatever their nature, are at bottom only manifestations of one and the same primordial agent. We can no longer question this general conclusion of all modern discoveries, Sénarmont explicitly says, though it is, as yet, impossible to formulate with precision its laws and its particular conditions. If this be true, and we hope we have proved it to be so, it is plain that those conditional particularities of which Sénarmont speaks, that is to say, those diversified manifestations of the sole agent to which he alludes, can depend only on differences in the motions which impel it. Now, the very existence of these differences necessarily implies a coördinating and regulating intelligence; but how much more extreme is the necessity for such a cause in chemical phenomena, which display such endless complications issuing from that primal energy to which every thing in the last analysis is reduced! We have seen that the variety of those stable and homogeneous energies known under the name of simple bodies, the number of which is now increased to sixty, depends on the variety of the vibrations that each one of these little worlds performs. This is the earliest intervention of a principle of difference. This principle does not merely determine the multiplication of simple bodies; it also acts in any one element with such intensity that the same element can acquire very unlike properties and attributes. What things are more heterogeneous than the diamond and charcoal, or than common phosphorus and amorphous phosphorus? Yet charcoal and diamond are chemically identical, just as the two sorts of phosphorus are. These cases of isomery, which are quite numerous, attest with the strongest evidence the excessive variability of which combinations of force are capable. When we see the same elements, combined in the same weight-proportions, produce sometimes harmless substances, sometimes terrible poisons, in one case evolve colorless or dingy products, in another brilliant hues, we become convinced that primal matter is of little consequence in comparison with the power of the weaver who arranges its threads, and knows beforehand what the aspect of the web will be. Besides, it is not alone in the whole that the formative principle is displayed; it shows forth also in the elements, considered individually, since every one of them exhibits tendencies, elective affinities, that bear witness to some obscure instinct toward harmonious completion.

There is not only a prodigious variety in the disposition of the atoms which make up molecules, and in the arrangement of the molecules among themselves, but this arrangement is governed, besides, by admirable geometric laws. The atoms that make up molecules are not heaped and flung together at random and in disorder; they enter into composition only in fixed proportions and in fixed *directions*. Marc-Antoine Gaudin has proved, in a late treatise devoted entirely to these refined inquiries, the existence of some of the most important laws in the geometry of atoms. This ingenious and persevering writer demonstrates that all chemical molecules, whether they are fitted to produce crystals or not, are formed by a symmetrical aggregation of atoms. The latter are arranged in equilibrium in two directions, perpendicular to each other, one parallel to the axis of grouping, and the other at right angles to that axis, so as always to compose a symmetrical figure. The most complicated bodies, so soon as they are brought under the law of definite proportions, and compose chemical species, are made up of molecules in which the atoms are grouped in prisms, in pyramids, in a word, in polyhedra more or less many-sided, but always of perfect regularity; so that, in this case, the differentiation is regulated with marvelous harmony.

We must now rise another degree, and pass from inorganic matter to living matter. What is it that distinguishes the latter from the former? When we make the answer depend on the results of direct experiment, nothing is easier than to establish the differential characteristics of living matter. In the first place, it is organized, that is, the anatomical elements, instead of being homogeneous and symmetrical in all points of their mass, are composed by the association of a certain number of different substances, in which carbon predominates, and which are termed immediate organic principles.[1] Then these elements grow. At no time the same throughout, as to the substance which makes them up, they are in a state of unceasing molecular renewal, of constant metamorphosis, of simultaneous and continuous assimilation and disassimilation. Besides, the various properties these elements may exhibit, contractility, neurility, and so on, are, in consequence of the growing state that characterizes them, in so unstable a condition of equilibrium that the slightest variation in the surrounding medium is enough to occasion some change in the expression of their activity; in other words, they have excessive excitability and irritability. Such, at least, is the region within which physiology is limited; but the fact which it does not clearly enough bring out, yet the thing which is the distinctive mark of life, is the harmonious seeking for each other of all these vital monads, the disposition of

---

[1] "The structure of chemical compounds is subject only to mathematical laws, which laws do not control that of organized matter. In germs and their products there exists a want of symmetry in their axes, which indicates a formative purpose, or, more properly, a creative omnipotence." —GAUDIN, "Architecture of the World of Atoms," p. 3.

biological energies to compose groups of which the end and the reason are found in what we call the individual. The differentiations of inorganic matter occur in molecules that are specific, in whatever bulk they are regarded. The differentiations of living matter take place only in individuals whose build and proportions are strictly determined. An iron bar, an iron crystal, and iron-dust, are all still iron. An organic substance fitted for life is nothing, whenever deprived of connection with an organism. It can display energy, can act, in a word, can be, so far as to be a living substance, only in virtue of taking place and rank in a certain whole, and assuming certain dependencies and connections with other more or less analogous substances. By itself it is not distinguished in essence from dead matter. It is raised to the rank and clothed with the dignity of life only from the time of its reception into that gathering of which the steps all move toward the same end, which is the functional action of the organism, and the perpetuation of the species.

What takes place in the ovule is a miniature image of what takes place in the universe. The differentiations occurring in that mucous drop are a copy of the differentiations unfolding and expanding in the ocean of the world. It is at first a microscopic mass, homogeneous, uniform in all its parts, a collection of energies identical with each other, and the group of which does not differ perceptibly from a drop of gelatine, hanging, hardly seen, from a needle's point. Yet soon a dull motion spontaneously stirs these nearly inert atoms, and this motion is expressed by a first condensation of the ovular or vitelline substance, which is the germinating vesicle. This passes off, but at the same time other vibrations arrange the molecules of this shapeless, transparent microcosm, in the order of more complicated groups. The vitelline substance swells toward the surface, where it forms the polar globules, while at the centre it thickens to produce the vitelline nucleus. This in turn cleaves and breaks into a great number of secondary nuclei, around each of which the ovular mass distributes itself while contracting. Instead of a single cell, the ovule, which has enlarged, is now found to contain a great number. These cells, called blastodermic, then tend to arrange themselves in two layers, two leaflets placed back to back, within which the elements of the embryo appear, and little by little develop, pursuing a continuous growth, in which forces becoming forms go on incessantly producing and multiplying new forces and new forms.

Now, these separations and distributions, these orderings and classifyings, these harmonies that are set up in the ovule to compose by slow degrees the structure of the embryo, reveal a principle of differentiation analogous to that which has caused the infinite variety of things we see come forth from the confused mass of cosmic energies. There is, as many biologists had felt assured, and as Coste has had the glory of clearly demonstrating in a work which is one of the noblest scientific monuments of this age, there is a force which gives reality, direction, life, to the forms of organized matter in the egg. All eggs are alike at first. There is a complete similitude in structure and substance between those which will produce a lion and those which will produce a mouse. The forms are identical, though the futures of those forms differ. It is, as Coste very well says, that "beneath that form, and beyond what the eye views, there is something which sight cannot reach, something which contains in itself the sufficient reason for all those differences now concealed under unity of configuration, and to become visible only later." This guiding idea, which Coste has brought forward, and which is admitted by all physiologists at this day, is as far from issuing out of the elementary forces of nutrition as the painter's picture is from being the creature of his palette.

Yet nothing in the ovule reveals its hidden and potent virtuality. Claude Bernard, who has repeated Coste's ideas on this subject, dwells strongly on the guiding force which is in the egg, and those *savants* who agree with Robin in denying this force, so far as it acts on the totality of elements in the embryo, regard it at least as shared, distributed, and acting in each of these elements separately, which, at bottom, is the same thing. We see, in any case, that there is in the inmost depth, and there dates from the most rudimentary sketch of the organized being, the fixed and formed idea of those differences in choice and those sympathies in work whose system shall build up the individual. The differential coefficient of organized matter is thus of a far higher order than that of mineral matter. It is this which is a distinct and peculiar result from the impotence which experimental science betrays more plainly every day, when attempting to convert physico-chemical activities into energies of the vital order. Even could this conversion really be effected, and it is not metaphysically impossible that it might be, the existence of a spiritual principle of differentiation would be in no wise put in doubt. Hitherto, at least, such a conversion seems beyond the reach of man.

Something that yet more completely baffles his research, while commanding too his highest admiration, is the supreme degree of complexity together with refinement of that energy which is the soul. Human thought is the sum of all the forces of Nature, because it assimilates them all, while distinguishing between them, by the work that it performs upon sensations. Sensations are to thought what food is to growth. Growth is not a result of feeding; thought is not a result of sensations. Nutrition, in shaping the living organs, determines the differentiation of the concrete forms in the individual's substance; thought, in shaping general ideas, determines the differentiation of the abstract forces in the world. Thus thinking energy is as much superior to sensations as nutritive energy is to aliments. In another order of thought, we might compare the soul to a paper covered with writing in sympathetic ink. At ordinary temperatures, the letters are unseen, but they appear in fine color whenever brought near the fire. So the soul has within itself dim marks and confused shapes, which sensation tints and brightens. We have seen that, in the mucous drop, a two hundred and fiftieth part of an inch through, called the ovule, the forces and tendencies of the whole nutritive and intellectual life of man lie prisoned and asleep. So, too in that force without form or extension which is the soul, there dwells a miniature picture of the whole universe, and, by some mystic grace of God, a dream, as it were, of that God himself. Thought consists in becoming acquainted with all the details of that picture in little, and unfolding its meaning. Thus, that which makes the whole reality of material things is form, and form, such as it is shown to us in the world, is at once a principle of differentiation and a principle of agreement; in other words, it is the work of an intelligence. Body and motion are mere phenomena. The first is only an image of substance, the last an image of action; but substance and action both are only effects of intelligent force, that is, of activity operating in view of a result. That activity, however, presents infinitely varied degrees of condensation, and we may say, with Maudsley: "One equivalent of chemical force corresponds to several equivalents of lower force; and one equivalent of vital force to several equivalents of chemical force." It is thus that modern science unties the Gordian knot of the composition of matter.

III.

A first exclusively analytical view of the world has led us to a first undeniable certainty, the existence of a principle of energy and motion. A second view of the universe, exclusively synthetic, leads us, as we have seen, to another certainty, which is the existence of a principle of differentiation and harmony. This principle is what is called mind. Thus mind is not substance, but it is the law of substance; it is not force, but it is the revealer of force. It is not life, but it makes life exist. It is not thought, but it is the consciousness of thought. A distinguished English *savant*, Carpenter, has said lately, with decisive clearness, "Mind is the sole and single source of power." In a word, it is not reality, yet in it and by it realities are defined and differentiated, and consequently exist. Instead of saying that mind is a property of matter, we should say that matter is a property of mind. Of all the properties of matter, in fact, there is not one, no, not a single one, which is not bestowed on it by mind. The true explanation, the only philosophy of Nature, is thus a kind of spiritualistic dynamism, very different from materialism, or from the mechanism of certain contemporary schools.

Materialism is false and imperfect, because it stops short at atoms, in which it localizes those properties for which atoms supply no cause, and because it neglects force and spirit, which are the only means we have, constituted as our souls are, of conceiving the activity and the appearings of beings. It is false and imperfect, because it stops halfway, and treats compound and resolvable factors as simple and irreducible ones; and because it professes to represent the world by shows, without attempting to explain the production of those shows. In a word, it sees the cause of diversity where it is not, and fails to see it where it does exist. The source of differentiations cannot be in energy itself; it must be in a principle apart from that energy, in a superior will and consciousness, of which we have, doubtless, only a dim and faulty idea, but as to which we can yet affirm that they have some analogy with the inner light which fills us, and which we shed forth from us, and which teaches us, by its mysterious contact with the outer world, the infinite order of the universe.[1]

The danger from materialism is not, as we usually incline to think, corruption of morals by degradation of the soul. Too much use, for censure's sake, has been made, against this system, of the seeming ease with which its professors have convinced themselves that they cut up by the roots the very principles of morality and duty. History proves, by examples too infamous, that barbarism and license are the privilege of no philosophic sect. The real enemies of society always have been, and always will be, the ignorant and the fanatical, and it must be frankly owned that, if these exist within the pale of materialism, there are quite enough of them outside. The danger in the doctrine which reverses the natural relation of things, and asserts that spirit is the product of matter, when in truth matter is a product of spirit, this danger is of another kind; materialism is fatal to the development of the experimental sciences themselves. If, in such a case, the example of men of genius might be appealed to, how eloquent would be the testimony of the two greatest physicists of this age, Ampère and Faraday, both so earnestly convinced, so religiously possessed by the reality of the unseen world! But there are other arguments. "All that we see of the world," says Pascal, "is but an imperceptible scratch in the vast range of Nature." The claim of

---

[1] "That cause, mould, or type, of all constitutions of beings," says De Rémusat, in a famous essay on this subject, "that general Nature, the original or principle of all natures, that force which fashions, specifies, and characterizes all these kinds of beings, cannot be conceived of as a constant property of any being, because the diversity between all these beings is what it has to account for. I look upon this as the strongest proof of the presence of a will and an intelligence exerting their power throughout all Nature."

mere experimentalism is that it may sentence men to the fixed and stubborn contemplation of this scratch. What folly! All the history of the development of the sciences proves that important discoveries all proceed from a different feeling, which is that of continuation of forces beyond the limits of observation, and of a harmony in relations, overruling the singularities and deformities of detached experiences. To hedge one's self within what can be computed, weighed, and demonstrated, to trust such evidence only, and bar one's self inside the prison of the senses, to hush or scorn the suggestions of the spirit, our only true light, because it is the spark of the flame that vivifies all—this is, deny it or not, the condition and the subject state of materialism. Only reason can conceive the fixity, the generality, and the universality of relations, and all *savants* admit that the destiny of science is to establish laws possessing these three characteristics; but to admit that is to confess by implication that partial, incoherent, imperfect, relative details must undergo a refining, a thorough conversion in the alembic of the mind, whence they issue, with so new an aspect and meaning, that what before seemed most important becomes as mere an accessory as it is possible to be, and that which looked most ephemeral takes its place among eternal things.

The conception of atoms dates from the highest antiquity. Leucippus and Democritus, the masters of Epicurus, several centuries before the Christian era, taught that matter is composed of invisible but indestructible corpuscles, the number of which is as boundless as the vastness of the space in which they are diffused. These corpuscles are solid, endowed with shape and motion. The difference of their forms regulates the difference of their movements, and consequently of their characteristics. The conception of a principle guiding these diversities, that is, of an intelligence as the supreme cause of differentiation, is not less ancient. "All was chaotic," Anaxagoras of Clazomene said; " an intelligence intervened, and regulated all." Plato, after defining matter as an existence very hard to understand, an eternal place, never perishing, and furnishing a stage for whatever begins to be, not the subject of sense and yet perceptible, and of which we only catch glimpses as in a dream, tells us that the supreme ruler "took this mass which was whirling in unchecked and unguided movement, and made order come out of disorder." And this ordering grows real in conformity with ideas, the prototypes of things, whose totality makes the divine essence itself. The world's activities are reflections of God's thoughts. To these two fundamental notions, that of atomism and that of idealism, Aristotle added a third, that of dynamism. As he holds, indeterminate matter, in the highest degree of abstraction, is without attributes. If it tends always toward form and action, that is because it contains a principle of power, a force. Force is, in Aristotle's view, the principle of form. The latter is actually existent. We have here the whole ancient philosophy regarding the world. Modern philosophy has taught us nothing different. Atomism, strengthened and widened by Descartes, and borrowed from him by Newton, is identical at bottom with that held by the teachers of Epicurus. In the same way, Leibnitz's dynamism is only a revival of Aristotle's. And, just as Descartes and Leibnitz reproduce the old Greek masters, contemporary science renews Descartes and Leibnitz.

"But what!" it will be said; "always repeating, never inventing, must that be the fixed doom of metaphysics?" Not so; these renewals contain continuous growth toward perfection. The old truth has been preserved, in its original sense, but it has been constantly illuminated and made exact in the lapse of time by happy efforts of speculative genius. Greek atomism left an immense chasm which Descartes filled by the conception of ether, the most marvelous of modern creations. Aristotle's dynamism was vague, and Leibnitz gave it precision by showing that the type and the fountain of force is and can be nothing else than mind. He lifted the conception of force to the conception of soul. And what has been done in our days? We have computed the motion, we have detected the action, of that subtile ether; we have proved the absolute imperishableness of force; we have shown by many instances the fundamental identity of the appetitive and elective powers of chemistry and crystallography with those which psychology reveals. Here is the future of science and of metaphysics. Both will henceforth follow in their development the very course they have held to since the first day; they have never, like Penelope, destroyed yesterday's work the day after. They have pursued the same end with continuous advance, that is, the conception of invisible principles, and of the ideal essence of things. This end will remain the ever-unattained goal of their ambition. The farther we shall advance, the more clearly and convincingly will they persist in defining those primal forces and elementary activities half guessed at from the very dawn of thought. Never false to themselves, they will always, at whatever point in history we appeal to them, represent the human soul unchanging in its nature, its powers, and its hopes. Let them never muse over the mournful question whether the work of the past will not vanish at some time without leaving a trace. All of it will survive, and from this confidence those who strive to increase the sum of knowledge draw their courage and consolation.

The conceptions of matter now entertained agree not only with the boldest deductions and most splendid discoveries of contemporary science, as well as with the oldest truths and the most instinctive faiths of humanity, but also with those loftier convictions, more precious and as solid, which form our moral and religious inheritance, and the crowning prerogative of our nature. The most advanced science rejects none of the traditions and objects to none of the great lasting sentiments of past ages. On the contrary, it fixes the stamp of certainty on truths hitherto lacking adequate proofs, and rescues from the attacks of skepticism all that it coveted as its prey. No proof of the soul's immortality is so strong as that we have drawn from the necessary simplicity and eternity of all the principles of force. Nothing bears witness so powerfully to the majestic reality of a God as the spectacle of those diversities, all harmonious, which rule the infinite range of forces, and bind in unity the ordered pulses of the world. Enough has been said to prove the truth that the moral greatness and the intellectual dignity of a nation must always be measured by the standard of the esteem and credit it accords to high metaphysical speculations, and chiefly to such as relate to the constitution of matter. Meditation on the constitution of matter is the best method of teaching us to know mind, and to understand that every thing must be referred to it, because from it every thing flows.

THE PHILOSOPHY OF NATURE, AND LEIBNITZ'S IDEAS.

WHILE science in our day is pouring unexpected floods of light upon the solution of those problems which are at once the highest and the most subtle in natural philosophy, the great systems of metaphysics become an interesting subject of review. Forgotten or despised by a science wholly devoted to experiment, given over to the routine judgment of unprogressive criticism, those systems had ceased to have any worth except as proofs and records of laborious study. Subjected to fresh investigation and searching exposition, they now reveal proportions worthy the attention of the *savant*, who may find in them conclusions expressed with a breadth that can cover the wider range of the results he has himself reached. A movement of this kind in favor of the philosophy of Leibnitz is just now taking place. The buried germs of that philosophy had long been slowly developing, under the brooding thought of later science, and we find them now breaking forth with singular power of life. The conception of spiritual and material principles formed by the Hanoverian thinker seeming indisputably the most probable and plausible one, we are forced to give up our settled and accepted ideas as to those things, and to adopt another, confessed by scientists and metaphysicians alike to be effective in removing many difficulties. Nor does that correspondence between the maxims of Leibnitz and the results of most modern research dwell in the general philosophy of Nature only; it reaches also to special branches of knowledge, which often exhibit the existence as facts of what were conjectures on the part of the author of the "New Essays." Thus the slow progress of these sciences has reached the revelation of truths seized by the thinker's rapid intuition. This consideration increases our admiration for that daring genius who pierces with so natural an ease to the knowledge of the secret springs of the world, as if he had won his way to communion with the absolute.

Leibnitz's intellect, indeed, could not tolerate either the geometrical exactness or the unyielding persistence displayed by that of Descartes. All the ideas of the latter are deduced by rule and method; all his systems are rigidly disposed in order; he reveres precise lines and clear drawing. Leibnitz has the ways of a colorist; he goes on without rule, or sequence, or control, almost by starts, flinging out his ideas here and there, as his fancy bids, whensoever and howsoever reflection or impulsive intuition hint them to him. Incessantly diverted from one thought to another, he expatiates on the various subjects that attract him, instead of arranging his conceptions in an orderly whole. For him, philosophy seems like a contrasting relief from the profound and tedious studies that employ his sustained attention and the controversies in which he displays extraordinary activity. He loves action and social intercourse. He aims at being a statesman. If he gives himself up to metaphysics, he handles the most intricate questions with simple ease, but in a manner indirectly, and solves them by deep sayings. Clearly that pursuit is not the great business of his life, but is its dignified amusement. In matter and in manner alike, Descartes and himself are opposed. They agree neither as to methods nor as to conclusions. They are at variance upon first causes, upon final causes, upon man, the world, the soul, and God. The demon of geometry, accused of having been the evil genius of Descartes, never tormented Leibnitz; his philosophy does not issue from that source. Nevertheless, that philosophy is a star that, after seeming eclipse, rises anew to illuminate us. In the light of its rays, it may be unwittingly, sciences gain unlooked-for power, and are invigorated by grand inspirations. Be its term of revolution long or brief, it will have been the guiding star, through all the course of its circuit, for the most useful and productive studies. We shall attempt to prove this assertion; but first we must renew the recollection of the principles lying at the foundation of Leibnitz's metaphysics, and the too-unfamiliar aggregate of his scientific teachings.

I.

Our senses are struck by an endless variety of perplexed and intertangled phenomena; our mind is a restless, limitless ocean, full to overflow of impressions, thoughts, and longings. By what means do we attain the conception of any single distinct thing in this measureless chaos? By unceasing action and reaction of the external upon ourselves, and of ourselves upon the external. We begin by dividing the *I* from the *not I*, and this process gives us the perception of a profound difference between these two terms. The *not I*, the external, impresses us at once, from the most general point of view, that of motions and forms, with something purely geometrical; but we also discern in it another, more hidden element, which Leibnitz discusses admirably; that is, resistance, spring, inward and latent force. At the bottom of those phenomenal shows, which Descartes reduces to what he calls material points, and to motion, the Hanoverian philosopher detects a very different notion, that of "force not myself," as Maine de Biran uses the expression, in virtue of which the external object resists the effort of will, limits and confines it, and reacts against our own force as strongly as our own force acts to surmount it. Whether this resistance makes itself known directly, in the immediate apperception of the effort put forth by the *I* outside of itself, or whether the mind clothes it in some other conception, that force is definitively conceived in the same way as the *I* is conceived, as a pure and absolute category, with no appreciable shape. This active force, Leibnitz holds, differs from bare force of which the schools talk, in this respect, that the entire power, or *faculty*, of the scholastics, is only the imminent possibility of action, which still requires, before passing into action, an impulse from without; but the active force we speak of intends a kind of *actuality* which holds a middle place between the power to act and the act itself, and takes effect as soon as the obstacle is removed. As a clear illustration, take the instance of a weight stretching the cord that holds it up, or of a strung bow. Or, again, we cannot possibly describe in what respect a body in motion, at each one of the points it successively occupies, differs from a body at rest, unless we add that at each of those points it *tends* to go onward.

The mind thus takes in, by the method of metaphysical abstraction, the primitive capacities of action, the actualities, the powers that give to matter its dynamic characteristics. Leibnitz considers these capacities, to which he also gives the name of *monads*, as real and absolute principles, the sum of which in Nature is always the same, while the quantity of motion in Nature is variable. Every sort of phenomenon resolves itself into these substantial unities, the number of which is infinite, and which are the only mode we have of conceiving bodies and souls. *Atoms of matter* are contrary to reason—apart from their being themselves made up of parts—because, however invincible the attachment of one part to another may be, that does not alter the fact of their diversity. There exist only *atoms of substance*, that is, real unities, absolutely devoid of parts, which are the sources of action, the first principles in the composition of things, and the last elements, so to speak, in the analysis of substances. These might be called, as Leibnitz calls them, *metaphysical points:* they possess some vitality, and a kind of perception; and *mathematical points* are the mode employed in using them to express the universe; but, when corporeal substances are compressed, the aggregate of their organs makes but one *physical point*, as we regard it. Thus physical points only seem to be indivisible, but are not really so; mathematical points are exact, but they are only modes of thought. Nothing is complete and real except metaphysical points, or points of substance (the *forms* or *souls* of Leibnitz), and without them no reality would exist, since without true units there can be no multitude.

Points of substance, or monads, without extension or form, are then truly the inner and specific forces of things. We can conceive them, but cannot shape their image. Just as we should be incapable of knowledge if we had not the signs of language, so, without the support of those representations to the senses furnished by body and motion, we must remain ignorant of force. They do not, however, help us to escape the inference that force is the reality of which body and motion are merely the concrete and sensible images, not intelligible ones. Briefly, there is something more in the world than a display of phenomena, something more than visible forms and express motion: there is energy, spring, concealed activity at rest, concentrated and condensed inner potency, ever ready to be translated into numberless appearances. Beyond perception and without extension, these mother-forces, fertile sources of all action and all life, compose, as Leibnitz teaches, the very essence of things.

How do these forces engender bodies and souls, and

what are the latter's mutual relations? On this subject Leibnitz develops completely original ideas. Souls are monads of more perfect kind and higher activity, the principles of all those forces that are specially translated into organization, life, thought, etc. There are souls everywhere—if not thinking souls, at least forces that have the power of occasioning appearances resembling those of life. Leibnitz thus holds that the number of souls is infinite, and that there is no portion of matter, how small soever it may be, in which a living actuality is not always found; but, just as the monads of mere matter are manifested by it, the monads of organized matter are manifested by organization. The perfection of the substance accords with, and is proportioned to, that of its original. While Descartes makes an essential separation between soul and body, Leibnitz cannot conceive of them apart. He says distinctly, in the "New Essays," "The soul is never separated from some kind of a body;" and he writes to Arnauld, "Our body is the matter, and our own soul is the form, of our substantial existence." We find exactly the same propositions in several of his works, especially in the "Monadology." The rational soul must be distinguished from the sentient soul. Animals, in the condition of germs, have only sentient souls; but, as soon as those germs are elected, and arrive at a perfect nature, their sentient souls are raised to the prerogative of reason.

The reasoning soul is, for Leibnitz, the source of all highest revelation. The foundation of things, as he holds, is everywhere the same, and we must judge of every thing according to that which is known to us, that is, the soul. Our *self* is, in fact, the only substance of which we have direct consciousness. The true unity we feel to exist in it we must attribute to other substances, just as we must judge of force, not as an object of the senses and the imagination, but in accordance with that type which we discover in the will. We can conceive of spiritual substance in an infinite number of various degrees, which may be either superior or inferior to the *self;* we can conceive of nothing active that is not similar to it. Since all our ideas proceed from profound reflection on ourselves, we could know nothing of being, if we did not find being in ourselves. This is the same as saying that the intellect contains in itself certain primordial notions, which are the starting-point and the condition of all others. In other words, it is declaring that ideas exist in the mind anterior to experience, dependent on the very constitution of that mind. Aristotle and Locke compared the soul to a blank tablet, on which the senses and experience proceed to inscribe their teachings. Leibnitz maintains that it originally holds the principles of many ideas and doctrines, which outward objects merely call into action at fitting times. With Plato, with St. Paul, when he declares that the law of God is written in our hearts, with Scaliger, who called them *seeds of eternity,* the author of "Monadology" admits these fundamental concepts of the understanding as the bases of all knowledge. He compares them to living fires, to luminous rays hidden within us, which the contact of sense and of outward objects brings to view, as sparks that leap out on striking flint with steel. And these flashes are visible more than in any other thing in the gift of perceiving the connection of things, that is, in the reason.

In what relation does the soul, this especially active monad, find itself to be with those monads of a lower order, the elements of the body? In Leibnitz's view, that organized mass by which the soul makes itself known, being of a nature very similar to it, acts in turn of its own accord, whenever the soul wills it, without any clashing between the laws of either, the spirits and the blood performing at such times exactly the required motions in correspondence with the soul's passions and perceptions. It is this mutual relation established beforehand in every substance in the universe which creates its general communion, and creates particularly the union between soul and body. We may hence understand how the soul has its seat in the body by near and direct presence, for it is in it as unity is in multitude. The soul, a thinking monad, acts in consonance with inferior but still vital monads, which, concurrently with it, are manifested by the organized substance in which thought has its seat. The soul is in relations with the lower activities of life, as they are with the still duller activities of mere matter, in a companionship which is not a dependence.

We must now rise higher, and study the relations and the communion between monads in the universe. Three principles, that of *preëstablished harmony*, that of *continuity*, and that of *the sufficient reason*, are here the basis of Leibnitz's philosophy. Preëstablished harmony expresses nothing else than the combination of all monads in the universe. Our mind perceives an infinity of relations among them, of which it does not grasp the physical necessity. It does not know why two monads act in concert, or the one upon the other, to bring about some special results. It cannot explain how monads of a lower order exert influence over those of a higher order, those of the body on those of the soul, and reciprocally. In a word, as Hume demonstrates, we perceive no logical and necessary connection between phenomena which follow each other in the successive relations of cause and effect. Yet we are certain that no single molecule in the world is alien to the rest, that not one is isolated from the whole, that all are conjoint and act together in the whirl of general existence. We remark that every effect depends on an infinity of causes, and that every cause has an infinity of effects. The concourse, the common action, the *consensus* of all these monads toward a regular order, manifestly prove an established harmony among their essential activities. There is a perfect concord, in virtue of which every substance, following its own laws, agrees with what all the others require. Leibnitz believes this harmony to cover something besides mere relations of causality. He sees in the relations of monads influences of the same kind as those the soul exerts over the body; he believes that they have an intuitive feeling one for the other, each having a kind of apperception of what is not itself. He believes that, having this reciprocal feeling, they exhibit a kind of irritability, attended by more or less consciousness, in respect to their mutual qualities. He even judges that, while they receive the harmonious impression of the complete world in which they are factors, they reflect it in a certain way, and express its law. Every substance, he says, is percipient and representative of the total world, according to its point of view and its impressions. A Persian poet had said before him, "Cleave an atom, and you will find in it a sun." In a word, monads, though each possessing in itself its peculiar principle of activity and direction, all act together in an ordered concert of energy. But what bond unites them? Are those relations we observe among them only relations in our own reason? Do mutual necessary relations among them exist? How does unity rule in the world? This is the absolutely unknown in our science, and is one of the arguments urged by Leibnitz to prove the existence of God. God makes the bond, the communion, among substances. Moreover, these substances, logically connected, though each performing its distinct part, tend toward one final end.

The law of continuity displays new, closer relations among monads, and fixes the place in the scale of their various conditions. Future characteristics are traced beforehand, and the marks of the past are always preserved in every substance. Thus every event issues from those that precede it. On the other hand, monads, in their infinite diversities, succeed each other without a break from the most rudimentary to the most perfect ones. That progression which we conceive of in the abstract quantities of mathematics exists among the real quantities of the world, which monads of every kind are. Force, life, will, are assigned in different proportions to all the degrees of that immeasurable series—in the lower ones dull and imperceptible, in the higher ones potent and fruitful. The passage of inferior monads to higher planes takes place gradually through a thousand-intermediate ones. The principles of bodies advance incessantly nearer to perfection, and do not differ essentially from those of the souls with which they are connected. Souls in their turn are numerous, and they too obey a law of progress. Thus there is a measureless quantity of degrees of life, some more or less dominant over others, from the faint and dull activity of the atom of sand up to the sovereign power of absolute mind. Descartes had said that all the facts of Nature follow on in connection like geometric truths. Leibnitz shows us a yet deeper and more universal order in things. Every thing is proportioned, analogous, harmonious: all is held, is continued, in unbroken interdependence. Thus we no longer recognize two distinct worlds, the natural and the spiritual one. Spiritual existences compose a part of one and the same series with corporeal ones. The only differences between them are differences of degree.

The principle of the "sufficient reason" discloses to us the strict economy of things. Nothing occurs in Nature without a reason, but she is not wasteful of her reasons. She always chooses the shortest ways. Magnificent in effects, miserly in causes, she produces the greatest amount of work with the least amount of force. The reasons of the world, Leibnitz holds, are hidden in something extramundane, which differs from the interdependence of states,

the series of substances, whose totality makes up the
world. We must rise, therefore, from physical or hypo-
thetical necessity, which determines the succeeding state
of the world accordantly with an anterior state, to absolute
or metaphysical necessity, of which we can give no account, and this last reason is the reason of all the others.
As a thoughtful interpreter of Leibnitz's teaching says,[1]
thought, will, are at the bottom of all things; phenomena,
in all their degrees, appear in the last result only as so
many refractions in the variously-disturbed media of sole
and universal light—light which shines most of all in our
own soul, because it is the focus in which are concentrated
the everywhere dispersed rays of that diffused effulgence.
From action to action, from power to power, we must thus
soar to a potency which at last suffices singly for itself—
that is, to perfect spontaneity.

In time, then, as in space, all things are subject to a
law of inflexible interdependence. This idea of beholding
the universe in the microcosm, of regarding the infinitely
great in the infinitely little, monads in incessant reciprocal
action, each part bearing the stamp of the absolute which
shines forth in the all, and this all moving onward in grand,
harmonious might toward an end of which our intelligence
can catch perchance but a dim glimpse, but which it feels
in deep conviction—this idea is the glory of Leibnitz. It
is determinism in its all-embracing fullness. Descartes, too,
had formed an image of the world accordantly with supreme
laws; but he had shut up those laws within the limits of
mechanism. Leibnitz beholds a grander sphere, and views,
beyond mechanism, energy, life, love, and good; he gazes
upon the true God in his magnificence. The God of Descartes
is number and force; the God of Leibnitz is life and beauty.
From his bosom all wells forth and radiates in floods of
eternal light, as thoughts emanate from our own existence.

[1] Ravaisson, "Philosophy in France in the Nineteenth Century."

II.

Leibnitz has thus led us on to the loftiest heights of thought, the furthest bounds of speculation. Let us now come down again with him to the special questions he has explored and transmitted to modern science, which still lacks the power to solve them all. We shall learn how serviceable that science has found the general principles settled by him as the grand laws of the world's order. Leibnitz has the clearest and strongest sense of the diffusibility of life. He defines exactly the characteristic which lies at its base, that is, the incessant molecular replacement of matter in the permanence of active forms, namely, of souls. He holds that the minutest portion of matter contains a world of creatures, lives, animated beings, actualities, souls. Every particle of matter is to be conceived of as a garden full of plants, or a pond full of fishes; but every twig of each plant, every limb of each animal, every drop in its humors, is again such a garden, or such a pond, full of decreasingly minute lives, similar in kind. All these bodies, he adds, move like rivers, in unresting flow. Portions pass into them, and pass out of them, incessantly. In this way the soul changes its bodies by very fine degrees, and is never suddenly stripped of its organs; vital properties are continuous, while the matter of life is transitory. Leibnitz conjectured, consequently, that some animals must have the faculty of multiplying by scission, like plants. The discovery of polyps by Trembley, the facts of the mode of increase in vorticelli, parameciæ, and bursars and opalines, since noticed, have justified the philosopher's guess.

Descartes regarded animals as machines, as soulless automata, made up of atoms the movements of which are coördinated in the manner of those of plants. He denied them intelligence, and supposed that the sensibility and instinct noticed in them might be explained by purely mechanical causes. Leibnitz does not admit that there are any specific differences between man and animals. He grants that they have a soul inferior to ours in being less rational, but still a rational soul, a soul fundamentally of the same essence as ours, a principle of activity quite other than the energies of the inorganic world. He considers it, moreover, equally indestructible and immortal with our own. Those, says Leibnitz, who conceive that an infinity of little living things exists in the smallest drop of water, as Leuwenhoeck's experiments prove, and who do not think it strange that matter should be filled everywhere with animated substances, will not think it strange either that there should be something animated in ashes, and that fire may transform a living being, may reduce it, instead of destroying it. Thus, life does not vanish. Only the arrangement and agreement of the monads are modified; the essences that compose them remain with their original and incorruptible properties, ready to reappear in other living things. That which never begins never perishes either. These reflections led Leibnitz to a very profound way of looking on the phenomenon of death. As life is not a breath coming suddenly and all at once to animate the body, death cannot be attributed to the sudden vanishing of such a breath. As generation is only the developing of an already-formed animal, corruption, or death, is only the enveloping of a living being which does not cease to remain living. Death takes place by degrees; it attacks first the imperceptible parts, and does not strike our attention until it has seized the whole being. And we do not see the gradual steps of that retrograding as we perceive those of the slow forward movement that constitutes birth. The facts of transformation and renewed life among insects, the return to life of men nearly frozen, drowned, or strangled, seem to Leibnitz a proof that death thus comes on by very slow degrees, and he advises medical science to attempt the task of bringing men to life again. Later science has confirmed these ideas. Life does dwell in the infinitely little; it holds its silent and secret flow under the "manifold disguises" Hamlet speaks of, eluding search while it still plays in every pulse, and finding its food in death.

Leibnitz also turns his attention to species, which he defines by generation in such sort that the being similar to another which comes from the same origin, or the same seed, is also of the same species. The various classes of beings appear to him only as ordinates of the same curve, and form but one chain, in which these classes, like so many links, hold so closely to each other that it is impossible to fix the point at which any one of them begins or ends. All species, he says with remarkable exactness, which border upon or occupy parts of the curve where it is bent or returned on itself, must be endowed with equivocal characteristics. Then, looking at the subject as a whole, and bringing it under the law of continuity, he arranges species, and beings generally, in an immense series, from man to the simplest existences; he holds that there is so close an approach between animals and vegetables that, taking the least perfect of the former and the most perfect of the latter, they can hardly be distinguished. It accords, too, with the superb harmony of the universe, with the grand plan as well as with the goodness of its Sovereign Architect, that the various kinds of creatures should rise by degrees toward his infinite perfection. Leibnitz admits the existence of creatures more perfect than ourselves, but of whom he confesses that we can have no clear conception. He also believes that in the series of existing things there are voids, *possible* things non-existent. The variation of species, several instances of which he examines, seems to him to be real, but not their transmutation; he is for limited variableness, that is, he allows the action of modifying circumstances within a wide range, yet does not go so far as to believe that they can transform the species. On examining the impressions of fishes and plants in the schists of Halle, Leibnitz, for the first time, perceived in those remains, not a sport of Nature, but testimonies to revolutions on the globe, and to the existence of faunas and floras that have perished. The "Protogæa," in which this important question is particularly and deeply studied, fixes the starting-point for modern geology and paleontology, and for all explanations, on the Plutonic theory, of the earth's crust. Hutton, Buffon, and Cuvier, drew inspiration for their labors from this sketch of Leibnitz.

He argues that, if it often happens in science that we fail in the power of distinctly marking differences, that results from our ignorance of both the minute parts and the inward structure of things, that is, the principles by which their fundamental nature might be accounted for. That want of knowledge obliges us to pronounce by guess on many phenomena, the full understanding of which is reserved for the future. Therefore he builds great hopes upon the use of the microscope, and upon comparative anatomy (the term is his own), in which he believes that the confirmation of many of his ideas will be found. Among other conjectures he distinctly foresees the function and importance of the spermatozoa, in making the assertion that it will be discovered how each sex supplies some organized thing in the phenomena of generation. And this assertion has a very just effect in correcting his theory of the syngenetic preformation of beings, or the incasement of germs, according to which all ova exist beforehand from the origin of the world, inclosed in that of the first representative of each species. That theory, proved to be erroneous by the whole result of observation in embryogeny, is thus erroneous, precisely because the organized element contributed by the male sex is indispensable to the growth of the embryo.

The classification of genera and species in the vegetable kingdom is a difficult task. Botanists in the seventeenth century thought that distinctions, founded on the shapes of the flower, made the nearest approach to the natural order in arranging a series of classes. Leibnitz judges that it would be best to make the comparison not only in respect to a single characteristic, such as that of the flower, which may after all be the most useful in arranging a convenient system, but also in respect to the characteristics of other parts in plants. He thus suggests the rule of subordination in characteristics, as a result of his ideas upon the harmony of beings.

Thus all these labors and hypotheses issue directly from Leibnitz's metaphysical conceptions as to the system of mundane elements. A still more direct outcome from them is the invention of the infinitesimal calculus. Were the calculus of itself nothing more than a splendid curiosity, even then it would be much to have discovered a means of working upon and with infinite quantities as with finite ones. Fortunately that method of calculation has found occasion in astronomy, mechanics, and physics, for applications so rich in results that those sciences have gained a new being from it. It is a new instrument, a new lever supplied to them for the highest researches. We thus learn the extent of Leibnitz's familiarity with the most difficult problems.

III.

What has been the influence of the metaphysics of Leibnitz over the great processes of advance in modern science, beginning with those of the last century? It is an old saying that the eighteenth century had no original philosophy; in fact, it lived on borrowed doctrines. It had among others one system of teaching proceeding from that of Leibnitz, and Diderot may be said to have been its true representative. At the first glance, that abounding and undisciplined mind seems devoid of the qualities of dogmatism and method which properly make the philosopher; but on a closer study we become aware that he did develop an exact and settled system, in which the ideas of Leibnitz hold a large place, and the principle of dynamism, the notion of mother-forces, governs. In the "Interpretation of Nature," in "D'Alembert's Dream," and in "Philosophical Truths as to Matter and Motion," Diderot shows himself a pure scholar of the Hanoverian thinker, rather a fanatical one even, since he goes so far as to write that Leibnitz by himself alone gives as great a fame to Germany as Plato, Aristotle, and Archimedes together confer on Greece. Diderot's dynamism, by which we mean his strong, full conviction of the activities of substance, exists also in the minds of Charles Bonnet, of Buffon, of Bordeu, and other famous naturalists of the same era. He inspired at that period a whole school of investigators and philosophers, some of whom found an excess of negations in Hume's doctrine, and others an excess of analysis in Condillac's system.

Buffon, like Leibnitz, sees in Nature arranged plans, continuous relations, regulated facts, ends everywhere foreseen, conforming to an order dictated by supreme control. Those *organic molecules* and those *penetrant forces* (immanent) which in his view compose life, and go on from one mould into another, to perpetuate it, are precisely Leibnitz's monads. The great ideas unfolded in the "Epochs of Nature," which, however disputable in some points, have had so real an influence over the later advances of geology, are for the most part borrowed from the "Protogæa." Buffon's general physiology is not less similar to that first pronounced by Leibnitz. Such is the fact also as to those of two of his famous contemporaries. Bordeu and Barthez, protesting at once against Cartesian geometrism, erroneously extended to comprise the phenomena of life, and against analysis pushed to extremes, as preached by Condillac and applied by his school, demonstrate and maintain vital forces in all their splendid independence of action and simplicity that cannot be further simplified. No doubt they exaggerate the weakness of mechanical explanations, and the perils of analysis, and it would be an error to suppose that later science has always pronounced them right. But it has at least justified them in holding the opinion advanced by Leibnitz in opposition to Descartes, namely, that life is a higher force which involves lower ones without dependence on them, that the organism is a system of energies in which not every thing takes place mechanically, that the forces which act in animals are essentially analogous to those which act in man, and that they all, consubstantial with organized matter, can come to act only in it and by it. It is thus that those two great physicians at the same time destroyed the medico-mechanics of Boerhaave and the animism of Stahl, and made the way ready for Bichat. Neither does the same recent science wholly confirm the conjectures risked by Charles Bonnet, by Telliamed, and more lately by Delamé-thérie, Lamarck, and Darwin, upon the connection of beings, the origin and transformation of species, conjectures of which Leibnitz had furnished the cautious outline; yet it would be unjust not to acknowledge that they have aided in giving a strong impulse to zoological researches.

So also Vicq-d'Azyr, and those other anatomists who lay the foundation of comparative anatomy, and examine the harmonious relations, the various connections, the dynamic adjustments of the organs, are faithful to the conceptions formed by Leibnitz as to Nature's plans. Goethe, who openly expressed his respect for Diderot, shows himself a follower of Leibnitz as well as of Spinoza, not only in his works on comparative anatomy, in which he points out the latent symmetry of living parts and examines fine proportions in bodies, but also in his general doctrines as to the world. He admits that all Nature is filled with forces, lives, and souls, a feeling most eloquently uttered in "Faust," in "Werther," in the "Poesies;" and, still more, he expressly approves of the "Monadology." In his magnificent funeral discourse upon Wieland (1812), he unfolds, in language that Leibnitz would not have refused to adopt, all the details of that belief he resorts to in explaining the immortality of thought, that is, of conscious monads. All that school distinctly supplies us with proof of the influence philosophic teachings exert over the mind of *savants*, and consequently over the advance of discoveries. We thus discern of what advantage it always is to guide researches and experiments by the loftier hints of speculative genius, and we perceive, too, the need there is for the consideration by philosophers of objective reasonings.

Our age has been too long neglectful of these important lessons. We have seen its philosophy take leave of science, to ally itself with literature and morals. While science and philosophy, continuing closely united, were destined, by the natural progress of things, to gain more intimate mutual intelligence, their divorce has retarded the moment of a reconcilement and good understanding, so highly desirable. No doubt, very well-written books, full of excellent thoughts, were still published among philosophic schools; no doubt, grand discoveries were still brought to light in the schools of science; but doctrines had vanished, and with them labored and fruitful meditation had ceased to exist. Science, departing from high thought, lost its dignity and contracted an empirical character. Philosophy, by dint of ignoring experimental facts, lost itself in the chimerical. The Cartesian spirit, even more perhaps than the spirit of Descartes, rose predominant, and urged metaphysicians to empty spiritualism, and physicists to sophistical materialism. While knowledge of mind was thus wasting itself in literary declamation, and knowledge of Nature in desultory research, idle discussions multiplied, oftener inspired by passion than by reason, giving weapons to the least noble purposes that passion suggests, and paralyzing the most praiseworthy undertakings of reason. At the present time this state of things is disappearing, and Leibnitz's philosophy, it seems, must be the strongest ally of all who long for a fruitful union between science and metaphysics. The highest minds in schools most widely apart give us grounds for indulging that hope. They do not rest satisfied with wishing for its fulfillment; they are laboring for that direct purpose, disregarding all impediments of prejudices or of objections.

The result most clearly ascertained by vivisections in experimental physiology, and by observations in microscopic anatomy, mainly through the labors of Claude Bernard and Charles Robin, is, that living beings are agglomerations of infinitely fine and delicate particles, real individualities, each endowed with characteristic and consubstantial properties. These active units, forms and forces in one, bring about, following upon manifold interminglings, the whole organization and the whole working of animal and vegetable parts. Animals and plants have ceased to be machines vivified by a power distinct from them, which possesses and moves them; they are systems of combined monads in which life is deeply lodged, and by which it expresses itself—they are marvelously ordered collections of minute springs, possessing certain innate tendencies. As Leibnitz had said, every living being is made up of an infinity of living beings. Now, these corpuscles, known to modern science as *anatomical elements*, have as their essential principle what Leibnitz described by the term "souls," forms of substance, essential powers, monads. In fact, that which gives their character to these primordial elements of life is dynamic actuality. Let us consider a dead cell and a living cell. What makes the difference between them? Nothing at all, either from the geometrical point of view, or from the physical or chemical one; nothing which may be detected by measurement, or balances, or reagents. The difference between them is, that the former is devoid of the activity which exists in the latter. That activity is a continuous inmost transmutation, by which the matter of the cell is incessantly renewed, without any modification of its morphological appearances or of its other properties. Life consists in this tide which flows deep through every element in the organization, in that virtue of instability which effects unceasing change in the matter of appearances, while the form and the force do not vary. It exists in those organic properties, pure forces, which are constant, while the organs, the visible forms, are passing. Therefore, in opposition to the belief of materialism, and in accordance with Leibnitz's views, matter, in such case, is merely the shifting envelope; the unchangeable base is force. In addition to nutrition, which has just been defined, other manifestations of life are, through organization, development, contractility, feeling, thought, will. These other aspects yield us the same demonstration. The utter impossibility of producing any thing organized with mere inorganic forces, the impotence of spontaneous generation in the first place, testifies that organization possesses a higher principle than that of the phenomena of the mineral kingdom: but organization is not the only thing that it is forbidden to attribute to the working of physico-chemical means; the same holds true of contractility, sensibility, and *a fortiori* of thought and will. The greater the development of experimental science, the more decided is the difference between these two orders of phenomena, which theory held might be confounded, the organic and the inorganic order, namely, and the more evident it becomes that the forces of life and those of a stone cannot be identified, even in their principle. The monads that engender cells are higher than those that slumber in the grain of sand, just as the coarsest portion of an animal is otherwise and more intricately complex than the most perfect crystal. Very clearly, if form, personality, thought, memory, will, all that makes up the life of self, and the self of life, persists in identity, while the matter of the organs suffers change and renewal, it must be because life consists in a system of activity essentially different from geometrical extension and from mass that has weight; it is because it is the peculiar property of a substance which involves physico-chemical action indeed, but involves besides that something quite different.

Every monad, says Leibnitz, has its principle, its essence, its law, and is not made subject to the will of external impulses. This is the very basis of the doctrines as to life enounced by Charles Robin. Instead of granting that the body is ruled by a vital principle which coördinates and guides physiological motions, he believes that, thanks to a complete concord in virtue of which every substance, obeying its own laws, assents to what other substances require, the effective working of the latter follows or attends the effective working of the former. The development of living beings, which consists in a progressive and ordered accumulation of anatomical elements, is explained, as he avers, not by one force which holds them under its guidance, but by the successive coming into view, in some sort the revelation, of elementary substances which express life, every one of those substances duly appearing when the conditions needed for its manifest existence concur.

But is life everywhere in the world, as Leibnitz insists? Undoubtedly, if by life is to be understood spontaneity of all things, activity peculiar to each monad. Or again, when we reflect that every portion whatever of substance virtually contains some aspiration toward life, since it is ready to enter as a component part into the constitution of a living being, we may surely say that every thing lives. But if by that word we mean to express special energies, of the nature of nutrition, sensibility, and will, then we must acknowledge that life belongs only to organized substances, that is, to a single category of monads. There no doubt is in the lowest monads, and those furthest removed from life, some dim tendency toward a determined order; but it seems to me erroneous, as yet, to view in this a conscious purpose. It is rather by a sort of reflex action that such monads exert their powers, under the influence of superior monads, exactly as the elements of the nerves, for instance, sometimes act on those of the muscles unwittingly to us, and in spite of us.

Another question, and one not less grave, here arises. The thinking soul, as Leibnitz holds, is a dominant monad, a solitary monad. Science seems not to authorize such an assertion. For science, in its highest interpretation, the soul is a concurrent power of monads, all of them sentient and intelligent, but in different degrees, which accounts for the variations in degrees of feeling and of reason. In one living being there exists no monad expressing self, in another self is only very vaguely perceived, in another again it is conceived in its fullness. In one and the same living being the soul is evidently manifold, because it shows itself under distinct aspects, as affection, feeling, intellect, will. Thus, far from being single and indivisible, it consists of a combination of monads which are not all equally perfect, some being found occurring in the lowest animals, others being characteristic of man exclusively. An intricate system of primordial forces, a concordant action of energies without extension, expressing themselves in the anatomical elements of the gray matter of the brain, and radiating thence by its peculiar virtue into the infinity of things, the human soul is like Milton's lion, half lion and half mud, and still struggling, under the moulding hand of the divine sculptor, to get free from chaos. Half spirit, half matter, our soul aspires to absolute purity: it is checked and fettered by the bonds of the body. The great mystery is to know how it releases itself from them when passing into eternity.

Leibnitz did not merely distinguish those virtues which he called substantial forms, or souls, and which are the properties of corpuscles endowed with life, such as we now know them; he drew a further distinction, in these corpuscles and in all bodies generally, between *mass* and *matter*. Now what he termed mass is the grouping of our geometric and mechanical properties, and matter is the association of our physico-chemical properties. Mass and matter belong to all bodies, soul does not belong to all. Yet it is perhaps allowable to regard as a quasi-vital thing that tendency of inorganic molecules to form regular groups in crystallization, and even that more general property they possess of always combining in definite proportions, assuming figures of the generating law of which chemistry is beginning to gain a glimpse. At all events, whatever may be the principles of those inward motions, of those harmonious struggles that have their seat in the inmost depths of substance, chemistry in our days is a copy of Leibnitz's thought in all its parts. In fact, it reduces those complicated phenomena that are the object of its study to simple elements known under the name of *atoms*, and having nothing but the name in common with those of Leucippus and of Descartes. Pure idealities, and yet the principles of all that is real, these atoms are distinguished and classified by functions that are absolutely dynamic. Chemistry proves the action in those atoms of primitive forces, which it designates by the term *atomicities*, and which it measures not by weight or motion, but by the direct product of the actual play of those forces. "The energy with which one body combines with another body," says Würtz, "is independent of the power it possesses to attract the latter. The first is atomicity, the last is affinity." Atomicities are capacities of action, powers of combination, immanent in atoms, or rather consubstantial with them. Such is the language at this day of the most authoritative chemists. They contemplate in bodies elective virtues, tendencies to saturation, appetencies which imply something prior and subsequent to motion, something like that which in us brings about action. Chemistry no longer dwells in appearances and sensible forms, in those brilliant shows which delight or dazzle the senses; it dwells in those mute forces, in those acting monads, the substances of substance, the matters of matter. Bodies are no longer characterized by their outward and momentary physiognomy alone; they are also characterized by that which is most secret within them, by the principle of their past and coming existence, by a spring which is as inwardly theirs as our soul is ours. That in them which strikes our senses is merely the veil of their real nature. Faraday and Dumas alike, Berthelot and Würtz too, here find the whole in a dynamic harmony. A distinguished English chemist, lately deceased, Graham, the discoverer of dialysis, even went so far as to conceive, under the name of *ultimates*, of certain principles yet simpler than atoms, real points of substance, the essence of which is determined by the kind of vibrations they are subjected to, and in its turn determines the various natures of bodies. Thus monads have become, in vital phenomena, anatomical elements with their consubstantial attributes, and, in chemic phenomena, atoms with their consubstantial attributes. Greek atomism and Cartesian atomism formed the conception of geometric and mechanical corpuscles; Leibnitz formed the conception of the principles of apparent activities, explainable neither by geometry nor by mechanics.

Let us last question the physical science of our own day, and we shall discover in it still the same ideas. It reduces every thing to vibrations, both those of what it terms material atoms, and those of what it calls ether. In its view, physical phenomena are explained by the system of motions of atoms and of the ether, and, since these motions may be transmuted into one another according to a mathematical law, it follows that relations of equivalence exist among the various manifestations of physical activity— that there is such a thing, for instance, as a mechanical equivalent of heat, a calorific equivalent of electricity, etc. Now, that internal motion revealed by analysis and induction, that corpuscular agitation which gives bodies the qualities without which they could not be perceived, namely, weight, color, heat, etc.—that motion, under every form, implies a moving principle, something simple and irreducible, a spontaneity similar to that Leibnitz conceives of in monads. What is that living force, that potential energy, that virtual energy, which physicists so often employ in their speculations, if it is not the same thing as metaphysical actualities, the intelligible cause of acts of force, of tendencies like those the soul feels within itself? Will it be said that all these manifold and varying aspects of physical force are derivative from the sheer mechanical force, whose sum in the universe is unchanging? But, then, why does motion become at one place heat, at another light, and still at another electricity? Must it not be because, besides those monads that are the spring of motion, others exist, whose special function, from the point of view of our sensibility, is to act on different perceptive capacities from those by which we cognize motion?

Under another aspect we recognize in our sciences of to-day some of the great thoughts of Leibnitz, thanks to which those sciences have gained a wholly new character: we allude to those logical formulas into which the mind condenses the materials of knowledge, those synthetic ideas which are the summary of grand inductions. After having shown how we must conceive of mind in Nature, we should point out how it is necessary to conceive Nature in mind, for our sensations, in undergoing elaboration by the mind in order to become knowledge, borrow, and borrow very much, from the peculiarities of the spiritual essence. Intellectual processes, says Charles Robin, form a whole with the rest of science, in such a way that history proves the exposition of a *general idea* to be proper, and to be admissible as equivalent or superior to the exposition of facts.

What, then, are these intellectual processes, these general ideas? These processes may be briefly stated as dialectics, either synthetic or intuitive, and these ideas as the concepts about form and force, of which we proceed to point out the chief ones. The idea of series is perhaps the most important. In contemplating mineral or chemical species, or in contemplating animal or vegetable species, the mind arranges them in a series. That is the form under which it conceives the *totality* of beings. It sets up a continuity among them, resembling that of series in the higher algebra. It ranges forces and qualities in an unbroken graduated progression, the effective cause of which is perfection, in this sense, that beings rise to a higher point in the scale just in the degree of their approach to the conditions of that which is perfect, to wit, intelligence. So luminous is this order, that Gerhardt effected a magnificent renovation in recent chemistry by bringing into it the idea of series. The real relations and the true characteristics of bodies have been settled with new exactness by that method. This conception stamps itself so forcibly on the *savant's* mind that he feels a tendency, as spontaneous as it is irresistible, to fill up the voids that he observes in the series, and to imagine rationally possible species in order to do it. In this way he sees beforehand the existence of some being unknown in reality, just as he foresees, in accordance with the laws of celestial mechanism, the existence of a planet never yet observed. This doctrine, which Leibnitz had deduced from the principle of continuity, and from that of the "sufficient reason," has been undeniably rich in results for the sciences. We name a late instance, taken from chemistry. "The synthesis of neutral fats," says Berthelot, "not only enables us to make artificially the fifteen or twenty natural fatty substances heretofore known, but allows us also to foresee the formation of some hundreds of millions of similar fatty bodies. . . . Every substance, every phenomenon, represents, we may say, one link involved in a more extended chain of similar and correlated substances and phenomena. . . . Without quitting the range of reasonable expectation, we may assume to conceive *the general types of all possible substances*, and to produce them."[1]

Another general idea is precisely that of *type*. We cannot define type better than by using the old expression, "creature of reason." In truth, it is a grouping together of elements which maintain themselves in an harmonious arrangement in such wise as to form a whole, conceived by the reason as perfect. Such ideal and rational creation, answering to certain conditions of fixity, necessity, and generality, becomes a pattern, a standard to which the mind refers and compares existing beings outside of itself. The mind thus has the power of using reality to abstract from it certain conditions which it groups in a higher, clearer, in brief, in a truer, order than that manifested in the outward world. We may add that the creation of types is an imperative need for the mind; it shows it in

[1] "Organic Chemistry," vol. ii., p. 800, *et seq.*

the sciences as well as in literature and the fine arts. It grasps reality only by referring it to such ideas, that is to say, to wholes in which the mutual relation of the parts is perfect. In chemistry, as in zoology and in botany, the type is the fundamental idea from the point of view of classifying. The great discoveries of our day, especially the late discoveries in organic chemistry, bring this strongly into view. They all issue from some speculative theory as to the peculiarly rational structure of things. The true philosophy of mind consists, perhaps, in the study of these fundamental conceptions of the understanding, as the true philosophy of Nature lies in the study of the primordial forces showing forth by the sensible phenomena of the world external to us. Thus, by a new path, we reach the confirmation of Leibnitz's ideas; for these general concepts, these logical expressions, these universals, on the one hand, furnish proof of those innate aptitudes in the mind upon which Leibnitz endeavored to construct mental philosophy; and, on the other, they imply in Nature a tendency toward development, toward metamorphosis and perfection, in other words, an intelligent force.

A brilliant school of mathematicians and physicists has lately pronounced against the doctrines the progress of which in the natural sciences we have just traced. Its disciples profess an exaggerated Cartesianism, denying any real existence to inner forces, to spontaneities, to actualities, to monads. It is an avowed return to geometrism, with all its strictnesses, and with all its illusions too. That school rejects attraction and affinity under the pretense that it is impossible to form any conception of those forces without imagining in matter a multitude of little hands hooking on to each other. It throws every thing into the shape of a formula, and asserts that any thing is chimerical which wants the capacity of being expressed mathematically. That school defines *force* as the product

PHILOSOPHY OF NATURE—LEIBNITZ'S IDEAS. 59

mg of mass multiplied by momentum, and *active force* as the product mv^2 of mass multiplied by the square of the velocity. Let us in the first place remark how highly unphilosophical it is to regard the most simple and irreducible things in the world as products, to confine within the strict limits of a one-term statement the living pulsations of the infinite and the absolute in things. In the next place, the attempt to define force by any calculation of figures seems like aping a man who should insist that the arrow-marks used in geometrical diagrams to denote the direction of forces were exact likenesses of the forces themselves. The cipher is the sign of quantity, the line that of motion. Force is something else than quantity, a very different thing from motion. But let us grant these definitions are proper: the question still remains, What are the causes that produce acceleration, velocity, resistance, in the mass? Now, it is impossible to avoid connecting these causes with some principle higher than geometrics, with a spontaneity more or less resembling that effort which in ourselves goes before action. We are thus always brought back, whether we would or not, to active monads, whose infinite varieties, infinite relations, and infinite interminglings, bring forth all. The accomplished writers we speak of will in vain strive to reduce to measured fractions of space and of time that which is in its essence the opposite of space and time—force; and the attempt is futile to prove that we have not a consciousness of the dynamic resistance of the elements of the world as clear as that which we have of our own individual effort to counterpoise it.

It is easy to point out the cause of such specious abuse of geometrical and mechanical considerations in natural philosophy. It grows out of ignorance of those biological facts by which the profound spontaneity, and the reality of forces consubstantial with bodies, are revealed in a special way. Geometry and mechanics, in their speculation, separate material points from forces, while biology teaches us to keep them bound together in an indestructible and necessary unity. The science of motions and of the forms they take, shows us only the outside of the energy of the universe. The science of life, on the contrary, unveils to us its throbbing heart and its splendid plan. Such is the measureless and priceless service it yields to knowledge and to discussion. Descartes, and those who attempt in our day to revive his system by deducing physics from mechanics, and physiology from physics, by explaining the higher through the lower, as Auguste Comte says, by forbidding any endeavor to conceive first principles by the aid of last principles—all those philosophers, whatever their merit in other respects, have misunderstood the lessons yielded by the living being in its twofold physiological and psychological relation. The evidences of soul making one and the same with life might have displayed to their view images of the soul and of life throughout the universe, instead of blind and misleading geometrism. They would have understood that ciphers and diagrams do not solve every thing, that computation is not the only method. That which does solve every thing is the soul, because it alone embraces every thing, or at least discovers in itself alone, rapt in abstraction, instinctive secret affinities with all. Besides, the certain and enduring fame of Descartes is great enough to permit us, without fear of dimming its deserved lustre, to pronounce sentence of impotence upon any attempts made in our day toward the introduction into natural philosophy of false principles borrowed from his teachings. The guidance and inspiration which modern biological science owes to them attest the increasing honor paid to the ideas of Leibnitz.[1]

[1] This article, written during the siege of Paris at the ambulance of Conflans, where I was serving as physician, having access only to a few

memoranda, is unfinished in several respects. Still it has an interest as the sketch of some ideas upon history and opinions which I have since unfolded at greater length. See particularly my essay entitled "Leibnitz, the Naturalist, Physiologist, and Physician" ("Comptes rendus of the Academy of Moral and Political Sciences," 1873).

THE GENERAL CONSTITUTION OF LIVING BEINGS.

PHYSICS, chemistry, and physiology, are making marvelous advances in our day, in their superficial range; but it is, perhaps, not so clearly remarked that they are at the same time rising in their aims and aspirations. In proportion as processes improve and doctrines grow established, Science takes fresh courage to attack lofty problems with new vigor, and boasts of bringing light and certainty to their solution. It takes up by exact methods and with very confident system the discussion of the most general and comprehensive questions. Owning no longer any limits to its investigation of the world of suns nor to its researches in the world of atoms; believing, too, that this twofold quest must yield up to it all the hidden things of matter and of spirit, no wonder that it is confident in its power to win by such inquiry the knowledge of all that has seemed hitherto a prize reserved to other capacities than its own. Whether warranted or unwarranted, this philosophic bent of modern science is in either case due to the influence of a multitude of discoveries full of interest in spite of their commonly abstract nature, full of rich instruction beneath the seeming barrenness of their details.

If every one carries about with him certain notions as to the conformation of the chief viscera of animals, few persons, even among the most enlightened, have a suspicion of the absorbing interest and the scope of our knowledge regarding the inner composition of organs, the structure and development of their deepest and most delicate parts, the curious properties of those infinitely tiny corpuscles that group together to make up living beings. The problems of life stand forth in such studies in all their grandeur, all their mystery and charm. The silent revelations of the microscope are here associated with the eloquent language of experiments on the animal frame. All the complexities of chemistry here give their aid to expositions which are but the more convincing for their extreme positiveness. And medicine itself, if it would escape stagnation, is forced to ask from such studies the key to riddles never answered by any power of empiricism. These words describe fully enough the interest that must attend a complete picture of the present condition of general anatomy.

I.

General anatomy has been created only of late days. Ancient anatomists, limiting their studies to the examination of the surface of organs, neglected to explore their depths. Besides, they were long forced to do without that instrument, most indispensable in this kind of investigation, the microscope. During the period beginning with Herophilus and Erasistratus, who flourished three hundred years before the Christian era, and who are the real founders of descriptive anatomy of the human body, extending down to Galen, and from Galen onward, including the time of Vesalius, the main subject of anatomy was formed nearly as a complete body. A great number of points that remained obscure were afterward cleared up by Bérenger de Carpi, Massa, Servet, Sylvius, who discovered the valves of the veins; Eustachi, who found the tube and valve named after him; Varolus, who examined the brain; Botal, Bauhin, Cesalpinus, Fabricius of Aquapendente, and a host of others, who, during the fifteenth and sixteenth centuries, produced in engraving magnificent plates of almost as great service to the advance of anatomical studies as the most successfully completed original researches. This acquired knowledge, already extensive, was improved in the seventeenth and eighteenth centuries by a succession of able men, whose names of themselves recall laborious lives and brilliant achievements. Harvey, in 1619, demonstrates the circulation of the blood; after him Wirsung points out the pancreatic duct; Pecquet, the thoracic duct; Rudbeck and Thomas Bartholin, the lymphatic conduits; Vieussens throws light upon the whole of neurology. Still later Ruysch, Albinus, Haller, Boerhaave, Winslow, Vicq-d'Azyr, unite the gains of their persistent investigations with those won by their predecessors.

To sum up all, the descriptive anatomy of the human body was in a state of remarkable completeness at the close of the eighteenth century. The outward arrangement, the shape and relations of the bones, muscles, nerves, vessels, and viscera, were settled in a positive manner, sufficient for the needs of the surgical art. Great was the amazement of old anatomists at that day when a man of genius arose, to tell them, and convince them, too, that merely the first half of anatomy was known, and that the coarser and more superficial part; and that another half, full of difficulties and surprises, invited investigation. This is exactly the fact as to general anatomy and Xavier Bichat, who is its founder. In truth, those organs known in their contour, their disposition, and locality, were but half known. Their texture, their inner composition, their delicate tissue, were all unknown. The essential properties of the membranes that make them up had not been analyzed. That is the aim of the new anatomy created by Bichat. A bold and fertile experimenter, as well as an able and clear-sighted observer, equally skilled in knowledge of the sound and of the unsound man, deep and lucid as a thinker, untiring and wonderfully fortunate in the methodical investigation of facts, deliberate and cautious in establishing principles, joining a broad and all-embracing view of things to a most just conviction of the dangers and difficulties of researches into organized being, a spirit at once very positive and very lofty, wanting neither boldness nor noble ambition, this great man was destined perhaps to give new and finished form to biology, had death not cut him off at the age of thirty-two. Yet his unfinished labors have sufficed to raise it to remarkable completeness by leading the way to the knowledge of living tissues. "All animals," says Bichat, "are a collection of various organs, which, while each performs one function, all concur, each in its own way, in the conservation of the whole. They are so many special machines in the general machine which makes the individual. Now these special machines are themselves made up by several tissues of very different kinds, and which really form the elements of those organs." Taking for his base the fact that these various tissues are nearly identical whether in some one animal or in another, Bichat had fairly the right to bestow on the science that studies them the name of general anatomy. Not satisfied with describing them exactly, he undertook the categorical analysis of their inmost properties. At the same time, he caught a glimpse of the function of the fundamental humors in the system.

Death did not suffer Bichat either to extend his discoveries in general anatomy, and apply them to pathology, or to draw out from them a new system of medicine. This was the work of another highly-endowed man, whose ardent disposition, amazing vigor of mind, and generalizing sagacity, made him one of the most original figures of this age. Broussais explained diseases by the alteration of the tissues. Rejecting the "imaginary entities" and "occult causes" of ancient medicine, looking for the mechanical action of morbid disturbances in the study of the functions while regular, fully understanding the value of deep, searching study into the properties of organized matter, this famous physician, by his work upon fevers, inflammations, and insanity, completely changed the teachings of his time. Reducing the essential attributes of living matter to one sole property, *irritability*, he endeavored to show how disturbances of the system depend on the increase or decrease of that. This was rather an hypothesis at a venture, which needed modification afterward; but he had gained so true an insight into the spring of vital phenomena, he had penetrated so deeply into the secret of all modes of organic activity, that the whole of medicine was illuminated by that proposition. Broussais had shown, at any rate, that disease does not occasion the appearance of new properties in the constituent parts of organs, but results from disorder in the intricate manifestation of usual properties. He had perceived that the laws of disease are only particular cases of those general laws governing the existence of animal tissues.

Blainville did not go beyond Bichat as regards the tissues, but he understood far better the action and organization of those liquid parts distinguished by the name of humors, and he added the knowledge of these to the acquisitions of general anatomy. He traced the coincident history of the tissues and the humors, both regarded as constituent and undivided parts of the system; and he threw new light upon the systems that are formed by the grouping of similar tissues. During the time of Blainville, that is, in the first third of this century, foreign *savants*, applying to the living tissues of animals the same method of observation applied by Mirbel to vegetable ones, discovered that all these tissues, far from being homogeneous, are made up by the interweaving of corpuscles different in form and kind, only visible under the microscope, and which are called anatomical elements. They brought to sight some of the cells, pores, and excessively small tubes, which thus group together to form the solid parts observable by the naked eye. Gruthuisen, Heusinger, Schleiden, Schwann, and others, thus unfolded the system of general anatomy expounded by Xavier Bichat.

Medicine of old had believed in the strangest doctrines as to the liquids of the system, and had connected them in the wildest ways with its theories upon health and disease. The Hippocratists and Galen, at a later time, supposed there were four humors, the blood, the phlegm, yellow bile, and black bile, whose due attempering supported health, while their disproportion or acridity occasioned diseases. Moderns were for a long time satisfied with these delusive views, and it was not until the eighteenth century that a true advance was made in the knowledge of the humors, thanks to the labors of the younger Rouelle. After him, Fourcroy, Vauquelin, Berzelius, Chevreul, Liebig, Dumas, Denis, etc., using the exact method of chemical investigations in the study of these interesting parts, grew acquainted with the chemical compounds, the *immediate principles* out of which they are formed. They also tried to detect and measure these principles in the organs and tissues of the system. Unfortunately, chemistry does not avail to solve all the problems of biology, and in our day we have acknowledged that chemical analysis must give precedence to anatomical analysis in researches into the composition of the machinery of the organism. In this way there came to be formed a more complete general anatomy than that of Bichat, one that embraced the study by method of animated beings, beginning with their most rudimentary component principles, and ending with those complex tissues which are the web of their organs.

II.

Every one knows how geologists decompose systems into rocks, and rocks into minerals, which are the primary elements of the earth's crust. Thus they distinguish in the igneous systems granite, syenite, gneiss, diorite, etc. They then reduce each one of these rocks to a certain number of immediate principles. Granite, for instance, will yield felspar, quartz, and mica. In like manner there are many degrees of complexity in the edifice of living beings, which are reduced by a series of analyses of a similar kind to a certain number of elements which are no less immediate principles, that is, fundamental chemical substances. Robin was one of the first to understand the need of organizing, systematically, our knowledge of these ingredients, these materials for all vital elaboration and all organic construction.

Ancient chemistry admitted, without question, that the humors and tissues of the system are made of water, oil, earth, and salt. They sometimes added sulphur, phlegm, and alkali. All this was quite vague and uninstructive. It has since been admitted that the number of immediate principles is considerably more extended, and that their composition is very intricate. The analyses of modern chemistry have settled the exact nature and the chief properties of these bodies, but have not yet reduced our knowledge of them to system. They have taught us that there exist in the system coloring matters, albuminoid ones, acids, salts, alkalies, alcohols, sugars, fats, and ethers. M. Robin, taking up certain hints of M. Chevreul, put the immediate principles in their true place, and classified them, while fixing their duty in the different parts of the system. These principles mark the passage from chemistry to biology. Regarded singly, in their molecular composition, their chemical function, and the transmutations they may undergo when influenced by reagents, they belong to chemistry. Looked at from the point of view of their number and their distribution in the living system, of the share they have in the growth of the animal's organs and fluids, of the peculiarities they present according to ages, species, and morbid conditions, they belong to general anatomy. Robin has pointed out how they become grouped and transformed in the cycle of life.[1]

The immediate principles, gathered in a fixed order, and with a peculiar structure, form corpuscles of different kinds, but always extremely fine and delicate, only visible with the aid of highly-magnifying microscopes, and which are called *anatomical elements*. These elements, placed in contact and intertangled in a thousand ways, form the tissues of the organs, and it is essentially in them that all the forces of the living being dwell. More complex than some of the infusoria (monads, amœbæ), they stand as tiny organisms composing in federation the organism of the individual. Thus the physiological simplifications of modern science have no other object than, by processes of sagacious analysis, to seize upon these active monads that are counted by myriads. These are the simple bodies of biology, not less indispensable for the clear rendering of vital facts than those which the genius of Lavoisier has the honor of discovering were to the understanding of chemical facts. Among the anatomical elements a distinction is made between cells, fibres, and tubes. Cells are spheroidal corpuscles, polyhedral or disk shaped, having very nearly equal dimensions in every direction, varying from five thousandths to one-tenth of the thousandth part of a metre. They are formed of a mass as a base, seldom having a cavity, but often with one or several nuclei distinguishable within it, which are sometimes provided with secondary nuclei. These elements are the ones most generally distributed through the system. The cellular shape belongs indeed to the red and white globules of the blood, to the elements of the bones and their marrow, to those of the central nerve-substance and the ganglions, to those of the

[1] *See*, on this subject, the introduction to my book on "The Humors."

epidermis, etc. The shape of the different cells varies very much in different species. Some of them even assume very odd forms. The multipolar cells of the central nerve-substance resemble polypi with singular arms. Others are star-shaped, others spindle-formed, etc. The fibres have the shape of a narrow ribbon, lengthened out and very thin, sometimes inclosing one or several nuclei. The fundamental elements of the muscles are fibres of two kinds: those of organic life, which are smooth, and varying in length between six-hundredths of one-thousandth of a millimetre and five-tenths of the same dimension; and those of the animal life, which are striated and very much smaller. The conjunctiva tissue and the elastic tissue are also made up from special fibres. Those elements having the shape of tubes are the perineura, which wraps the primal elements of the nerve-tubes in the nerves of animal life, and in the white filaments of the great sympathetic nerve; the myolemma, which surrounds the primal fibres of the muscles of animal life; the capillary vessels, the tubes of the glands, and the parenchyma, and last the nerve-tubes. These latter, which make up the larger part of the nerves, have a diameter varying from one-hundredth of a millimetre to one ten-thousandth of that dimension. Mirbel wrote, in 1835, that the cells or "utricles" are so many living individuals, each enjoying the property of growing, of multiplying, of certain limited modifications, working in common for the building up of the plant of which they become themselves constituent materials. He added, as Turpin had already expressed it in 1818, that the plant is thus a *collective being*. We can now say the same thing of the animal. It too is a collective being, made up by the agglomeration of the fibres, tubes, and cells, which we have just described. We are only federations of anatomical elements.

Until the time of Robin, the anatomical elements had

THE GENERAL CONSTITUTION OF LIVING BEINGS. 71

been more or less confounded with the tissues. Neither their function nor their biological characteristics had been defined. Phenomena had been explained without ascending to those corpuscles which are the seat of their beginning. This *savant* regarded them for the first time as properly forming the subject of a special branch of anatomy. Besides, he discovered a certain number of them which had till then escaped microscopic observation—the perineura in the nerves, the medullocele and myeloplax in the marrow of the bones; he disclosed the unknown functions of several others, such as the leucocytes, the nerve-cellules of the ganglia, the different epithelia; in a word, he shed new light upon the history of all by describing the peculiarities of their origin and development.

Nothing is more instructive and attractive than the study of the anatomical elements. They are invisible to our eyes, but they are not the less the glowing centres in which the fire of life burns. It is in and by them that it begins and grows; it is in them that those fundamental attributes one after another appear, which occasion the highest manifestations of animal existence. Real microcosms, each living with its own self-subsisting life, they are endowed with essential properties which explain all vital acts. Their composition from immediate principles is quite complex. It is as inconstant as their structure is delicate: subject to an incessant molecular renewal, assimilating constantly new materials, and constantly getting rid of a part of their substance, they are in a state of permanent transmutation. This perpetual renovation is exactly *nutrition*, the positive mark of organized beings. No life without nutrition. The lowly vibrio nourishes itself as the most complete mammal does; the meanest mould-spot as the gigantic cedar. All other properties of living bodies are subordinated to this one, which is their first condition, and the most specific sign of life. Another characteristic of the anatomical elements is *evolution*, quite distinct from nutrition. These little bodies, at the instant when they make their appearance, are not like what they are about to be at a later time. The more remotely from the moment of their birth we consider them, the more different is the aspect we observe them to present from that they formerly had. They gain a larger bulk, and complicate themselves with new parts, with more perfect forms, which will vanish in their turn, so that every element thus describes a curve of evolution, of which the apex, representing the full-grown state, is reached more or less rapidly.

If nutrition and evolution belong to all anatomical elements, contractility is the privileged mark of a very small number among them. It is peculiar to muscular fibres, in which it presents two modes: In the striated muscular fibres of animal life, it is sudden and quick; in the smooth fibres of organic life, it takes place slowly. It is upon this property that all movement and locomotion depend, since it is that which gives force to the muscles.

Innervation is the peculiarity of the nerve-elements. Its manifestations are complex and diversified, but it is specially marked above all by this fact, that, far from limiting its play to a local action, it radiates from a distance and carries its influence far along. The nerve-cell, in fact, finds in the nerve-tubes issuing from it, in the congenerate cell which is appended to it, either conducting apparatus, designed to carry off the force which it produces, or a true receiving apparatus, designed to store up that force, and propel it at a distance under another form. A real electro-dynamic pair, as M. Luys has so well expressed it, the nerve arrangement thus reduced to its simplest expression, itself engenders the force which it transmits afar. It conducts, receives, and transforms it in the manner of those machines for electric transmission which represent, in the apparatus for generating electricity, the emitting cell in the interposed wire, the nerve-tube, and in the cell placed at the other end of the tube the receiving apparatus intended to record and to translate into a new form the original impulse. This force, sometimes centripetal, in the form of sensitiveness, sometimes centrifugal, in the shape of thought, is also both at once as an impulse to movement. But the most characteristic thing there is in these acts of innervation is, their spontaneousness. The nerve-cells have the property of retaining the impression of outward agents that have affected them, and of remaining for a greater or less length of time in that condition in which they have been artificially placed. Thus, in the physical order, light imparts to bodies it has touched for a moment a real activity, and makes them *phosphorescent* for a longer or shorter time. This fitness to keep external impressions stored up, which is the privilege almost exclusively of the nerve-cells, may continue in the latent state an indefinite time, may at length be lost, and not reveal itself promptly except under the evoking power of the first impression, or, it may be, under that of the surrounding cells, which are in some sort new centres of secondary stimulations. Just as we see bodies which had become phosphorescent by effect of exposure to the sun insensibly lose that property, and regain it by the help of some other source of phosphorescence— heat, for example—so the receptivity of cells may be restored either under the influence of the first cause, or that of some other source of stimulation. Let us remark once more, and this is precisely the most important point in cerebral innervation, that cells once agitated by contact with outward impressions do not stop with this. The state in which they find themselves after their impregnation by the outward impression, and which M. Luys compares to phosphorescence, spreads on and imparts itself, and proceeds, by a succession of intermediate agitations, to arouse the beginning of action in new groups of cells situated at other poles, and which combine with the first in exciting in their turn new impulses. Such are the chief noticeable ways in which innervation makes its appearance and fulfills its action; a property which, rudimentary, and hardly to be detected in the lower animals, rises in the higher ones, and lifts them, too, to so lofty a degree of perfection. Whatever may be, as to the rest, the first cause of the most striking acts of our life, of the affections and the intellect, we feel, will, imagine, and understand, only through the means of these nerve-corpuscles distributed through our system, and endowed with that power, not paralleled elsewhere, of receiving, transmitting, perceiving, storing away, and modifying impressions.

This, then, is one first and fundamental lesson yielded by the study of the anatomical elements; the play of animal organisms is reduced to four simple essential modes of action: nutrition, evolution, contractility, and innervation. At once distinct and combined, sometimes intricately intermingled, sometimes visibly separate, consubstantial with those anatomical elements by which their existence is made known, capable of putting on various and manifold appearances, these properties are the springs of all living mechanisms. In machines produced by man's industry, one single force goes through many forms to accomplish the most various effects. In animals, several different forces have for their business, in the midst of a thousand entanglements and intricacies, to insure the perpetuation of the species through the full working of the individual.

We are thus led to speak of the generation of the anatomical elements. This question is one of twofold gravity: In the first place, it abounds in difficulties of every kind, so extremely subtile are the observations in the case, so prompt the senses to be misled, so ready the mind to be deceived. Then it borders on the most formidable problems, not merely of general anatomy, but also of natural philosophy, since it is mixed with the study of the production of organized beings generally. Robin's researches have contributed in large measure to the advance of knowledge as to these obscure phenomena.

Every organized substance, which is nourished and developed, effects the appearance of new anatomical elements in its neighborhood. It tends to create new forms and new activity about it. One element may engender another like it by segmentation, that is, by breaking up into two or several parts. In cells with nuclei, we observe first the breaking up of the nucleus, and then the *individualization* of the contents of the cell about the little secondary nuclei thus formed. So a cell is the point of origin of three or four new cells, each of which becomes the seat of exactly the same phenomenon. There is, in this case, a sort of partitioning off effected in the contents of the cell in the course of its growth. A second mode of production of anatomical elements is *gemmation*. In this case there forms at one of the points of the parent element a bulge, or hernia, from which results another element distinct from the first. And this proceeding, like that of segmentation, is much more like a reproduction than a birth.

Let us consider the third mode. In this the anatomical elements are born in full completeness within and at the expense of a living liquid, issuing from already-existing anatomical elements. This liquid, called *blastema*, is made up of immediate principles, which proceed from a transudation of the organized substance, into the interstices of which it flows. The blastema is eminently the fertilizing liquid, the secret region in which are condensed the creative forces of life, making themselves evident by a continuous elaboration of cells, fibres, and tubes, which are the rudiments of tissues and organs. In it a very tiny nucleus at first makes its appearance, which little by little envelops itself with solidified matter, that ends by gaining a fixed shape and a special structure. The elements of the tissue of plants form in the same way within a mucilaginous liquid called *cambium*, and in which the most improved instruments detect nothing but shapeless matter. There are as many different blastemas as there are tissues; in other words, the anatomical elements of each tissue exude between them those generative fluids whence similar elements spring. We shall presently have occasion to notice some interesting instances of this.

This hatching of living molecules in the mass of blastema, proved by Robin's numberless experiments, confirmed by those of many other *savants*,[1] is a true *spontaneous generation*. In fact, organized corpuscles are here developed without germs or parents, in the midst of a liquid in which, a few moments earlier, nothing would authorize us to foretell their appearance. Only this liquid results from a living organism, that is, one whose elementary particles are themselves in course of ceaseless molecular renewal. Beyond these facts we have not been able to prove absolutely that beings, even microscopic ones, can be produced simply by the concurrence of physico-chemical forces. The numerous experiments which have occasioned within a few years so hot and passionate controversies, prove that a liquid or an infusion observed in the vessels of a laboratory remains absolutely barren as long as it is guarded from contact with germs and spores conveyed by the atmosphere. This result, demonstrated by M. Pasteur, demolishes all the arguments called up in support of heterogenesis.

The three modes of birth that we have just examined are the very modes of generation of living beings, since these invariably begin by anatomical elements. To give a clearer idea of these very curious operations of Nature, let us see what takes place in the organized granule which is

[1] *See* the late works of Messrs. Onimus, Feltz, and others.

the starting-point of the formation and development of the embryo, that is, in the ovule. We shall there point out these three modes at work.

The ovule is a little globule, from one to two tenths of a millimetre in diameter, that is, as large as a grain of sand that can but just be seen. It is made up of an enveloping sphere, called the vitelline membrane, in which is found a semi-liquid gelatinous matter, to which the name of *vitellus*[1] is given. The vitellus in its turn presents a sort of nucleus which is the *germinating vesicle*, or that of *Purkinje*. Thus the ovule offers to view at the outset the marks of a true cell, but it gains, while developing, a structure and dimensions that soon distinguish it from one, and make of it a special organ. When it has reached the period of maturity, the germinating vesicle disappears, and its substance mingles with that of the vitellus. At the same time the latter shrinks upon itself, and contracts. There comes between it and the wall of the vitelline membrane a space which fills up with a clear liquid. It is at this moment that the phenomenon of *fecundation* occurs, which is owing to the penetration of the spermatozoa, which make their way into the newly-formed space that we have mentioned. Then the vitellus loses shape, and for several minutes goes through a series of very varied gyratory motions, which Robin has studied. Simultaneously the spermatozoa—which are, as Robin has proved, true anatomical elements proceeding from male ovules, analogous to the embryonic cells of the female ovules—dissolve, and thus mingle the substance of one parent with that of the other, which they impregnate. There is then remarked a very curious fact, also discovered and studied

---

[1] Birds' eggs contain their ovule in the centre, the development of which, instead of taking place by means of materials provided directly by the mother, is made at the expense of materials contained in the egg, that is, the white and the yelk.

by Robin, the production of *polar globules*. These globules are little prominences which rise by *gemmation* on the surface of the vitellus. They mark the point at which the depression of the latter, and then its breaking up, will afterward begin. At the same time a new nucleus, the vitelline nucleus, is born complete, by spontaneous generation, in the depths of the primitive mass. This nucleus breaks up and divides into several nuclei, about which the substance of the vitellus forms separate groups, and there thus arise cells which proceed, by ranging themselves close against the wall of the vitelline membrane, to form another membrane, called the *blastoderma*. This segmentation of the vitellus, discovered in 1824 by Prévost and Dumas, is exceedingly important, seeing that the first elements of the embryo proceed immediately from blastodermic cells. It must be remarked that in insects and spiders, as Robin has discovered, the vitellus does not split up. In these little beings the cells of the blastoderma are formed by gemmation of the surface portion of the vitellus; that is to say, the polar globules, instead of being developed at one single point of the latter, make their appearance over its whole surface, to compose the blastodermic membrane. In brief, the essential mechanism of generation is reduced to the following succession of phenomena, taking place in the depths of the ovule or of the egg within a time which varies from twelve to twenty-four hours: 1. The disappearance of the germinating vesicle; 2. Shrinking of the vitellus; 3. Penetration by the spermatozoa; 4. Loss of form and gyration by the vitellus; 5. Production of the polar globules by gemmation; 6. Origin of the vitelline nucleus by genesis; 7. Splitting up of the vitellus; 8. Composition of the blastoderma; 9. Formation of the embryonic dot; 10. Appearance of the first definite elements of the embryo. As we see, the new being, formed of well-constituted anatomical elements, has received none of them from its mother. The materials that have acted together in the gradual production of these elements have come to it only molecule by molecule, through the enveloping membranes.

Robin's doctrine with regard to the production of anatomical elements within blastemas is not accepted by some German physicians, who persist in maintaining the *cellular theory*, established in vegetable physiology about 1838 by Schleiden, and extended later by Schwann to animal physiology. This theory admits that all the anatomical elements of animals proceed from a succession of direct transformations of the cell. One single primordial cell is the source of the most dissimilar elements, nerve-elements, muscle-elements, etc. The cell springs from the cell by *proliferation;* the other elements spring from it by *metamorphosis*. The most complex organism thus results, through a series of varied transfigurations, from one simple rudimentary ovule. It is, as we see, the doctrine of Lamarck and of Darwin, applied to the genesis of the embryo. The question is important. It has lately given rise to celebrated discussions, and perhaps it is as well to consider it briefly here.

Omnis cellula e cellula, say the partisans of Schwann's theory. That might be readily granted, if the system contained none but similar cells; but there is in it a great number of elements so distinct that the mind cannot comprehend how some of them could be emitted by the rest. It refuses to allow, for instance, that leucocytes, which water attacks and acetic acid dissolves, proceed, by *proliferation*, either from neuclei of cellular tissue or from epithelial nuclei, which those reagents do not affect. We can hardly believe that sons are so very unlike their fathers. We can form no idea how muscular fibres and nerve-tubes can issue from globules that bear no resemblance whatever to them, either as regards composition or as regards properties. Besides, such a relationship has never been directly proved. It is very plainly seen that cells which have become individualized by splitting up, are the seat of a division which gives rise to other cells; but that only occurs when the mother-cells have gained or exceeded their complete development and their regular dimensions. Now this fact, which has been taken as the starting-point of the cellular theory, is a mere phenomenon of evolution, and not a fact of production. The inventors of that theory, for want of observing closely and continuously enough, have quite as widely misunderstood what takes place when we see certain anatomical elements succeed to others of a different kind, as in the case of the liquefaction of one set of elements, and then the formation of a blastema in which the second set is produced. This is a real genesis by substitution, as Robin calls it, and not a direct emission, a proliferation, as is taught in the schools across the Rhine. In this case there are several phases which have escaped the observation of the too systematic doctors of Berlin and Wurzburg, but which French *savants* have settled in a way not to be gainsaid, not being blinded, like the former, by a preconceived idea. What these same Germans call *endogenous generation*, that is, generation within a cell, is quite as much an exceptional mode of production of anatomical elements, but one that in no way contradicts those we have enumerated, and in no way avails to prop up Schwann's theory. The cellular theory is a doctrine as delusive as it is convenient and attractive. It is one of the numerous mistakes introduced into German science by that philosophy of Nature so highly relished by the contemporaries of Schelling and Oken, and of which the traces are to be found in the works of many eminent *savants* of Germany even at this day. Flattering as it is to that inclination by which we are led to the desire to confound things the most disparate in one chimerical unity, it is not surprising that such a philosophy should so long have imposed upon minds that took every thing to be real except the reality itself.

Some biologists of the same school have been led by a similar mistake to the notion of a supposed property inherent in living tissues, the peculiarity of which is the power they have of setting up action under the most varying influences. They have given this property the name of *irritability*, the same peculiarity formerly regarded by Broussais as a specific one, and used by him as the mainstay of his theory. This irritability, neither specific nor spontaneous, is nothing else than the manifestation of one of the five fundamental properties of organized substance. At least it is always reducible to that, as Robin has shown, and could not from any point of view be regarded as a new property. The anatomical elements are in a state of incessant transformation, and therefore the least thing may disturb their equilibrium, and bring about what is called irritation. Let a single atom of their mass experience a derangement of any kind, the remainder of them undergoes its reaction, and all the properties of the element are differently affected. Heat, cold, electricity, chemical substances, in a word, any causes that can affect the molecular condition of the elements, thus act on organized substance. It is the instability in a system of such restless and fleeting changes which makes it so quick to feel all influences, so irritable; but, we repeat, irritants call forth in it nothing more than the exhibition of the properties we have mentioned.

"Cleave an atom," the Persian poet says, "and you will find in it a sun." So the anatomical element, examined in its deepest recesses, yields us the magnificent vision of life. It unveils for us its secret machinery, its hidden energies, its latent springs, its concealed forces; teachings full of light, which have transformed the conceptions of philosophy regarding the world of life.

III.

Thus we are brought back again, after a rather long circuit, to the *tissues* of Bichat. In fact, it is by the piling together or the interlacing in a thousand cross-ways that these tissues are formed, and they in turn mingle to compose organs. The study of the tissues, or *histology*, is no doubt that portion of anatomy which, by its amazing and priceless revelations, has most strongly attracted contemporary physicians and physiologists. The number of anatomical elements that come together to make up a given portion of tissue, could no more be computed than that of the grains of sand on the sea-shore. When we think that these elements, having the shape of cells, tubes, and fibres, are measured by thousandths of the thousandth part of a metre, it is clear that a shred of skin or muscle, a bit of brain or bone, contains immense quantities of them. However, this question is only one of secondary interest. What it is important to know is, the arrangement of these elements and the order in which they combine to compose the tissue; in a word, it is the *texture* of it. Apart from the tissue-*products*, which result from merely bringing anatomical elements of the same kind into contact, all the other tissues present one sort of element called *fundamental*, because it predominates, and gives the tissue its chief properties, while also it is associated with other sorts, which are called *accessory*. Tissue-products thus present the simplest degree of texture, and in their normal condition contain no vessels. Of this number are the epidermis or epithelial tissue, the tissue of nails and horns, which are formed wholly of epithelial cells, the crystalline tissue, which is made up of fibres arranged in concentric layers, etc. The other tissues, that is, by far the majority of the whole, present a very complicated texture. Several distinct sorts of anatomical elements are in these associated in definite grouping. The part fulfilled by the tissue is the sum of the properties inherent in each sort of element, while the characteristics of the fundamental element predominate. The accessory elements in a manner restrain the too great activity of this latter, and thus take part in giving to the tissue properties of a secondary order indeed, but indispensable to the discharge of its duty, which is thus the result of manifold properties. When the texture of these organic webs is studied under a microscope, we are often astonished at the prodigious complexity they exhibit. Nothing is so curious as the disposition and arrangement of all these tiny centres of life, some round, others polyhedric, others thread-like, others again tubular, and all so small that the humblest flesh-worm is a monster beside them. Sometimes the fibres are tangled inextricably, like dense ivy around an aged trunk; sometimes there is a singular net, formed by the capillaries with fine meshes, in which the cells crowd and crush themselves out of shape. Sometimes we find clusters in which little bladders are arranged along a crooked channel; sometimes there are layers, piled one on another, resembling geological strata. In a word, the arrangement of the elements is exceedingly diversified, and, if we might say that the tissues are words in which anatomical elements stand for the letters, it must be added that the order of the latter is much more complicated than is the case with the terms of spoken language, and very differently too.

The nerve-tissue, the real masterpiece of vital force, has been well understood only since histology has disclosed to us all the elements of that fragile whitish pulp. The structure of the ganglia, the connections they have with the nerves, the difference between nerve-tubes and nerve-cells, have been made out by Robin. He it was, too, who discovered the lymphatic vessels of the brain-substance. These lymphatics encircle the blood-vessels traversing the central nerve-tissues in such a way that the latter are completely sheathed in the former. The lymph circulates with its globules between the inner surface of the lymphatic and the outer surface of the capillary, which occupies the centre. The texture of the marrow of the bones, the placenta, the umbilical vesicle, the skin, the arteries, the pancreas, has been illuminated with strong light by the investigations of the same observer. It may even be said that, of the thirty tissues of the system, there is not one whose nature is not better understood through his labors. And this work performed has suggested another to him: we mean the comparison of the same organic parts with each other at different times in their existence; that is to say, the establishment of general comparative anatomy. In this vast field of histological comparison, so little explored before his time, Robin has collected many precious truths for the general science of biology.

We have seen that the normal tissues of the organism consist of a fundamental anatomical element and of a certain number of accessory elements. Medical art has gained wholly unexpected light from the discovery of this order of facts. The works of modern micrographers, particularly those of Hannover, Lebert, Virchow, Robin, Broca, Follin, etc., have proved, in fact, that all morbid growths, and especially those known under the names of tumors, cysts, polypi, cancers, tubercles, and scirrhous growths, proceed merely from the superabundant, excessive formation of some one of these accessory elements. It is now demonstrated that those new formations, so often repulsive in appearance, and concealing the seeds of death, contain nothing which is foreign to the organization in its sound state, and are not characterized by any peculiar substance produced under the influence of the disease. They are due sometimes to *hypergenesis*, that is, to an unusual collection of some accessory element taking part in the regular composition of the tissue in which they are developed; sometimes to the *heterotopy* of some other element, that is, to the appearance of that element where it is not usually produced. Cancer, for instance, that terrible cancer, gnawing and spreading, is wholly composed—who would have believed it?—of an excessive development of epithelial cells identical with those of our skin, or differing from them only by slight peculiarities whose origin is easily explained. Phthisis, that terrible scourge which decimates our race, is caused by the development of a matter called tuberculous, composed of epithelial embryoplastic nuclei, become granular and fatty, and mixed with spindle-shaped bodies, all of them elements that are formed in the system in the usual state. The lungs are thus attacked and destroyed by products of a cheesy appearance, made by the effect of the same law that governs normal products, but under different conditions. *Heterotopy* discloses to us other phenomena equally extraordinary. There have been found in the ovary cysts containing in their inner wall a true skin, furnished with papillæ, epidermis, hairy follicles, hairs, and perspiratory glands. Teeth have even been found developing in the abdomen. All these organs are accidentally produced in those regions, having by fortuitous concourse found the circumstances favorable to their appearance all existing there. Robin has remarked, in the neighborhood of certain glands of the body, the formation of small masses consisting wholly of tissue identical with that of the breast. So, too, late experiments by Ollier and Goujon, confirming those of Flourens, have taught us that bones may be produced at any points in the system to which periosteum or fresh marrow is taken, in the stomach, for instance. This singular production of bony substance has not yet been observed taking place spontaneously, but it is easy to effect it by experiment on animals.

The formation of the tissue of a scar is nothing else than a renovation of the layer-tissue of the skin; and all the tissues, excepting one only, may thus be renewed in the system, when they have been destroyed in it by any process, and they are reproduced in accordance with the same rules that govern their appearance and their development in the embryo state. Robin, who has expressed this law, extends it to the production of morbid tissues also. Besides the restoration of the tissues, the naturalist notes also that of some organs. The famous experiments of Spallanzani have placed beyond question the reproduction of the limbs and tail of the salamander. The restoration of the tails of lizards has been always known, only that no vertebræ had been remarked in the newly-formed appendage. Charles Legros has lately found that vertebræ do appear in it at the end of two years after amputation. He has also effected the complete reproduction of the eyes and of a part of the head of salamanders, from which he had cut off the entire head with scissors, only sparing the brain. He has also procured the new growth of a tail in dormice; but he did not succeed in keeping the animals long enough to give the vertebræ time to make their appearance within the organ.

These phenomena show us one and the same law governing the various exhibitions of the power of evolution, in disease as in health. We find in the facts, already well known, of animal-grafting, other remarkable proofs of that power. Bert's experiments have shown, from a new point of view, how certain animal organs may be removed from place, and transferred to a part of the system which is not their original home, and may yet continue living there. We may even transfer and graft tissues from one kind of animal upon another kind; we may inject the blood-globules of one animal into the veins of an animal of another species, and these globules in that new place discharge their peculiar function. There are cases in which animals, and men also, brought by loss of blood into a state of seeming death, have been restored to life by the transfusion of blood from a being of the same species of either sex; we know, moreover, that calves' blood and lambs' blood have been injected into the veins of men who have lived after it; that the case has been the same in the instance of the transfusion of human blood into a dog, of that from a sheep and a calf into a dog, from a calf to a sheep and a chamois, and in the case of transfusion from a dog, a rabbit, or a Guinea-pig, to a hen and a cock. These phenomena of physiology, added to the results of anatomical observations, leave no doubt as to the specific identity of the elements in the entire animal series.

This acknowledged identity in the solids extends also to the liquids of the living system, and these liquids are parts not less indispensable for the complete effect of vital phenomena. Formed by the mixture of very many immediate principles dissolved by each other's help in water, and holding suspended often one, two, or three kinds of anatomical elements, the humors are more complicated than those elements, while they are less so than the tissues. For a long time the exclusive property of chemists, the study of the humors, thanks to Robin, has once more taken its natural and proper place in the series of anatomical studies. These moving organs are studied with the same system, by the same processes, and in the same spirit of subordination to physiological and pathological experiences, as the firm and immovable organs placed in a fixed position.

Robin has thus done for the humors what he had already done for immediate principles and anatomical elements. He has put them in their true place, has classified them and pointed out their function in the generality of organic acts. He divides animal liquids into three classes: the *constituent humors*, the *secretions*, and the *excretions*. And there is a positive satisfaction for the mind in the picture he gives us of the relations of these three classes in the system of vital operations. The constituent humors, the blood, chyle, and lymph, conveying throughout into the inmost parts of the tissues and organs those materials of nutrition designed to be assimilated, and that oxygen fitted to aid the work of assimilation, are eminently the vivifying fluids. They bathe the whole system, they pour into it ceaselessly new stores of strength and warmth, they maintain it in its harmonious and perfect working. They are true organic *media*, intervening between the external medium surrounding the individual, and the anatomical elements lodged deep within the body. They are organized, and have the faculty of nutrition, that is, their substance is molecularly renewed in a continuous way. While the secretions, and the excretions particularly, are liquids devoid of life, made by the glands and the parenchyma at the expense of the blood, the blood, so to speak, creates itself with the materials it receives as well by way of the lungs as by that of the whole digestive canal. The blood is a laboratory in which the most varied and elusive transformations take place, in very minute intervals of time—so minute that it is impossible for the biologist's vision to seize all their phases, and follow their headlong successive course. The whole of chemistry of which we have any knowledge unfolds itself in this laboratory; but another chemistry also moves there in incessant action, of whose laws we can but gain a glimpse. In fact, those immediate principles which pass into the blood in the form of fatty substance, of sugary and of albuminoid matter, and pass out of it under the form of cholesterine, leucine, tyrosine, urea, creatine, etc., do not pass instantly from one state to another. During all the course of combustion sustained by breathing they undergo a thousand isomeric modifications and specific changes, of which we know nothing. We seize only the beginning and the end of the phenomenon, but the middle course of it evades our view.

Not one organic molecule in it is identical with itself for two successive instants. There is going on there, in those myriads of capillaries, a work of which we have no conception. These metamorphoses are real chemical equations in action, they are life's mathematical series, analogous to those studied by the infinitesimal calculus. When shall the Leibnitz come who will reveal to us the analytical processes we may apply to that burning blood?

However that may be, this mobility of the sanguine fluid is precisely what makes it capable of undergoing modifications of every kind under the influence of miasmatic matters sometimes contained in the air. The albuminoid substance, which is the fundamental part of the blood-compound, readily comes into union with poisonous molecules originating without, and, when one point is once affected, the change passes on from neighbor to neighbor, molecule to molecule, throughout the mass. The blood, and after it the most unstable tissues, thus suffer an isomeric modification which unfits them to discharge their normal functions, and often induces death. In the instance of cholera, especially, the albumen of the blood undergoes a transformation which makes it unable to remain united with the water that keeps it fluid, and brings about its coagulation in the vessels. The fatal consequence is the stoppage of circulation, respiration, and all other vital actions. Robin has also developed very forcibly the idea that there is no such thing as virus, but merely humors grown virulent, which are to healthy humors what common and noxious phosphorus is to red harmless phosphorus, and we know that these two bodies have the same chemical nature. No doubt the secret of virulent and contagious or epidemic diseases, so numerous and so formidable, is nevertheless still undiscovered, but at least we shall now know the direction that it is proper to give to researches, and the true meaning of those that may be made.

The case with morbid humors is the same as with morbid tissues. They are derived from healthy humors by similar processes, and they contain no principles foreign to the system—only they are produced in places where they should not be produced, and in a proportion which accounts for the disorders they bring on. The fluids of the various dropsies, for instance, proceed from hypergenesis of normal serous products, which are extracted from the blood by serous membranes, such as the pleura and the peritoneum. Pus is formed by a blastema issuing from the subcutaneous cellular tissue, and within which the white globules originate.[1] The contents of the various liquid cysts are similarly produced at the expense of the blood-plasma by a true hypersecretion. These morbid humors do not rid the system of some subtile and noxious principle, as it used to be taught; they form under the effect of an alteration of the blood, of some disturbance of circulation, or of irregularity in the acts either of secretion or of excretion.

Ancient physiology and ancient medicine have by turns preached solidism and humorism, that is to say, the exclusive predominance either of the solids or of the fluids, in the effecting of vital phenomena. Neither of these systems is sustained by facts. The tissues and the humors play equally active and important parts in the organism, and disease has its source in the alterations which occur in the latter, as well as in disturbances affecting the

---

[1] Some authors who had heretofore believed that globules of pus grow by proliferation out of the elements of the tissue called the conjunctive, have of late found themselves obliged to give up that explanation, which conformed too to the cellular theory, and they have adopted another extremely ingenious one, which consists in assuming that these globules come from the blood, without, however, having ever proved how they are produced in that blood. Besides, they forget too to explain how, in certain cases, collections of pus form in which there are five or six times as many leucocytes as there were in the whole mass of blood that served to form them.

former. In other words, there are diseases of humors, diseases of tissues, and diseases of anatomical elements; but this diversity vanishes when we ascend to the common cause of all morbid phenomena, when we descry the efficient and inmost source of the disturbances, that is, the quantitative or qualitative modification of the immediate principles. Thus we come back to our starting-point, and find at the end of our study the proofs of the interest connected with the subject of its beginning. In fact, real and positive experimental medicine sets out from normal immediate principles, and rises by successive degrees from the knowledge of these to the understanding of anatomical elements, tissues, humors, organs, systems. It begins with those immediate principles that are toxic, disease-producing, and medicinal; and it discovers the law of various pathogenic irregularities, as it does that of healing effects. All the animal organs and all the liquids of the system resolving themselves into immediate principles; all the metamorphoses of health and disease reducing themselves to transformations of immediate principles; all the effects of poisoning or of healing ending in the action of foreign principles upon normal principles; in a word, the most complex acts of life, whether regular or disordered, being explained, in the last analysis, by immediate principles—we may form an idea of the great importance of these. The instant that medical researches are ruled and guided by that necessity of referring facts to such a starting-point, the instant that experiments and observations converge toward that light, every thing becomes orderly, every thing finds its place, every thing gains significance. Uncertainties vanish. Science advances with regularity, and practice with assurance. In this manner general anatomy exerts an influence of a constant and wholesome kind upon the increasingly rapid progress of medicine properly so called.

IV.

What has gone before is merely an exposition of facts and phenomena of which the discovery is due, in almost all instances, to the use of the microscope, connected with the suggestions of a superior intellect. The great majority of the public knows Robin only in this way, and readily assumes that all the merit of that *savant* consists in his labors in micrography. It pictures him as a man inured to tedious and minute details, not rising above them, leaving the eye-piece of his instrument only on compulsion, with little heed for philosophizing, and systematically indifferent to doctrines. In fact, many micrographers are persons of that kind, and that is the most usual effect of too devoted an intimacy with things infinitely little. By an uncommon exception, the reverse of all this has been Robin's fate. Persistent attention to minute and tiresome realities has enlarged his mind, while enlightening it, to such a degree that his works have contributed as greatly to the advance of ideas as to the progress of facts.

Robin cherishes the thought that biology might be recast and reformed by method, that is, by the introduction of severe logic into studies upon life. Borrowing the ideas of Blainville, Auguste Comte, and Chevreul, upon this difficult subject, adding to them the fruit of his own reflections, he has reduced the mass of biological knowledge to system, in a manner that is probably definite and final. He has, in part, brought into it the same order which is employed in the simpler sciences, in chemistry, for instance, an order which consists in beginning with the most elementary, and thence ascending to the most complex. Robin puts at the foundation of biological studies the immediate principles which are the starting-point of all organization, being also the most simple compounds that exist in the organism. This division of the subject bears the name of *stœchiology*. Afterward comes the study of anatomical elements, or *elementology*. These elements, formed by the bringing into contact and the blending of immediate principles of the three classes, visible only under the microscope, and showing themselves under the form of cells, fibres, and tubes, are endowed, as we have said, with elementary vital properties: nutrition, generation, evolution, contractility, and innervation. The science of the humors, or *hygrology*, is placed at a higher degree. The organic liquids, in fact, are formed by the dissolving in water of a certain number of immediate principles, and they hold anatomical elements suspended in them. The tissues, the study of which constitutes *histology*, are more complex. They proceed from the association and intertangling of anatomical elements. With the exception of those that are called products, they all contain several kinds of anatomical elements. *Homœomerology* treats of the systems formed by the assembling of parts identical in tissue (the nervous system, the bony system). In the higher degrees comes the study of organs, then that of apparatus. Such is the methodical gradation of the parts, the totality of which is the subject of anatomy. If we add that these parts, which represent the different complications of organized matter, may be studied not only from the anatomical or static point of view strictly so called, but also from the physiological and therapeutic point of view, that is to say, in their course of action and in their relations to the media, we shall have indicated the complete frame of the science.

This, for Robin and for most biologists, is the general constitution of biology; but this system is rather a plan and a method than a doctrine. We do not learn by it either what life is in itself, or what notion we must form of the regular succession and the concordant connection of phenomena, the dedication of organs to the performance of defined acts, the permanence of types; in short, all the striking and remarkable characteristics which give so distinct an expression to organized beings. These questions have been handled by Robin with a logical exposition as original as it is learned.

Claude Bernard has written a very admirable book,[1] in which he expounds, under the name of *determinism*, the doctrine which establishes the indissoluble combination of all the conditions necessary to production of the phenomena of life. In it he demonstrates that these phenomena are rigidly fore-defined, in the sense that they are produced according to fixed and unchanging laws, as express as those which govern the mineral world, and that no intermeddling of caprice could disturb the order imposed by these laws. For the illustrious physiologist there is no such thing as a *vital principle* any more than there is a *mineral principle*, that is, an entity distinct from the phenomena themselves. Yet he admits that, from the moment of the appearance of the earliest elements of the embryo, the evolution of these phenomena does obey a law or a premeditated idea, governing by anticipation the phases of the coming existence. In a late and very remarkable work,[2] Robin has unfolded ideas quite different from these. The distinguished anatomist, supported by the views of modern embryogeny as it has been established by the Prévosts, Dumas, Coste, Reichert, and Bary, and by himself, sees in the harmony and unity of the organism the spontaneous result of the concourse of those energies peculiar to each anatomical element. He finds in it the necessary *consensus* of the unconquerable tendencies of these myriads of monads, each having by itself its part and its direction, and this view reveals to him in an unexpected light the solution of the diffi-

[1] "Introduction to Experimental Medicine," 8vo, 1867.
[2] "On the Appropriation of the Organic Parts and the Organism to the Accomplishment of Ordained Actions," 8vo, 1869.

cult questions that we have enumerated above. In his view, the ordering and adjustment of the parts flow from the very fact of the gradual formation of those parts, and of the properties inherent in them. He shows how an explanation is to be found in the simultaneous operation of properties consubstantial with the elements, in the logical connection of generative, evolutionary, and nutritive acts, of all that had been heretofore attributed to the presence of a so-called vital principle.

The hypothesis of a vital principle which coördinates and rules the phenomena of life seems to contradict the fact, in this sense, that it is in the first place impossible to fix the exact moment at which this principle intervenes. We have the ovule—that is, a mere simple anatomical element, containing the vitellus. That ovule is already endowed with life while it is still dependent on the ovary. By an uninterrupted and inevitable chain of progress other anatomical elements unfold in it, in an ordained sequence, from the moment that it ceases to be part of the ovary until the moment that the embryo is formed. This latter comes forth in the embryonic dot in the same way as the vitelline nucleus does in the vitellus. Each element, by the very fact of its existence and of the performance of the part peculiar to it, here becomes the condition of existence of other elements necessarily appearing in the medium which it has engendered, and conducting themselves as it has done. Therefore, at what instant and in what way could a vital principle intervene in this series of engenderings?

It being known that the whole function of the vitellus is to present in succession those conditions required for the genesis of the different elements of the embryo, and that these are parts of one whole process, it is plain that, if one of the acts of development be hindered or modified, it will no longer go on in a regular manner. Experience entirely confirms this. The slightest causes, the least deviations, whether spontaneous or occasioned, in the arrangement of the blastodermic or the embryonic cells, endanger the regular growth of the new individual, by inducing either the production of monstrosities or the death of the germ. When that is checked in its evolution, its natural envelopes continue theirs, and we find the growth of what is called a mole. In fact, the idea must be clearly fixed that the cells we have been speaking of have absolutely only a single function and a single power: that of providing the conditions required for the growth of the earliest organs of the embryo, namely, the dorsal and ventral layers. These layers are, in their turn, the starting-point for the dorsal cord, which ends in the appearance of the two halves of the central nerve-axis. Then come, after the vertebral cartilages, the eyes and auditory vesicles, the heart, the veins, the blood, etc. Every one of these organs becomes, on making its appearance, the cause of the generation of the next, so that, if any circumstance disturbs or puts an end to the production or the development of the former, the latter either does not show itself, or else comes out as a monstrosity. In the case of trout, salmon, and pike, seventy or eighty per cent. of the eggs, artificially fertilized, die. Lereboullet, to whom we are indebted for this investigation, also points out that out of a hundred eggs hatched the number of monsters produced varies between two and five. The human being is subject to the same accidents. In three thousand births, there are always at least two hundred still-born in Paris and half as many in the rest of France, and among a hundred still-born an average is found of one monster not viable. Independently of the still-born, we find in the human race a number of congenital anomalies, which, though they do not threaten life, do often shorten it and make it difficult, by interfering with the regular exercise of its functions. Cretinism, idiocy, deaf-

and-dumbness, hydrocephale, double spine, extrophy of the bladder, imperforate state or absence of the latter vessel, anomalies of the heart, the genital organs, etc., are thus irregular actions of the power of evolution as common as they are painful.

These facts seem to prove the futility of that hypothesis of a moulding principle controlling the ovule and the embryo, and fashioning them after its will, in conformity with a premeditated law. They prove too that the birth of the new being consists in a series of births upon births, instead of being effected, as some naturalists have supposed, by the successive transformation of parts preëxisting in the ovule. That doctrine of the encasement of germs, or of *syngenetic preformation*, by which it is conceded that the germs of all coming generations were contained in one primordial egg, that is to say, that the ovule contains potentially every thing that will exist later in the organism—that theory, maintained by Leibnitz, Kant, and several other philosophers and naturalists, seems therefore to be in opposition to observations on the production of the embryo.

Very clearly the phenomena of evolution and of organization are subject to a law which is expressed by the limits fixed to evolution, and by the form fixed for the organs. This law is not invariable, as the study of diseases and of monstrosities shows; and, even if it were so, nothing gives authority for supposing that it has an origin anterior or exterior to living beings, any more than for inferring it from the mechanism of atoms. Very clearly, in the succession of anatomical growths, there is a gradual creation, and in the series of physiological functions there is a distinct direction; but what boldness it is to infer thence the existence of a creating idea and of a directing idea! Have we any right thus to assign objective reality to the abstractions of our mind? Besides, in what manner, and by what mode of comparison with known things, could we represent the influence of such ideas upon organic materials? The intrinsic, sufficient, and determining cause of vital phenomena, we are forced to confess, after the demonstration Robin gives of them, lies in the properties themselves of organized substance. These phenomena are equations of a very high order, infinitely complicated formulas, of which these properties are the first factors, which we cannot reduce. In a word, anatomical elements have in themselves their principles of action and direction, exactly as the mineral molecules which form crystals have in themselves the principle of the harmony which they produce. The external form, that is to say, the contour, just as the internal form, that is, the organization, is the consequence of spontaneous principles of energy peculiar to the ultimate particles of life. As to the *principle of these principles*, their first cause, impenetrable darkness hides it from our sight.

No doubt, when we cast the first glance on the totality of animated beings, it is with difficulty that we resist the thought that a breath as intelligent as mighty has communicated itself to them, impregnates, vivifies, and urges them in a course of which it knows the end (*mens agitat molem*). Seeing the most perfect and delicate organs grow out of a coarse and shapeless-looking pulp, we are almost irresistibly driven to look on high for the workman of that amazing fabrication. But if the mind be ever so little penetrating, it must soon give up its first momentary illusion in presence of the testimony of facts. If it takes the trouble to go to the bottom of things, and to exhaust their details; if it chooses to follow step by step the development of life in the ovule and the embryo, to study the functions of the system, in healthy animals and in diseased animals, it will recognize the spontaneity and the activity of the natural forces acting in themselves and by themselves in eternal continuous movement. The clear perception of faint and commencing activities rising to the condition of harmonious systems, and unfolding into productive energies, will be a complete revelation to it. This new mode of regarding things, by which we set out from the small, the imperfect, and the relative, to reach the great, the perfect, and the absolute, will seem like a reminder of the philosophy of Leibnitz. The especial virtues of elementary corpuscles engendering a whole superior to them, by those very virtues, will recall to the mind his *monadology*. It will conceive of unity in combination and not in confusion. All that is and lives on the surface of our planet will rise before it in distinct vision as the result of numberless and complicated groupings of simple phenomena, in which the consubstantiality of form and of force is manifest. "In eternal despair of knowing either the beginning or the end," as Pascal says, the mind will be content with grasping the most certain and defined appearances. By no means dogmatic, equally impotent to understand, in either case, in what way life and thought can proceed from an aggregation of atoms, or from a supernatural cause, it will hold itself wisely balanced as regards these formidable problems. This, at least, is the last lesson and the positive command of experimental science.[1]

Science has, at any rate, revealed many secrets to us. To show organic matter, shapeless and rudimentary in the blastemas, combining, organizing, evolving, and ordering itself in a thousand ways; to form by successive degrees anatomical elements, humors, tissues, and organs; to point out the elementary and irreducible properties, linking, mingling, working in, to effect by their spring the accomplishment of the highest operations; to display the connection of all the acts taking place in the development of

[1] The reader is reminded that this was written at the beginning of 1870. Since then, my mind has found its way out of these uncertainties.

embryos as in perfect life; and to gain a glimpse of the mechanism of disturbances of every kind—the effect of this is to give ample gratification for the present, and noble hopes for the future, in regard to the understanding of the animal system.

LIGHT AND LIFE.

The organized being that we observe on the surface of the globe does not subsist solely by the nourishment absorbed, sometimes in the form of aliment, sometimes in that of atmospheric air; it needs, besides, heat, electricity, and light, which are like a secret and life-giving spring for the world. Its organs are subject to the twofold influence of an inner medium, represented by the humors moistening its tissues, and of an outer medium, composed of all those subtile and fluid agents with which space is filled. This close interdependence of beings and of the media in which they are immersed, too plain to have quite escaped notice, yet too complex for analysis by science in its infancy, has been brought in our day under piercing and methodical investigation, yielding results of remarkable interest. Light especially takes a part in this combination deserving deep study. Whether organic existence in its simplest expression and its lowest degree be considered, or whether we regard it in its highest functions, the influence of light upon it strikes us in the most strange and unlooked-for relations. Lovely forms and vivid colors, the hidden harmonies of life as well as its dazzling brightness and bloom, alike claim mysterious connection with that golden mist diffused by the sun over the world.

From this point of view, modern science finds reason in the simple worship paid by primitive man. It helps us to understand the divine honors given to the star of day among the earliest civilized nations, and the pathetic terror those childlike races suffered when, at evening, they saw the crimson globe, that was the source for them of all power and all splendor, slowly disappear in the horizon. That pious idolatry, far from being a mere utterance of gratitude for the wealth of fertility scattered by the sun over earth, was a homage, too, to the comforting source of brightness and joy, revealing the natural affinity between man and light. The Vedas, the Orphic hymns, and other remains of the earliest religions, are full of this feeling, which appears again in many poets and philosophers of antiquity, Lucretius and Pliny among others. Dante, invoking so often "the divine and piercing light," crowns his poem by a hymn which more than any thing else is a symbolic description of the supreme brightness. On the other hand, laborers, gardeners, physicians, unite in bearing witness to the beneficial effects of light. Naturalists and philosophers, too, in all ages, impressed with the power of the sun, have described its manifold effects. Alexander Humboldt, following Goethe and Lavoisier, often notices its various influences. Yet it was not until the middle of the eighteenth century that so rich a subject of study began to attract serious experimental research; and such are the difficulties of this grand and complex problem, that its solution is only partly reached, in spite of a long series of attempts. Great deficiencies remain to be supplied, and many vaguely-known points to be cleared up; nor has an effort even been made as yet to systematize all the groups of results gained. The latter task we propose to attempt here, with the purpose of showing by a remarkable instance the manner of evolving knowledge through the power of the experimental method, the sequent, cumulative, and mutually-supporting character of well-conducted experiments, and their endless wealth of instruction; in a word, the process adopted by eminent men in the great art of wresting her secrets from living Nature.

I.

Plants gain their nourishment by the absorption through their roots of certain substances from the soil, and by the decomposition through their green portions, of a particular gas contained in the atmosphere—carbonic-acid gas. They decompose this gas into carbon, which they assimilate, and oxygen, which they reject. Now, this phenomenon, which is the vegetable's mode of respiration, can only be accomplished with the assistance of solar light.

Charles Bonnet, of Geneva, who began his career by experimenting on plants, and left this attractive subject, to devote himself to philosophy, only in consequence of a serious affection of his sight, was the first to detect this joint work, about the middle of the eighteenth century. He remarked that vegetables grow vertically, and tend toward the sun, in whatever position the seed may have been planted in the earth. He proved the generality of the fact that, in dark places, plants always turn toward the point whence light comes. He discovered, too, that plants immersed in water release bubbles of gas under the influence of sunlight. In 1771, Priestley, in England, tried another experiment. He let a candle burn in a confined space till the light went out, that is, until the contained air grew unfit for combustion. Then he placed the green parts of a fresh plant in the inclosure, and at the end of ten days the air had become sufficiently purified to permit the relighting of the candle. Thus he proved that plants replace gas made impure by combustion with a combustible gas; but he also observed that at certain times the reverse phenomenon seems to result. Ten years later, the Dutch physician, Ingenhousz, succeeded in explaining this apparent contradiction. "I had but just begun these experiments," says that skillful naturalist, "when a most interesting scene revealed itself to my eyes: I observed that not only do plants have the power of clearing impure air in six days or longer, as

Priestley's experiments seem to point out, but that they discharge this important duty in a few hours, and in the most thorough way; that this singular operation is not due at all to vegetation, but to the effect of sunlight; that it does not begin until the sun has been some time above the horizon; that it ceases entirely during the darkness of night; that plants shaded by high buildings or by other plants do not complete this function, that is, they do not purify the air, but that, on the contrary, they exhale an injurious atmosphere, and really shed poison into the air about us; that the production of pure air begins to diminish with the decline of day, and ceases completely at sunset; that all plants corrupt the surrounding air during the night; and that not all portions of the plant take part in the purification of the air, but only the leaves and green branches."

How do this transformation of impure air into pure air under the influence of sunlight, and the reverse process during darkness, take place? Senebier, the countryman and friend of Bonnet, gives us the answer. Applying to the problem the late discoveries of Lavoisier, he showed that the impure air absorbed and decomposed in the daytime by plants is nothing more than the carbonic acid thrown off by a burning candle or a breathing animal, and that the pure air which results from this decomposition is oxygen. He proved besides that the gas released by vegetables during the night is also carbonic acid, and consequently that the respiration of plants in the night-time is the reverse of that in the daytime. He also demonstrated that heat cannot supply the place of light in these processes. Thus the nature of the phenomenon was explained, but it remained to be learned what relation exists between the volume of carbonic acid absorbed and that of the oxygen released. Another Genevese, Théodore de Saussure, proved that the quantity of oxygen released is less than that of carbonic acid absorbed, and at the same time that a part of the oxygen retained by the plant is replaced by nitrogen thrown off; and supposed that this nitrogen was furnished by the substance of the plant itself. This function of the green portions of vegetables is, moreover, performed with great rapidity and energy. Boussingault, who has made some remarkable experiments on this subject, filled a vessel of water with vine-leaves, placed it in the sun, and sent a current of carbonic acid through it; on its passing out, he collected nothing but pure oxygen. It is calculated that a leaf of nenuphar gives out in this way during the summer more than sixty-six gallons of oxygen.

In 1848 Cloëz and Gratiolet contributed new facts. They showed that aquatic plants follow the same course during the day as others, but that at night they are at rest, and give rise to no release of carbonic acid. They proved the powerful, instantaneous action of solar light on vegetable respiration. If a few leaves of *potamogeton* or of *nayas* are put into a gauge full of water saturated with carbonic acid, as soon as the apparatus is placed in the sun, an immense number of light bubbles, of almost pure oxygen, are seen to detach themselves from the surface of the leaves. The shadow of a slight cloud, crossing the sky, suffices to check their disengagement at once, followed by sudden activity after it has passed. By intercepting the solar beam with a screen, the alternations of quickness and slowness in the production of gas-bubbles may be very plainly seen, according as the plant receives the rays or not. Water-plants show other interesting peculiarities. Diffused light has no power to excite the production of carbonic acid, unless the phenomenon has been first called forth by direct sunlight. Still further, the solar influence having once been applied, the evolution of carbonic acid continues even in darkness. The vegetable keeps up at night its mode of breathing by day. The living force of solar light, therefore, can be fixed and stored away in living plants, as

Van Tieghem, the discoverer of this curious property, very well remarks, to act afterward in complete darkness, and exhaust itself by slow degrees, through transformation into equivalent chemical energy. It appears to lodge itself in phosphorescent sulphur, to reappear under the form of less intense radiations; it hoards itself up in paper, starch, and porcelain, to come forth anew, after a greater or less lapse of time, through its action on the salts of silver. The peculiarity residing in these green cells of vegetables, then, is not an isolated one: it is a special instance of the general property, inherent in many bodies, of retaining, within their mass, in some unknown form, a part of the vibrations that fall upon them, and of preserving them through transformation, to be afterward emitted, either in the state of luminous radiations, or in the condition of chemical or mechanical energy. The great principle of the transformation of forces thus holds good in the vegetable kingdom. And we end with the remark that these facts of persistent activity, called out by an initial excitement, lend support to the idea that living forces hold a close connection with the molecular structure of bodies, and may even be the determinate expression of that structure. We cannot conceive manifold energy in a mathematical and irreducible atom; but in a molecule, made up of a certain number of atoms, we can fancy dynamic figures of a very complex order.

We have thus far regarded only the action of white light, the effect of the totality of rays sent us by the sun; but this light is not simple. It is composed of a great number of radiations, of distinct colors and properties. When white light is decomposed by the prism, we obtain seven groups of visible rays, of unequal refractive power, violet, indigo, blue, green, yellow, orange, and red. The spectrum or ribbon of colors thus obtained widens and spreads out by invisible radiations. Beyond the red, there exist radiations of dark heat, or calorific rays, and, outside of the violet, radiations which are called chemical or ultra-violet rays. The first affect the thermometer, the last occasion energetic reactions in chemical compounds. What is their influence upon vegetation? Does solar light act by its colored rays, its heat-rays, or its chemical rays?

The question has been subjected to many important experiments, and is, perhaps, not yet determined. Daubeny, in 1836, was the first to watch the respiration of plants in colored glasses, and he found that the volume of oxygen released is always less in the colored rays than in white light. The orange rays appeared to him most energetic; the blue rays coming next. A few years later, Gardner, in Virginia, exposed young, feeble plants, from two to three inches long, to the different rays of the spectrum, and observed that they regained a green color with a maximum rapidity under the action of the yellow rays and those nearest them. In one of his experiments, green color was produced, under the yellow rays, in three hours and a half; under orange rays, in four hours and a half; and under the blue, only after eighteen hours. Thus it is seen that the highest force of solar action corresponds neither with the maximum of heat, which is placed at the extremity of the red, nor with the maximum of chemical intensity, situated in the violet, at the other edge of the spectrum. Those radiations which are most active, from a chemical point of view, are the ones which have the least influence over the phenomena of vegetable life.

Mr. Draper, at present a professor in the New York University, and the author of a very remarkable history of the "Intellectual Development of Europe," undertook new and more accurate experiments about the same time. He placed blades of grass in tubes filled with water which was charged with carbonic gas, and exposed these tubes, near each other, to the different rays of the solar spectrum. Then, measuring the quantity of oxygen gas disengaged in each one of these little vessels, he proved that the largest production of gas occurred in the tubes exposed to the yellow and green light; the next, in the orange and red rays. In 1848, Cloëz and Gratiolet discovered the singular fact that the action of light on vegetation is more powerful when it passes through roughened glass than when transmitted through transparent glass. Julius Sachs, more lately, conceived the idea of measuring the degree of intensity of light-action upon aquatic plants, by counting the number of gas-bubbles released by a cutting of a branch exposed to the sun in water charged with carbonic acid. He thus observed that the bubbles thrown off under the influence of orange light are very little less numerous than under white light, while the branch put under blue light throws out about twenty times less. These experiments are decisive. Neither the chemical nor the calorific rays of the solar beam act on plants. The luminous rays only, and chiefly the yellow and the orange, have that property. To these clearly-settled results, Cailletet added a new fact, that green light acts on vegetation in the same way as darkness. He assigns this reason for the feebleness of vegetation bathed in green light under the shade of large trees. It is true, this discovery of Cailletet has been warmly questioned recently, but it has found defenders too, Bert among others; and we shall find soon that it harmonizes with the whole system of the actions of light in the two kingdoms of life.[1]

A year ago, science had gone thus far, when a very distinguished botanist, Prillieux, published the result of a course of experiments made with an entirely different purpose, and taking up the study of the action of light from a new point of view. Resting on the twofold consideration that the distinctly-colored rays are not equally luminous,

---

[1] Bert ascertained that green light stops the motions of sensitive plants.

and that those of the greatest illuminating power are also those which act with most energy on plants, Prillieux undertook to examine what influence will be exercised on plants by rays different in color, but known to be equal in intensity, and whether this influence differs in the case of different colors, or is the same, provided they do not vary in illuminating power. The long and conscientious researches of this experimenter led him to the conclusion that rays of different colors act with equal force on the green parts of plants, and produce an equal release of gas, when they have the like luminous intensity. He holds that all luminous rays effect the reduction of carbonic acid by vegetables in proportion to their illuminating power, whatever their refrangibility may be. If the yellow and orange rays are more active in this respect, it is because their luminous glare is much greater than that of the extreme rays.

The luminous rays also promote the production of green tissue, the green matter of all vegetables. Gardeners blanch certain plants by raising them in the dark. They thus obtain plants of a pale yellow, spindling, without strength or crispness. They are attacked by a true chlorosis, and waste away, as if sprung from barren sand. The sun also aids the transpiration of plants, and the constant renewal of healthy moisture in their tissues. On failure of the evaporation of moisture, the plant tends to grow dropsical, and its leaves fall, from weakness of the stem.

This love of plants for light, which is one of the most imperious needs of their existence, displays itself also in other interesting phenomena, which show that solar rays are, in very truth, the fertilizer that produces color. The corolla of vegetable species growing at great heights on mountains has livelier colors than that of species that spring in low spots. The sun's rays, in fact, pass more easily through the clear atmosphere that bathes high summits.

The hue of certain flowers even varies according to the altitude. Thus the corolla of the *Anthyllis vulneraria* shades down from white to pale red and vivid purple. In general, the vegetation of open, well-lighted places is richer in color and development than that of regions not accessible to the sun. The *nelumbium* and the *bougainvillœa* will not thrive in English greenhouses, though heat is abundantly supplied them, but they unfold completely under the clear sky of Montpellier. Some flowers originally white afterward deepen in color by the direct action of light. Thus *Cheiranthus cameleo* has a flower at first whitish, afterward yellow, and, at last, a violet-red. The *Stylidium fruticosum* has petals which are pale yellow at first, and grow pink. The *Œnothera tetraptera* passes through white, pink, and red colors successively. The flowers of the *Cobœa scandens* are green the first day, and violet the next. The *Hibiscus mutabilis* bears a flower which opens at morning with a white hue, and grows red during the day. The flower-buds of the *Agapanthus umbellatus* are white when they begin to unclose, and afterward take on a blue tint. If, at the moment of leaving its spathe, the flower is wrapped in black paper, intercepting the light, it remains white, but regains its color in the sun. Edmond Becquerel remarked that if a slip of red flowering *crassida* is allowed to bloom in a dimly-lighted room, the petals take a tint half yellow, half pink, at the base. Exposure to sunlight for some hours occasions a red tinge in all the corollas of these little flowers. If some parts of the plant are protected by a covering of blackened paper, the flowers thus hidden keep the faint color which they had in the dim light of the room. The tints of fruits in the same way develop under the healthy action of daylight, and the rule extends to those principles of every nature which give taste and odor to the different parts of the plant.

Flowers, fruits, and leaves, then, are elaborated by the help of luminous vibrations. Their tissue holds the sun's rays. Those charming colors, those fragrant perfumes, and delicious flavors, all the innocent pleasures the vegetable kingdom yields us, owe their creation to light. The subtile working of these wonderful operations eludes us, as does that which guides the fleeting diffusion and thousand-fold refractions displayed by the imposing spectacle of the dawn; but is it nothing to gain a glimpse of those primal laws, and to possess even a twilight ray upon these magnificent phenomena?

II.

Light exerts a mechanical influence on vegetables. The sleep of flowers, the bending of their stems, the nutation of heliotropic plants, the inter-cellular movements of chlorophyll, offer proofs of an extremely delicate sensitiveness of certain plants in this respect. Pliny mentions the plant called the sunflower, which always looks toward the sun, and steadily follows its motion. He notices, too, that the lupin always follows the sun in its daily movement, and points out the hour for laborers. Tessier, at the end of the last century, took up the study of these phenomena, and inferred in a general way that the stems of plants always turn toward the light, and bend over, if necessary, to receive it. He noted, too, that leaves tend to turn toward the side whence daylight comes. Payer made more exact experiments. He tried them with young stems of common garden cresses grown on damp cotton in the dark. These stems have the property of curving and turning quickly when placed in a room lighted only from one side or in a box receiving light on one wall only. The upper part of the stem curves first, the lower part remaining straight. By a second movement the top erects and the bottom bends over, so that the plant, though leaning, becomes almost rectilinear again. When put in a room receiving light from two windows, the following results are noticed: If the openings are on the same side admitting light equally, the stem bends in the direction of the middle of the angle formed by these two beams; if one of the two windows admits more light than the other, the stem leans toward it; if the windows are opposite each other, the stem stands erect, when light comes equally from both sides, and, if it does not, turns toward the stronger rays. Payer discovered, moreover, that the part of the irradiating light most active in its effects corresponds in this case to the violet and the blue. The red, orange, yellow, and green rays do not seem to produce any movement in plants. Gardner carried the investigation still further. He sowed turnips, and let them develop in the dark to two or three inches in length. Then he threw the solar spectrum by a prism on this little field. The plants inclined toward a common axis. Those exposed to the red, orange, yellow, and green rays, leaned toward the deep blue, while the part lighted by violet bent in the opposite direction. Thus the crop took the appearance of a wheat-field bowing under two contrary winds. The turnips placed in the violet-blue region looked toward the prism. Gardner thus determined, as Payer had done, that the most refrangible rays are those which effect the bending of the young stems. He proved also that the plants grow erect again in the dark.

These experiments, repeated and varied in many ways by Dutrochet and Guillemin, uniformly gave like results, but the phenomenon itself still remains almost unexplained. This remark also applies to the very singular facts of the twisting of running plants. The stems of these plants, in twining about their supports, usually curl from the left to the right. Others follow the contrary course, and some twist indifferently in either way. Charles Darwin inferred, from his investigation, that light has an effect on this phenomenon. If twining plants are put in a room near a window, the tip of their stalk takes longer to complete the half-circuit during which it turns toward the darker part of the room than that which is described nearer the window. Thus, one of them having gone through a whole turn in five hours and twenty minutes, the half-circle toward the window employed a little less than an hour, while the other was not traversed in less than four hours and a half. Duchartre placed some China yams in full vegetation in a garden, and others in a completely dark cellar. The stems of the plants uniformly lost in the dark the power of twisting around their supporting sticks. Those exposed to the sun presented one portion twisting, but, when put in the cellar, they shot out straight stems. Yet some twining plants are known that seem to be independent of light in twisting.

The sleep of plants, in connection with light particularly, is still less understood. The flowers and leaves of certain vegetables droop and wither at fixed hours. The corolla closes, and after quiet inaction the plant again expands. In others, the corolla droops and dies without closing. In others still, as the convolvulus, the closing of the flower occurs only once, and its sleep marks its death. Linnæus noted the hours of opening and shutting in certain plants, and thus arranged what has been called Flora's clock; but the relations of these closings with the intensity of light have not yet been scientifically determined.

The green coloring of vegetable leaves and stems is due to a special substance called chlorophyll, which forms microscopic granulations contained in the cells which make up these stems and leaves. These grains are more or less numerous in every cell, and it is their number as well as intensity of color that determines the tint of the plant's tissues. Sometimes they are closely pressed together, covering the whole inner surface of the cell; sometimes the quantity is smaller, and they are separate. Now, it has lately been discovered that in the latter case, under the influence of light, the green corpuscles we speak of undergo very singular changes of position. Some twelve years ago, Boehm noticed for the first time that in certain unctuous plants the grains of chlorophyll gather at one point of the wall of the cells under the action of the sun. He remarked that the phenomenon does not take place in the dark, nor in the red rays. The flat sheet made up of a single layer of cells, without epidermis, which composes the leaves of mosses, seemed to Famintzin the most suitable for this delicate kind of observations. He followed the movements, that take place in these sheets, by microscopic study. During the day the green coloring-grains are scattered about the upper and lower parts of the leaf-cells. At night, on the contrary, they accumulate toward the lateral walls. The blue rays affect them like white light; the yellow and the red ones keep the chlorophyll in the position it takes at night. The order of activity in the rays seems, then, to differ in this case from that in the phenomena of respiration. The researches of Borodine, Prillieux, and Roze, proved that these movements of coloring-corpuscles within the cells occur in almost all cryptogamous plants, and in a certain number of phanerogamous ones. The lately-published experiments of Roze show that in mosses the grains of chlorophyll are connected by very slender threads of plasma, and may suggest the idea that these threads are the cause of the changes of position just described. Perhaps there is some real relation between them; but it must not be forgotten that these movements of the plasmatic matter inside the cell take place by day and night, and that light has no marked effect on them. The green particles, on the contrary, creep over the walls of the cell, and move toward the lightest part as zoospores and some infusoria do.

Biot relates that in 1807, while at Formentera, employed in the work of extending the meridional arc, he devoted his leisure hours to the analysis of the gas contained in the swimming-bladder of fishes living at different depths in the sea. The oxygen required for these analyses was furnished him by the leaves of the *Cactus opuntia*, which he exposed in water to sunlight, under hand-glasses, ingeniously applying the discovery of Ingenhousz and Senebier. It occurred to him one day to expose these leaves, in a dark place, to the illumination thrown by lamps placed in the focus of three large reflectors, used for night-signals in the great triangulation. He threw the light from three of these reflectors on the cactus-leaves. The eye, placed in this concentration of light, must have been struck blind, Biot says. The experiment, kept up for an hour, did not cause the release of a single gas-bubble. The glass was then taken into the diffused light outside the hut. The sun was not shining, but the evolution of gas took place at once with great rapidity. Biot is a little surprised at the result, and concludes that artificial light is impotent to do what solar light can. The labors of Prillieux and other contemporary botanists have proved that all light acts on the respiration of plants, provided only it is not too powerful. In Biot's case artificial light had no effect, because it was far too intense.

III.

Lavoisier somewhere says: "Organization, voluntary movement, life, exist only at the surface of the earth, in places exposed to light. One might say that the fable of Prometheus's torch was the expression of a philosophic truth that the ancients had not overlooked. Without light, Nature was without life; she was inanimate and dead. A benevolent God, bringing light, diffused over the earth's surface organization, feeling, and thought." These words are essentially true. All organic activity was very clearly at first borrowed from the sun, and if the earth has since stored away and made its own a quantity of energy, that sometimes suffices to produce of itself that which originally proceeded from solar stimulus, it must not be forgotten that those living forces, of startling and complex aspects, sometimes our pitiless enemies, often our docile servants, have descended, and are still descending, upon our planet, from the inexhaustible sun. The study of animal life shows us by striking instances the physiological efficacy of light, and the immaterial chain, it may be called, which links existences with the fiery and abounding heart of the known universe.

In plants, as we have seen, respiration at night is the reverse of that by day. There are infusoria which behave, under the influence of light, exactly like the green portions of plants. These microscopic animalcula are developed in fine weather in stagnant water, and in breathing produce oxygen at the expense of the carbonic acid contained in the liquid. Morren saw that the oxygenation of the water occasioned by these little beings varied very perceptibly in the course of twenty-four hours. It is at the minimum at sunrise, and reaches its maximum toward four in the afternoon. If the sky is overcast, or the animalcula disappear, the phenomenon is suspended. This is only an exception. Animals breathe at night in the same way as in the daytime, only less energetically. Day and night they burn carbon within their tissues, and form carbonic acid, only the activity of the phenomenon is much greater in light than in darkness.

Light quickens vital movements in animals, especially the act of nutrition, and darkness checks them. This fact, long known and applied in practical agriculture, is expressly noted by Columella. He recommends the process of fattening fowls by rearing them in small, dark cages. The laborer, to fatten his cattle, shuts them up in stables lighted by small, low windows. In the half-light of these prisons the work of disassimilation goes on slowly, and the nutritive substances, instead of being consumed in the circulating fluid, more readily accumulate in the organs. In the same way, for the sake of developing enormous fat livers in geese, they are put into dark cellars, kept entirely quiet, and crammed with meal.

Animals waste away as plants do. The absence of light sometimes makes them lose vigor, sometimes entirely changes them, and modifies their organization in the way least favorable to the full exercise of their vital powers. Those that live in caverns are like plants growing in cellars. In certain underground lakes of Lower Carniola we find very singular reptiles resembling salamanders, called proteans. They are nearly white, and have only the rudiments of eyes. If exposed to light they seem to suffer, and their skin takes a color. It is very likely that these beings have not always lived in the darkness to which they are now confined, and that the prolonged absence of light has destroyed the color of their skins and their visual organs. Beings thus deprived of day are exposed to all the weaknesses and ill effects of chlorosis and impoverishment of the blood. They grow puffy, like the colorless mushroom, unconscious of the healthy contact of luminous radiance.

William Edwards, to whom science owes so many researches into the action of natural agents, studied, about 1820, the influence exercised by light on the development of animals. He placed frogs'-eggs in two vessels filled with water, one of which was transparent, and the other made impermeable to light by a covering of black paper. The eggs exposed to light developed regularly; those in the dark vessel yielded nothing but rudiments of embryos. Then he put tadpoles in large vessels, some transparent, others shielded from the light. The tadpoles that were shone upon, soon underwent the change into the adult form, while the others either continued in the tadpole condition or passed into the state of perfect frogs with great difficulty. Thirty years later, Moleschott performed some hundreds of experiments in examining how light modifies the quantity of carbonic acid thrown off in respiration. Operating on frogs, he found that the volume of gas exhaled by daylight exceeds by one-fourth the volume thrown off in darkness. He established, in a general way, that the production of carbonic acid increases in proportion to the intensity of light. Thus, with an intensity represented by 3.27, he obtained 1 of carbonic acid, and, with an intensity of 7.38, he obtained 1.18. The same physiologist thinks that in batrachians the intensity of light is communicated partly by the skin, partly by the eyes.

Jules Béclard made more thorough researches. Common flies'-eggs, taken from the same group, and placed at the same time under differently-colored glasses, all produce worms. But if the worms, hatched under the different glasses, are compared at the end of four or five days, perceptible differences may be seen among them. Those most developed correspond with the violet and blue ray; those hatched under the green ray are far less advanced; while the red, yellow, and white rays exert an intermediate action. A long series of experiments on birds satisfied Béclard that the quantity of carbonic acid thrown out in breathing, during a given time, is not sensibly modified by the different colors of the glasses the animals are placed under. It is the same with small mammifers, such as mice; but it is to be observed in this case that the skin is covered either with hair or feathers, and the light does not strike the surface. The same physiologist examined also the influence of the differently-colored rays of the spectrum on frogs. Under the green ray, the same weight of frogs produces in the same period of time a greater quantity of carbonic acid than under the red ray. The difference may be a half greater; it is usually a third or a fourth greater; but if the skin is afterward taken off the frogs, and they are replaced under the same conditions, the result alters. The amount of carbonic acid thrown out by the flayed frogs is greater in red than in green light. A few experiments tried by Béclard on the exhalation of the vapor of water by the skin show that in the dark, temperature and weight being alike, frogs lose by evaporation a half or a third less moisture than under white light. In the violet ray the quantity of moisture lost by the animal is perceptibly the same as in white light.

Light acts directly on the iris of almost all animals, and thus produces contraction of the pupil, while heat produces the reverse phenomena. This stimulus is observed in eyes that have been separated for some time from the body, as Brown-Séquard has shown.

Bert lately took up some very curious experiments on the preference of animals for differently-colored rays. He took some of those almost microscopic crustacea, common enough in our fresh waters, the daphne-fleas, remarkable for their eager way of hurrying toward light. A number of these insects were put into a glass vessel, well darkened, and a spectrum of the ray then thrown into it. The daphnes were dispersed about the dark vessel. As soon as the spectrum colors appeared, they began to move, and gathered in the course of the luminous track, but, when a screen was interposed, they scattered again. At first all the colors of the spectrum attracted them, but it was soon noticed that they hurried much more toward the yellow and green, and even moved away a little if these rays were quickly replaced by the violet. In the yellow, green, and orange parts of the spectrum there was a thronging and remarkable attraction. A pretty large number of these little beings were remarked in the red, too, a certain number in the blue, and some, fewer in proportion to the distance, in the most refrangible portions of the violet and ultra-violet. For these insects, as for ourselves, the most luminous part of the spectrum was also the most agreeable. They behaved in it as a man would do who, if he wished to read in a spectrum thrown about him, would approach the yellow and avoid the violet. This proves, in the first place, that these insects see all the luminous rays that we see ourselves. Do they perceive the colorific and chemic rays, that is to say, the ultra-red and ultra-violet ones, which do not affect our retina? Bert's experiments enable us to answer that they do not. That physiologist is even led to assert that, with regard to light and the different rays, all animals experience the same impressions that man does.

Let us now look at the influence of light upon the color of the skin in animals, noticing first the being which presents the strangest peculiarities in this respect, the chameleon. This animal, indeed, experiences very frequent modifications of color in the course of the same day. From Aristotle, who attributed these changes to a swelling of the skin, and Theophrastus, who assigned fear as their cause, to Wallisniéri, who supposes them to result from the movement of humors toward the surface of the animal's body, the most different opinions have been expressed on this subject. Milne-Edwards, thirty years ago, explained them by the successive inequalities in the proportions of the two substances, one yellowish and the other violet, which color the skin of the reptile, inequalities due to the changes in volume of the very flattened cells that contain these substances. Bruck, renewing these researches, proves that the chameleon's colors follow from the manifold dispersion of solar light in the colored cells, that is to say, from the production of the same phenomenon remarked in soap-bubbles and all very thin plates. Its colors, then, come from the play of sunlight among the yellow and violet substances distributed very curiously under its wrinkled skin. It passes from orange to yellow, from green to blue, through a series of wavering and rainbow-like shades, determined by the state of the light's radiation. Darkness blanches it, twilight gives it the most delicate marbled tints, the sun turns it dark. A part of the skin bruised or rubbed remains black, without growing white in the dark. Bruck satisfied himself, moreover, that temperature does not affect these phenomena.

The influence of light and of the surrounding color on the tint of fish and shell-fish was long ago observed. These creatures change their shade with that of the bottom they live on. Georges Pouchet, a late student of these phenomena, found that in such a case light does not act on the skin directly, but on the retina of the eye, which, through the great sympathetic nerve, transmits the modifying influences of luminous vibrations from without to the colored cells of the epidermis. Turbots, for instance, placed on a white and a black bottom alternately, become dark or light. But, if their eyes are put out, they do not change color.

All animals having fur or feathers are darker and more highly colored on the back than on the belly, and their colors are more intense in summer than in winter. Night-butterflies never have the vivid tints of those that fly by day, and among the latter those of spring have clearer, brighter shades than the autumn ones. Night-birds, in the same way, have dark plumage, and the downiness of their coverings contrasts with the stiffness of that in those that fly by day. Shells secluded under rocks wear pale shades, compared with those that drink in the light. We have spoken above of cave-animals. What a distinction between those of cold regions and those of equatorial countries! The coloring of birds, mammals, and reptiles, peopling the vast forests or dwelling on the banks of the great rivers in the torrid zone, is dazzling in its splendor. At the north we find gray tints, dead and of little variety, usually close upon white, by reason of the almost constant reflection from snow.

Not only the color of organized beings, but their shape, too, is linked with the action of light, or rather of climate. The flora of the globe gain increasing perfection as we go from the poles toward the equator. The nearer these beings approach the highest degree of heat and light, the more lavishly are richness, splendor, and beauty, bestowed on them. The energy and glory of life, perfect forms as well as brilliant arraying, are the distinguishing mark of the various and manifold races in tropical regions, giving this privileged world its characteristic aspect. Nature is here grandly imposing in the radiance of her virginity, unsullied and unsubdued by man's presence and arts. A pure emanation from the sun, she here lives wild and splendid, gazing unshrinkingly, like the Alpine eagle, on the eternal and sublime source which inundate her with heat and glow. Look, now, at the region of the pole! A few dwarfish shrubs, a few stunted and herbaceous plants, compose all its flora. Its animals have a pale covering and downy feathers; its insects, sombre tints. All around them are the utmost limits of life—ice invades every thing, the sea alone still breeds a few acalephs, some zoophytes, and other low rudimentary organizations. The sun comes aslant and seldom. At the equator he darts his fires, and gives himself without stint to the happy Eden of his predilection.

IV.

It remains to note the relations of light to that being most sensitive to its influence, and best able to express its effects, man himself. The new-born child seeks the day by instinct, and turns to the side whence light comes, and, if this spontaneous movement of the infant's eyes is thwarted, strabismus may be the consequence.

Of all our organs the eye is the one that light especially affects. Through the eyes come all direct notions of the outer world, and all impressions of an æsthetic kind. Now, the excitability of the retina shows variations of every kind. Prisoners confined in dark cells have been known to acquire the power of seeing distinctly in them, while their eyes also become sensitive to the slightest changes in the intensity of light. In 1766 Lavoisier, in studying certain questions upon the lighting of Paris, which had been given for competition by the Academy of Sciences, found, after several attempts, that his sight wanted the necessary sensitiveness for observing the relative intensities of the different flames he wished to compare. He had a room hung with black, and shut himself up in it for six weeks in utter darkness. At the end of that time his sensitiveness of sight was such that he could distinguish the faintest differences. It is very dangerous, too, to pass suddenly from a dark place into a strong flood of light. The tyrant Dionysius had a building made with bright, whitewashed walls, and would order wretches, after long seclusion from light, to be suddenly brought into it. The contrast struck them blind. Xenophon relates that many Greek soldiers lost their sight from reflections off the snow in crossing the mountains of Armenia. All travelers who have visited the polar regions have often seen like results produced by the glare of the snow. When the impression of light on the eye is sudden and overpowering, the retina suffers most. If it is less powerful, but longer continued, the humors of the eye are affected. The phenomenon called sunstroke results from the action of light, and not, as is often supposed, from excessively high temperature. It sometimes occurs in the moderately warm season of spring; or a very intense artificial light, and particularly the electric light, may occasion it. The violet and the ultra-violet parts of the sunbeam seem to be the cause of this action, for screens of uranium glass, that absorb these portions, protect the eyes of experimenters occupied in studying the electric light. This disorder is a true inflammation.

The action of light on the human skin is manifest. It browns and tans the teguments, by stimulating the production of the coloring-matters they contain. The parts of the body usually bare, as the skin of the face and hands, are darker than others. In the same region, country-people are more tanned than town residents. In latitudes not far apart, the inhabitants of the same country vary in complexion in a measure perceptibly related to the intensity of solar light. In Europe three varieties of color in the skin are distinctly marked: olive-brown, with black hair, beard, and eyes; chestnut, with tawny beard and bluish eyes; blond, with fair, light beard and sky-blue eyes. White skins show more readily alterations occasioned by light and heat; but, though less striking, facts of variation in color are observable in others. The Scytho-Arabic race has but half its representatives in Europe and Central Asia, while the remainder passes down to the Indian Ocean, continuing to show the gradual rising heat of climate by deepening brown complexions. The Himalayan Hindoos are almost white; those of the Deccan, of Coromandel, Malabar, and Ceylon, are darker than some negro tribes. The Arabs, olive and almost fair in Armenia and Syria, are deep-brown in Yemen and Muscat. The Egyptians, as we go from the mouths of the Nile up-stream toward its source, present an ascending chromatic scale, from white to black, and the same is true of the Tuariks on the southern side of Mount Atlas, who are only light-olive, while their brethren in the interior of Africa are black. The ancient monuments of Egypt show us a fact equally significant. The men are always depicted of a reddish brown; they lived in the open air, while the women, kept shut up, have a pale-yellow complexion. Barrow asserts that the Mantchoo Tartars have grown whiter during their abode in China. Rémusat, Pallas, and Gutzlaff, speak of the Chinese women as remarkable for a European fairness. The Jewesses of Cairo or Syria, always hidden under veils or in their houses, have a pallid, dead color. In the yellow races of the Sumatra Sound and the Maldives, the women, always covered up, are pale like tallow. We know, too, that the Esquimaux bleach during their long winter. These phenomena, no doubt, are the results of several influences acting at once, and light does not play the sole part in them. Heat and other conditions of the medium probably have a share in these operations of color. Still, the peculiar and powerful effect of luminous radiation as a part of them is beyond dispute.

The whole system of organic functions shares in the benefits of light. Darkness seems to favor the preponderance of the lymphatic system, a susceptibility to catarrh in the mucous membranes, flaccidity of the soft parts, swellings and distortions of the bony system, etc. Miners and workmen employed in ill-lighted shops are exposed to all these causes of physiological suffering. We may notice, with regard to this, that certain rays of the solar beam affect animals like darkness; among others, the orange light, which, according to Bert, hurts the development of batrachians. Now, if this light is injurious to animals, it is not so to plants, as we have seen. In exchange, green light, which is hurtful to vegetables, is extremely favorable to animals. There is a kind of opposition and balance, then, as respects luminous affinities, between the two great kingdoms of life. White light, as Dubrunfaut says, seems to split up under the influence of living beings into two complementary groups, a green group and an orange group, which exhibit in Nature antagonistic properties. It is quite certain that green light is a very lively and healthful stimulant for our functions, and that, for that reason, spring is the favored and enchanted season.

The correspondence between perfection of forms and heightening of luminous intensity proves true in the human race as in others. Æsthetics, agreeing with ethnography, demonstrate that light tends to develop the different parts of the body in true and harmonious proportion. Humboldt, that nice observer, says, speaking of the Chaymas: "The men and women have very muscular bodies, but plump, with rounded forms. It is needless to add that I have never seen a single one with any natural deformity. I will say the same of so many thousands of Caribs, Muycas, Mexican and Peruvian Indians, whom we have observed during five years. These bodily deformities and misgrowths are extremely rare in certain races of men, especially among people who have a deep-colored skin." No doubt there is a great difficulty in conceiving how light can model—can exert a plastic power. Yet, reflecting on its tonic effect on the outer tegument, and its general influence over the functions, we may assign it the part of distributing the vital movement orderly and harmoniously throughout the whole of the organs. Men who live naked are in a perpetual bath of light. None of the parts of their bodies are withdrawn from the vivifying action of solar radiation. Thence follows an equilibrium which secures regularity in function and development.

It is commonly said that an ordained causality rules the operations of matter, and that free spontaneity is the privilege of those of spirit. It might well be said on this subject that, in many cases, the causes acting in matter elude us, and, not less often, the causes which act in spirit overpower us; but it is not our task to elucidate that terrible antithesis of law, when the genius of Kant failed in it. We would only ask it to be observed how great an influence light has on the system of the intellectual functions. The soul finds in it the least deceiving of the consolations it seeks for the eternal sadness of our destiny—the bitter melancholy of life. Thought, fettered and dumb in a dark place, springs into freedom and spirit at evening, in a room brilliant with light. We cannot shun the sad moods caused by gloomy and rainy weather, nor resist the impulse of joy given by the spectacle of a brilliant day. Here we must confess our slavery—yet a slavery to be welcomed, that yields only delights. And why should we not join in the chorus of all animate and inanimate things, which, at the touch of light, quiver, and thrill, and betray in a thousand languages the magical, rapturous stimulus of that contact? By instinct, and spontaneously, we seek it everywhere, always happiest when it is found. In some sort, it suffices us. And what a part it plays, what a charm it gives, in works of poetry and art!

This is not the place to unfold that attractive and hardly-opened chapter of æsthetics—to demonstrate the relation between the atmosphere and art, by interrogating the climates of the globe and the great masters of all ages, not following a system of empirical analogies and far-fetched suggestions, but led by strict physiology and rigid optic laws. A charming picture would unfold in tracing the countless and changeful aspects of the sky, and all the caprices of light and air in their influence over the moral and physical nature of painters, poets, and musicians. The ever-varying face of the sun, the fires of dawn and sunset, the opalescent play of air, the shimmer of twilight, the blue, green, shifting hues and iridescent gleams of sea or mountain—all these things find a destined answer in the inmost and unconscious ongrowings of life, as in the soul of one who looks understandingly at Nature's works. In it they reveal and transform themselves by subtilest thrills, tender and creative. He who shall detect these—shall link, range, and embrace them in their wonderfully complex unity—will render a great service to science and to art. He will not make the artist an automaton, nor prove man the copy of a plant, drawing all its virtues from the soil it springs in, but he will lay his hand upon the mechanism, as yet scarcely guessed, moving a whole system of mighty combinations of energy.

HEAT AND LIFE.

The full solution of the question of heat and life could only be reached by simultaneous concurrence of physics, chemistry, and biology. Ancient physiology treated of animal heat empirically, but was unable to explain its origin. That result required the discoveries of Lavoisier and the more modern researches of thermo-chemistry. After revealing the source of that heat, it was important to show how it was disposed of; and this is taught us by thermo-dynamics. And, in conclusion, only the most delicate physiological experiments could settle the modifications that take place in living beings, when subjected to the influence of a temperature either above or below that they possess normally. Medicine and hygiene already benefit by the indications yielded by pure science upon this subject. It is admitted that the study of the variations of animal heat in diseases is of the highest consequence for their comprehension, and that both diagnosis and prognosis receive unexpected light from it.

An inquiry into calorific phenomena, undertaken from various separate and independent points of view, for the solution of questions that seemed at first sight to have no mutual connection whatever, has thus obtained a body of truths which enter into combination almost of their own accord at the present time, and are found to contain the secret of a great problem in natural philosophy. A minute and extended analysis has thus resulted in an instructive synthesis, which is one of the most signal acquisitions of the experimental method.

I.

All animals have a temperature above that of the gaseous or fluid media in which they live; that is to say, they all possess the faculty of producing heat. Warm-blooded animals maintain an almost constant temperature in all latitudes and all climates. Thus, in polar regions, man, mammals, and birds, mark only one or two degrees less than they do at the tropics. The mean temperature of birds is 41° (cent.), and that of mammals 37°. Those animals called cold-blooded produce heat also, though in a less degree; but their temperature follows the variations of that of the surrounding medium, keeping, however, a temperature a few degrees higher than it. In reptiles, this excess varies from 5° to half a degree; in fish and insects, it is still smaller; and, in the wholly inferior species, it rarely reaches half a degree. In fine, with animals that vary in temperature, the power of resistance to external causes of refrigeration increases in proportion to the perfection of the organization. It is observed, too, that in these beings vital activity and the force of respiration have a direct relation to the thermometric state; thus, in a medium of 7°, lizards consume eight times less oxygen than at 23°. With animals of constant temperature, the reverse is the case; the colder it is, the more active is their respiration: a man, for instance, who, in summer, consumes only a fraction over an ounce of oxygen an hour, in winter consumes more than an ounce and a half. Apart from the state of the surrounding medium, many different circumstances exert a perceptible influence on animal heat, and produce tolerably regular variations in it. The seasons, the times of day, sleep, digestion, mode of nourishment, age, etc., are thus constant modifiers of intensity of combustion in breathing; but there are such order and harmony, such foresight, one may say, in the organization of the system, that its temperature continues definitively nearly the same in the physiological state.

The temperature of the human body, at the root of the tongue or under the armpit, is about $37°$ (cent.); this figure expresses the mean found in taking the temperatures of different points of the body, for there are certain slight variations in this respect in passing from one organ to another. The skin is the coolest part, and the more so the nearer we come to the extremities. The temperature rises, on the contrary, with increasing depth of penetration into the organism: cavities are much warmer than surfaces. The brain is cooler than the viscera of the trunk, and the cellular tissue cooler than the muscles. Nor does the blood have the same temperature in all parts of the body. The labors of Davy and Becquerel established the fact that the blood is warmer the nearer to the heart examinations are made. Claude Bernard measured, by methods of equal ingenuity and exactness, the temperature of deep vessels and the cavities of the heart. He showed that blood, in passing out from the kidneys, is warmer than when it enters, and the same is true of blood passing through the liver. He ascertained, too, that the vital fluid is chilled in going through the lungs, and consequently the temperature of the left cavities of the heart is lower than that of the right, by an average of two-tenths of a degree. The last fact clearly proves that the lungs are not the furnace of animal heat, and that the blood, in the act of revivification, grows cool instead of warm.

Ancient physiologists supposed that life has the power of producing heat; they conceived of a kind of calorific force in organized beings. Galen imagined that heat is innate in the heart—the chemic-physicians attributed it to fermentations, the mechanic-physicians to frictions. Time has dispelled these errors of supposition, and it is proved now that the heat of animals proceeds from chemical reactions taking place in the interior of the system. Lavoisier must be credited with the demonstration of this truth by experiment. As early as 1777 he discovered that air, passing through the lungs, undergoes a decomposition identical with that which takes place in the combustion of coal. Now, in the latter phenomenon, heat is thrown off; "therefore," says Lavoisier, "there must be a like release of heat in the interior of the lungs, during the interval between inspiration and expiration, and it is doubtless this caloric, diffusing itself with the blood throughout the animal economy, which keeps up a constant heat in it. There is, then, a constant relation between the heat of the living being and the quantity of air introduced into the lungs, to be there converted into carbonic acid." Such is the first capital fact brought to light by the creator of modern chemistry; but he did not rest there. He undertook to examine whether the heat theoretically produced in a given time by the formation of a certain amount of carbonic acid, that is to say, by the combustion of a certain quantity of carbon in the organism, is exactly equal to the amount of heat developed by the animal in a corresponding time. This quantity was estimated by the weight of ice melted by the animal placed in a calorimeter. Lavoisier ascertained in this way that such equality does not exist, nor was he long surprised at this, for he soon discovered that, of one hundred parts of atmospheric oxygen absorbed, only eighty-one are thrown off by the breath in the form of carbonic acid. He concluded then, from this observation, that the phenomenon is not a simple one, that a part of the oxygen (nine per cent.) is consumed in burning hydrogen, to form the vapor of water contained in the expired air. Animal heat must be accounted for, then, by a double combustion—of carbon first, then of hydrogen—and respiration regarded as throwing off out of the animal carbonic acid and vapor of water.

Lavoisier's experiments have been repeated and varied, and his conclusions discussed in many ways for nearly a hundred years. Several experimenters have corrected or perfected some points, but the general doctrine has not been shaken by the recognition of its secondary and very subtile difficulties, several of which still puzzle physiologists. It is, indeed, undeniable that the greater part of the reactions which occur in the system, with the production of heat, do bring out, as a result, the exhalation of watery vapor and carbonic acid from the lungs; but these two gases cannot arise from a direct combustion of hydrogen and carbon, because the system does not contain such substances in a free state. They represent really only the close of a succession of transformations, often distinct from combustions, properly so called. On the other hand, these are not the only residue of the chemical operations performed in the vital furnace. Besides the water and carbonic acid thrown off by animals in breathing, which are like the smoke of this elaboration of nutrition, they excrete by other channels certain principles which are, as it were, the scoriæ. Now, these principles of disassimilation, among which should be noted urea, uric acid, creatine, cholesterine, etc., could not be results of pure combustion, and they denote that the circulating current is the seat of extremely manifold reactions, the laws of which we are only beginning to gain a glimpse of.

The latest advances of chemistry allow us, indeed, to follow the linked sequence of the gradual transformations of nutritive substances into the cycle of vital operations. It is well, at the outset, to fix exactly the seat of these phenomena. They take place in all the points of the system traversed by the capillary vessels. The glands, the muscles, the viscera, in brief, all the organs, are in a state of constant burning—they are every instant receiving oxygen, which brings about alterations of various kinds in the depth of their substance. In a word, every organ breathes at all its points at once, and breathes in its special way. Certain physiologists of the present day are wrong in localizing the phenomena of breathing in the capillary vessels. They are merely the channels of transfer for oxygen, which, by exosmosis, penetrates their thin walls, and then effects, by direct contact with the smallest particles of the organized mass, the chemical action which keeps up the fire of life. It is easy to prove this by placing any tissue, lately detached from the body, in an oxygenated medium. We remark in this case an escape of carbonic acid, together with a development of heat, and this possibility of breathing outside the system proves clearly that such act can be accurately compared, as Lavoisier thought, to the combustion of any substance. The only difference is with regard to intensity. While a candle or a bit of wood burns rapidly, with a flame, the combustible materials of organic pulp unite with oxygen in a more slow and quiet manner, less violently and manifestly.

The blood, which flows and reflows incessantly in the most slender vessels of our bodies, and charges itself full with oxygen every time the chest heaves, is composed of very various substances. It contains mineral salts, such as chlorures, sulphates, phosphates of potassium, soda, lime, magnesia, coloring-matters, fatty particles, neutral substances of the nature of starch, and nitrogenized products, such as albumen and fibrin. The salts undergo slight changes in the torrent of circulation; they are eliminated by the chief emunctories. The neutral matters of the nature of starch are converted into glycogene and fat. The fatty particles undergo in the blood only such oxidizations as produce certain derivatives of the same order. And, last, the nitrogenized products are made over into fibrin, musculin, ossëin, pepsin, pancreatin, compounds all differing very slightly. It is the first portion of the chemical process which is effected in the principal fluid of the body. All these materials, elaborated at different points of the circulating current, and designed to be assimilated, are destroyed in the very organs in which they had been fixed. The glycogene is transformed into sugar, which is burned, yielding water and carbonic acid; the fatty acids are partly eliminated by the skin, and partly burned. As to the plastic matters which form the web of the tissues, we know little about the chemical relation which connects these with their products of destruction—urea, creatine, cholesterine, uric acid, and xanthine. Such is a rapid sketch of the principal chemical phenomena which, taking place throughout the entire system, kindle everywhere an evolution of more or less intense heat. There is no central organ, then, for feeding the vital fire—every anatomical element performs its share; and, if a nearly uniform temperature exists throughout the body, it is because the blood diffuses heat regularly into the various parts it bathes.

Now, how can the amount of heat to which these reactions may give rise be ascertained? Lavoisier arrived at it in a very simple manner. After comparing the oxygen absorbed by the animal with the carbonic acid and watery vapor thrown off, he deduced the weight of the carbon and hydrogen burned, by assuming that the formation of carbonic acid and of water produces in the system the same amount of heat that it would produce if taking place by means of free carbon and hydrogen. This is very nearly the result he obtained: A man weighing 132 pounds burns in 24 hours, at the average temperature of Paris, very nearly 11 ounces of carbon, and $\frac{11}{4}$ of an ounce of hydrogen, and thus develops 3,297 heat-units. During the same period he loses through his lungs and skin $2\frac{3}{4}$ pounds of watery vapor, which take from him 697 heat-units. There remain, then, nearly 2,600 heat-units to account for. Other analogous estimates have been made, and physiologists have deduced from them the conclusion that a man of average weight produces in our climate 3,250 heat-units every day; that is to say, a sufficient amount of heat to raise seven gallons of water to the boiling-point. These figures, though approximations, give a sufficiently clear notion of the power of the animal economy to generate heat.

Of late years the question has been taken up again with more exactness, thanks to the views of a new science called "heat-chemistry," which occupies itself with chemical phenomena in their relations to heat. Heat-chemistry, by the aid of very delicate apparatus for measuring heat, ascertains the number of heat-units developed or absorbed by bodies entering into combination, beginning with the noted experiments of Favre and Silbermann. Berthelot, who has made profound researches into this subject, reduces the sources of animal heat to five varieties of transformation: first, the effects resulting from the fixation of oxygen with different organic principles; then, the production of carbonic acid by oxidization; then, the production of water; in the fourth place, the formation of carbonic acid by decomposition; and, last, hydrations and dehydrations. The learned chemist attempted to show how the numbers obtained in the study of the heat of combustion of the different organic acids, alcohols, etc., might be applied to the compounds burned in the animal organism; but, while admitting the theoretic verity of the analogies he establishes, we cannot refrain from remarking that their practical verification is exceedingly delicate and difficult. How can we measure, at any one point of the system, the heat produced by a fleeting reaction occurring in the inmost depths of a tissue that must be lacerated to be examined?

If thermo-chemistry seems not to throw much light on physiology on this side, it reveals to it on another sources of heat that had hitherto escaped notice. Berthelot shows that carbonic acid in the system is not always formed by oxidization of carbon, but sometimes proceeds from decomposition absorbing heat. We know that alimentary substances are reducible to three fundamental types—fats, hydrates of carbon (sugars, fecula, starch), and the albuminoids. Now, the fats, in decomposing and combining with water, as it occurs under the influence of the pancreatic juice, evolve heat; and so it is with the hydrates of carbon, independent of any oxidization. And albuminous substances, too, produce very clear calorific phenomena, when their combination with water takes place with its consequent various decompositions. These facts, noted by Berthelot, must have their place in the minute and exact calculation of animal heat, which it is perhaps as yet too early to undertake. At any rate, this heat originates in the totality of those chemical transformations which are going on unceasingly in the depths of the animal organs, and are bringing about the continual renovation of the whole organized substance; in other words, nutrition; but why that nutrition—why that perpetual production of heat in the living machine?

We have now the means of answering this question, which involves the secret of one of Nature's most beautiful arrangements. The heat produced by animals is the source of all their movements; in other words, the mechanical labor they perform is a mere simple transformation of the activity of heat they develop. They do not create motive force by any voluntary operation, which would be one of the prerogatives of life; they draw it from the calorific energy stored up in the organs traversed by the blood. Besides, there is a fixed relation between the quantity of heat that disappears and the mechanical labor that appears. Yet it is to be remarked that, if all motion by living beings is a transformation of animal heat, that heat is not wholly transformed into motion. It is partly wasted by transpiration through the skin, by touch, and especially by radiation; it is used in keeping up to a constant point the temperature of the animal, subjected to many causes of refrigeration.

The mechanical labor performed by an animal is very complex. Independently of visible muscular motions, there are all the changes of place in the interior organs, the continual passage of the blood, the contractions and dilatations of a great number of parts. Now, these actions are only possible in so far as the phenomena of breathing are taking place in the active region. Prevent arterial blood from coming to the muscle, that is to say, prevent combustion taking place, and consequent heat evolving in it, and, although the structure of the organ suffers no harm, it loses its contractile power. Mere compression of the supplying artery of the muscle, so as to check the flow of blood in it, causes the organ to grow cool and lose its power. The labors of Hirn and Béclard have clearly established the relations between heat and muscular motion. Later experiments by Onimus have fixed, with equal precision, the efficiency of heat through the movements of circulation.

We have said that the heat-producing power of aliments will be the more considerable in proportion as they contain a greater quantity of elements that need a large supply of oxygen for their combustion. Therefore, meat and fats repair the losses of the system much more speedily than vegetable substances. The latter are suitable for the inhabitants of warm countries who do not require to produce heat, which the atmosphere supplies them with abundantly. The inhabitants of cold regions, on the contrary, whose accessions of heat ought to be as continual as energetic, are urged by instinct to use meats and fats, which throw out great heat in their combustion. For instance, it is a physiological necessity that the Lapps should feed on the oil of cetacea, as it is a necessity for men of the tropics to consume only very light food. The activity of respiratory combustion and the kind of alimentation thus vary with climate, so that there is always a certain proportion maintained between the thermic state of the surrounding medium and that of the animal furnace. In like manner, in the same climate, persons who perform great mechanical labor must eat more than those who put forth but little movement. This fact, long ago observed, has received of late the clearest and surest demonstration. Yet, perhaps, it is not kept sufficiently in view in the management of public alimentation. Many examples prove the benefit that industry would derive from increasing, in all possible ways, the amount of meat used in laborers' meals. Quite recently, at a manufacturing establishment of the Tarn, M. Talabot has improved the strength and sanitary condition of his workmen by giving them meat in abundance. Under the influence of a diet almost wholly vegetable, each laborer lost on an average fifteen days' work a year through fatigue or sickness. As soon as the use of meat was adopted, the average loss for each man per year was not over three days. Often enough, it must be owned, alcohol is only the workman's means of remedying the want of heat-producing elements in his food; a deceitful remedy, which buoys up the system for a time, only to sap it afterward with alarming subtilty. One of the best preventives of the abuse of alcohol would certainly be the lessening of the cost of meat.

From the point of view of the relation between heat and motion, the living being may thus be compared to an inanimate motor, as a steam-engine. In both cases, heat is engendered by combustion, and transformed into mechanical work by a system of organs more or less complex. In both cases it is at first in a state of tension, and yields motion in proportion as it is demanded for the performance of certain work. Only, the living being is the far more perfect machine. While the best-made steam-engines only utilize $\frac{18}{100}$ of the disposable force, the muscular system of man, according to Hirn, accounts for $\frac{18}{100}$. On the other hand, the animated motor has this peculiarity, that its sources of heat and its mechanical arrangements are intimately commingled, that its heat is produced by organs in motion with a sort of general diffusion, and that the machine itself becomes in turn transformed within itself into heat; an incredible complication, of which science has succeeded in unraveling the simple laws only by dint of the united efforts and resources of physics, chemistry, and biology.

As some physiologists hold, heat must not only be the source of motion in the system, but must also undergo transformation into nervous activity. The functional action of the brain must be a labor, exactly like that of the biceps. Mind itself should be regarded as engendered by heat. Late experiments by Valentin, Lombard, Byasson, and especially Schiff, would seem to prove, it is thought, that there is a proportional and constant relation between the energy of nervous functions and the heat of the parts in which they are effected. Gavarret boldly concludes, from his researches, that heat has the same relations to the nervous system that it has to the muscular system; only, in the case of the muscles, the force produced exhibits itself externally by visible phenomena, while in that of the nerves it is exhausted internally in profound molecular action, which eludes any exact measurement. A given sum of heat developed in the system would thus be on one side a mechanical equivalent, and on the other a psychological equivalent. Gavarret, who is a cautious *savant* and true to experimental methods, doubtless does not go so far as to maintain that thought and feeling can be estimated in heat-units; he even asserts that there is no common measure between intelligence and heat; but less timid physiologists are not wanting who reduce every kind of vital manifestation to the strict laws of thermo-dynamics. A few succinct remarks may perhaps show that such physiologists err.

A comparison between the muscular and the nervous systems from the point of view of their connection with heat is a bold one for many reasons. Between nerve and muscle there exists this enormous difference—that the former is endowed with a spontaneity denied to the latter. Muscular fibre never contracts of its own accord; it needs a stimulus—its energy is borrowed. The nerve-cell, on the contrary, has in itself an ever-present, never-exhausted power of action, the energy of which is its peculiar property. Both evidently derive the principle of the activity that marks them from the same external and internal media; but, while the muscle, a mechanical organ, is limited to the obedient transformation of the force assigned to it, under the form of heat, into a measurable amount of work, the nerve, a vital organ, remains impenetrable and inaccessible to our calculations, and exerts its characteristic and sovereign powers in its own way, through a series of operations that escape all estimates of their force and heat. On the part of the muscular system, every thing can be measured; on the part of the nervous system, nothing. Impressions, sensations, affections, thoughts, desires, pleasures, and pains, make up a world withdrawn from the common conditions of determination. That superior force which, ruling all the highest animal activities, decides, suspends, checks, and governs the very transformation of heat into movement; which, asserting its independence within us, call it by whatever name we may—soul, will, or freedom—remains the most undeniable, though the most mysterious, certainty of our consciousness—this force protests against the degradation of cerebral life to mechanism. Such is the conviction, moreover, of Claude Bernard and of Helmholtz.

II.

Independently of the slight and usual variations that heat may present in the same species, and those it exhibits in passing from one zoological group to another, we may consider the changes it undergoes in the same individual, influenced by the various disturbances of the system. Although it remains almost insensible to modifications of the surrounding temperature, it is not the same when the complete equilibrium of the organs is affected. The concord between the different parts of the organism and the functions they discharge is so perfect that the least trouble is reflected among them, and sends disorder everywhere. The nervous system, charged with keeping up harmonious communication between all points of the living being, first takes note of the change befalling, and transmits its abnormal impression into all quarters. It is not the generator, but it is the regulator, of animal heat; that is to say, it directs and in a manner oversees its production and diffusion according to the varying needs of the system. Every lesion or affection of this system reacts on the physiological processes, and particularly on the evolution of heat. By cutting the filament of the great sympathetic nerve on only one side of a rabbit's neck, Claude Bernard produced an elevation of temperature of several degrees on that side. The blood flows toward the point where the action of the nervous system is suspended under any influence whatever, bringing with it an increase of heating force. At a point where the reverse occurs, the vessels contract, and the temperature falls.

Imperfect nutrition and fasting act on the animal heat, but not directly. The organism keeps up to its normal degree of temperature till it has exhausted its reserved store of combustible substances. Then it cools slowly down to a much lower degree. Thus, a rabbit, starved by

Chasset, showed the first day a warmth of 38° 4' (cent.); two days before its death, 38° 1'; the evening before, 37° 5'; and at the moment of death, 27°. By placing it in a warm medium the moment it was about to die, the apparent activity of its functions was restored for a little while; but the renewal is of brief duration: the anatomical elements have absolutely lost their spring.

The hand of an invalid suffering from inflammation of the chest, or from an attack of fever, is burning; that of one affected by serious asthma, or by emphysema, is as cold to the touch as marble. This is because animal heat varies greatly in different pathological states. Sometimes it rises, sometimes it falls; and the morbid influence is scarcely ever compatible with the body's degree of normal temperature. In Hippocrates's time, when examination of the pulse was not yet practised, the increase of temperature was the only element in the commonest of maladies, fever. Galen defines it quite simply as an extraordinary heat (*calor præternaturalis substantia febrium*). The ancients did not err. It has been admitted and proved in our days that the elevation of the animal heat is just the specific character of the febrile condition. On the one hand, there is never any fever when the temperature continues at the normal degree; on the other, the rapidity of the pulse may reach the utmost limits, without any febrile movement, as is seen in hysteria. Whenever the bodily heat exceeds 38° (cent.), it may be affirmed that there is fever; and, whenever it falls below 36°, there is what is termed algidity. So that the normal heat varies within the narrow range of scarcely two degrees. Beyond these limits, that is, above 38° and below 36°, the temperature points out some morbid trouble. In common intermittent fever, it rises two or three hours before the chill, reaches a maximum at the close of it, and then falls. Acute and decided inflammations, such as pneumonia, pleurisy, bronchitis, erysipelas, etc., are marked by a period of thirty-six hours, or about two days, during which the heat rises slowly to 41°. Toward the third day, this heat decreases, ready to reappear in exacerbations of from half a degree to a degree, during three or seven days, at the end of which time the disorder has run its course. When the temperature gradually rises after the third day, a fatal result may be expected. Persistent heat in that case is the precursor of death. Eruptive fevers, like small-pox, scarlatina, and measles, present very important phenomena of heat. In these heat begins with the attack of the malady, and increases till the cutaneous eruption occurs. It keeps up at a maximum, which reaches $42\tfrac{1}{2}°$ (in scarlatina), till the eruption is complete; then it begins a declining course, variable with the phases of the eruption, which finishes either with scaling off as in scarlatina, or suppuration as in small-pox. And the temperature rises also in several surgical affections, bringing on a more or less inflamed and feverish condition. This is observed in wounds, and generally in every kind of traumatism, in tetanus, aneurisms, etc. In the case of strangulated hernia and of burns, and in most cases of poisoning, on the other hand, it declines in a remarkable way.

Very plainly this rising and falling of animal warmth in diseases can only be attributed to a corresponding state occurring in the energy of respiratory combustion. We do not yet exactly know the cause of these variations, that is, the mechanism by which the morbid influences stimulate or check the active production of heat. Some physicians see in it the effect of fermentations occasioned in the blood by certain microscopic beings, such as bacteria and vibriones, which may perhaps be supposed to be the fact in most febrile maladies. Others assume that, in local inflammations, it is the inflamed organ which communicates heat to the whole body, as a furnace does in a confined space. To others the disturbance seems rather to have a nervous origin, since the nerves, as we have seen, are the regulators of thermic action.

The use of the thermometer is the only exact method of measuring the temperature in disease. Swammerdam, in the middle of the seventeenth century, seems to have been the first to have the idea of it. De Haën and Hunter, in the last century, used it in their medical practice, but its employment at the sick-bed has really only come into importance in our day, thanks to the labors of Bouilland, Gavarret, Roger, Hirtz, and Charcot, in France; Bärensprung, Traube, and especially Wunderlich, in Germany. These physicians were not content with proving that the temperature in illness rises several degrees; they followed the variations of the thermometer day by day, hour by hour, in the different phases of the pathologic movements. They discovered that the curves of these oscillations furnish constant types for each disease, which are modified in a regular manner, according as the disease has been left to itself or treated by one or another medicine. By the study of these pathologic curves of heat the course of diseases may be followed, and valuable indications noted in diagnosis or prognosis. In hæmorrhage of the brain, for instance, the temperature falls to 36° or even 35°, while, in the attack that takes the form of apoplexy, it continues nearly at 38°. These two disorders, quite distinct in their treatment and cure, yet often give rise to a confusion, which the thermometer will hereafter permit us to avoid. Granular meningitis is distinguished from simple meningitis by the same method; in the former the temperature does not rise, notwithstanding the extreme rapidity of the pulse, but in the latter the thermometer marks 40° or 41°.

In every case we see what advantage practical medicine may gain from the physical sciences, what precision and safety it attains by the employment of its means, in proportion to the morbid symptoms. We may add that the future of diagnosis is to be found partly here. By the banishment from medical examination of the often-uncertain judgment of the senses, by substituting as far as possible for personal and arbitary conclusions, as well as for the feeling, always more or less confused, of the physician, the plain and impassive indications of an exact instrument, we do away with the causes that impede the methodical interpretation of the evil in question. Moreover, these instruments often reveal peculiarities that elude direct observation. They repair the omissions, correct the mistakes, guide the activity, multiply the power of our imperfect senses. From this point of view, the study, by the thermometer, of variations of animal heat in diseases, thermometric clinic, as it is called, is one of the most indisputable onward steps in medicine.

III.

After having seen how internal heat is produced in animals, how it expends itself in them, and undergoes change into mechanical work, in fine, what spontaneous or occasional changes it passes through in them, we should study the influence of external heat on the same animals, and the various phenomena resulting from the rise or fall of temperature in the medium they live in. Quite recent researches have thrown light on these questions. Boerhaave had made some experiments, not sufficiently exact, however, on the subject. Berger and Delaroche, at the beginning of this century, undertook new ones, which gained celebrity in the schools of physiology. They placed animals in stoves containing air heated to different degrees of temperature, and noted the effects produced on life by thermic influences. The conclusion from their researches was, that all animals have the power of resisting heat for a certain length of time, and that the duration of resistance varies with the species. Small animals yield after a moderate time to a temperature of 45° to 50° (cent.). Larger ones endure heat better. Cold-blooded animals and the larvæ of insects resist more energetically than warm-blooded animals; but the reverse is the case with fully-developed insects.

Delaroche and Berger studied the human subject, too, from the same point of view, and ascertained that the effect produced varies with individuals. Thus from 49° to 58° the stove grew insupportable to Delaroche himself, who became ill from the experiment, while Berger was scarcely fatigued by it. On the other hand, Berger could remain only seven minutes in a medium heated to 87°, while Blagden staid twelve minutes in it. In tropical countries the heat often rises during the day above 40° without troubling the natives. At the Cape of Good Hope the thermometer marks 43°. Yet sometimes such a heat is murderous. It is related, among other cases, that in the month of June, 1738, in the streets of Charleston, several persons died under the influence of 41°. In Africa our soldiers are often known to be attacked with madness and to die in making a long march, under the rays of a burning sun, but here the influence of light is combined with that of heat. Duhamel mentions the account of several servant-girls of a baker, who could remain without any inconvenience at all for nearly ten minutes in an oven heated to the necessary degree for baking bread. The experiment has since been repeated. There is nothing contradictory in these facts. An animal can endure for some time a temperature much higher than its own, because the very profuse transpiration which occurs in such a case prevents the heating of the organs; yet, as we shall see, so soon as the internal heat really rises a few degrees above the normal figure, life is no longer possible.

The study of these phenomena had scarcely been carried further, when in 1842 Claude Bernard devoted to it certain researches, which he resumed and finished last year, and of which he has just published the results. This physiologist used a pine box, divided into two parts by a grating, on which the animal subjected to the experiment is placed. The box rests on a cast-iron plate, and the whole is arranged on a furnace which warms the air of the apparatus more or less. A window, placed in the side of the box, allows the head of the animal to be fixed outside of it at will. Examining animals, subjected under these conditions to the influence of air more or less warm, Bernard verified the first observations of Berger and Delaroche, and made new and more important ones. Boerhaave had given as the cause of death the application of hot air to the lungs, preventing the cooling of the blood. Bernard showed by experiments that hot air, acting on the skin, creates a rise of temperature more rapidly fatal than when this fluid is merely introduced into the pulmonary vessels. He proved also that, when the hot air is damp, the phenomena take a more rapid course, and death occurs much more quickly and at a lower temperature, than in dry air. This difference must result from the fact that dampness promotes a rise in temperature.

When an animal is subjected to the poisoning effects of heat, it presents a series of uniform and characteristic phenomena. It is at first a little disturbed, then panting, its movements of respiration and circulation accelerate, it grows slowly hotter through the circulation, which, carrying the blood continually from the surface to the centre, bears heat also along with it, then at a given moment it falls into convulsions, the beating of its heart ceases, and it dies uttering a cry. By means of the thermometer it is noted that the temperature of the animal, in every case, is higher by four or five degrees (cent.) than the figure which represents the normal warmth. Thus at first the animal is excited, its functions seem to be performed with fresh vigor, very much as, in the first rays of April sunshine, the pulsations of life in all beings become more rapid; but this stimulus is only fleeting, and soon, when it reaches a certain degree, this heat gives place to the cold of death. Bernard carefully examined animals dying under these conditions, and the first phenomenon that struck him was the rapidity with which corpse-like rigidity came on. The heart grew suddenly insensible to any stimulus; effused spots appeared at several points on the skin. The heat fixed in coagulation the soft matter that composes the muscular fibres. These had the look of being struck with lightning. On the other hand, the arterial blood of the animal grew black, ill-supplied with oxygen, overloaded with carbonic acid, and assumed the look of venous blood. Yet in this state the blood has not lost its physiological properties, and under the influence of a new supply of oxygen can regain its normal state, and grow ruddy again. The heat, provided the degree be not too elevated, only promotes activity in sanguine combustion, without changing the blood. Nor does the nervous system either appear to suffer much. The element most deeply affected is muscle; *heat is a poison of the muscular system*, like sulpho-cyanuret of potassium, and the upas-antiar. It is the loss of the vital properties of this system which, by bringing about rigidity of the muscles, then the stoppage of circulation, and consequently of respiration, is a necessary cause of death. This destruction of the contractile muscular fibre occurs toward 37° or 39° in cold-blooded animals, toward 43° or 44° in mammals, toward 46° or 48° in birds, that is, speaking generally, at a temperature five or six degrees higher than the natural temperature of the animal. Bernard calls attention to the fact that in no case is it allowable to suppose that life opposes a kind of resistance to the excessive heating; on the contrary, vital movement tends to quicken it, and that may be readily understood. The internal heat produced by the animal unites with the acquired heat, and the renewal of the blood, which is the condition of the heating, then occurs with much greater activity. Let us add that quite lately Demarquay applied this toxic action of heat on the muscles in the happiest manner, and without suspecting it. He cured patients suffering from those frightful muscular contractions which characterize tetanus, by subjecting them to the influence of caloric, and making them take very hot air-baths. The rise of temperature in the tetanized muscles was sufficient to modify them, and restore them to a healthy state. Here the poison worked a cure.

Such are the effects on animals of the elevation of temperature. Let us now see what becomes of them when immersed in cold media. Some curious facts with respect to the freezing of certain animals have long been known. During his voyage to Iceland, in 1828 or 1829, Gaimard, having exposed in the open air a box filled with earth in which toads were put, opening it after a certain time, found the reptiles frozen, hard and brittle; but they could be restored to life when put in warm water. Many ancient authors cite similar cases, and we can almost bring ourselves to understand how a great English physiologist might for a moment have given them the whimsical interpretation that he did. John Hunter fancied it might be possible to prolong life indefinitely by placing a man in a very cold climate, and there subjecting him to periodical freezing. The man, he said, would perhaps live a thousand years, if, at the end of every ten years, he were frozen for a hundred, then thawed out at the end of the term for ten years more, and so continuously. "Like all inventors," Hunter adds, "I expected to make my fortune by this scheme, but an experiment completely undeceived me." Putting carp into a freezing mixture, he observed, in fact, that, after being entirely frozen, they were dead, past recovery. The case is the same with all other animals, as the late and very remarkable experiments of F. A. Pouchet have proved.

The influence of cold on organized beings varies, according as we regard superior animals or the inferior species. In general, it may be said that it requires a very low surrounding temperature to chill many animals, because the vital heat they develop resists the process with energy. Yet the mammals of arctic regions, in spite of their thick coat of fur, can only brave the temperature of the pole —sometimes equal to 40° (cent.) below zero, the freezing-point of mercury—by living under the snow where they make their lair. The Esquimaux, too, dig huts in it, where they pass their wretched days. When the organism can neither react nor protect itself against temperatures so low, death by freezing quickly overtakes it. The body is stiffened, and retains afterward a state of remarkable incorruptibility. Every one knows the story of the antediluvian mammoths discovered in the polar ice, where they had been buried, as fresh as animals just dead. While heat destroys the tissues, cold preserves them.

Through what mechanical means does cold become mortal? It seems to act on the nervous system. Travelers relate that in polar regions an unconquerable disposition to sleep overcomes men attacked by very low temperatures. On the icy shores of Terra del Fuego, Solander said to his companions, "Whoever sits down falls asleep, and whoever falls asleep never wakes again." This inclination is so overpowering that many of his attendants gave up to it, and he himself sank down for a moment on the snow. It is said that, during the winter of 1700, two thousand soldiers of Charles XII.'s army perished in the sleep to which they surrendered, under the influence of cold. Its action on the nervous centres, however, is only secondary and consequent on another phenomenon, studied by Pouchet, which reveals this as the secret of death. When the temperature of the interior of the body sinks to 10° or 12° below zero (cent.), the cold freezes the blood more or less, thoroughly disorganizing its globules, and it is this alteration which, either at once or when the blood beomes fluid again, destroys all the vital functions. Larrey relates the case of Sureau, chief apothecary of the French army in Russia, who, when chilled to freezing by a painful march in the snow, did not die until the moment they began to restore warmth. Experiments on animals show that they keep themselves alive as long as they are maintained in a state of half congelation, and die whenever their temperature and circulation are so far restored as to permit the blood-globules, disorganized by cold, to be diffused throughout the vessels. Death occurs, therefore, whenever the quantity of these globules is sufficient to produce a considerable disturbance in the system, that is, whenever the frozen part is at all extensive. An animal entirely frozen, and consequently containing in its congealed blood no globules but those unfit for life, is dead, without possibility of resurrection. Thawing it only restores a soft, flaccid, discolored body, with opaque eyes. If freezing only attacks a limb, it becomes gangrenous, and is destroyed. Pouchet deduced from these examinations a judicious, practical conclusion. If it is true that, in cases of partial freezing, the death of the individual is due to the disorganized globules reëntering the circulation and corrupting the blood, it is plain that, the more sudden the invasion of these globules is, the more rapidly death will supervene. It follows, that, by resisting this invasion, by means of ligatures, or extremely slow thawing, we might succeed in preventing the poisoning. The diseased globules which, pouring in a flood into the heart and lungs, would imperil life by the sudden alteration of the blood, will apparently disturb it merely in an unimportant way, if they are dropped into the blood by slow degrees.

Thus the late researches of experimental physiology explain for us the effects of heat and cold, regarded as toxic agents. The former is a poison of the muscular fibre, the latter a poison of the blood-globules. The case is the same with heat as with the other elements of the cosmic medium, in which the animated being lives. It infolds the most contradictory powers, like the tender flower, spoken of by Friar Lawrence, in "Romeo and Juliet," from which may be distilled both safety and danger. It can by turns support health, heal disease, or inflict death.

Man is, then, the weak plaything of all those silent forces that surround and press upon him. In vain he enslaves them; he cannot escape the inflexible laws that subject the equilibrium of life to that of the lowest physico-chemical conditions. He has at least the consolation of knowing these laws, and guiding his existence so as to soften their severity as far as possible. When Nature crushes him, she is unconscious of it, unconscious of herself: man, so small, is greater than these blind greatnesses, because his peculiar greatness is consciousness. The subject we have been studying is a grand proof of this; but its full, imposing interest would not be understood, were we to end without giving the answer to the last question it suggests. Whence comes this heat developed by chemical phenomena in the living system? It comes from aliments, which, in the last resort, are all drawn from plants, and they have borrowed it from the sun. When the vegetables, whose combustion takes place within the animal, there throw off a certain amount of potential energy, as heat, they do but transmit it to the force which the sun has supplied them with. It is, then, a portion of solar radiation, stored up at first by the plant, which the animal makes disposable and converts to use, whether for resisting cold or for securing the regular play of his motive functions. Thus we may say, with exact truth, the sun is the inexhaustible source, as it is the perpetual spring, of life. From this point of view, science confirms the intuitions of oldest date, and man's poetic dreams in the childhood of the race. Reason completes the instructions of its long experience by harmonious agreement with the simple and natural sentiment felt by the first of men, when for the first time they looked on the splendor of day.

ELECTRICITY AND LIFE.

GALVANI discovered, in 1794, that the muscles of animals experience contractions in contact with certain metals. In his view, this contact merely calls out the discharge of a fluid inherent in the animals themselves. The fact was not to be contested, but its explanation was. Lively discussions in the schools of physiology followed—fortunately, with a clear understanding that the difficulty could only be determined by experiments. A vast number were made, the name of Volta being connected with the most remarkable of them. Alexander Volta maintained, in opposition to Galvani, that the electricity which produces contractions in the muscles, far from originating in those organs, is introduced by the metals used in the process. In proof of this he constructed, in 1800, the pile that bears his name, and which is an arrangement in which the connection of two different metals becomes an abundant source of the electric fluid. Galvani and Volta were two men of distinguished genius, who thoroughly understood physics and physiology, and advanced nothing heedlessly. Their discoveries were the point of departure for one of the most admirable movements in all the history of science, a movement which is still most active, and is the more remarkable because it resulted but yesterday, as it were, in the complete demonstration that Galvani and Volta were both in the right. Science to-day proves that there is an electricity peculiar to animals, as Galvani declared. It decides also that electricity produced by external causes has an influence over animals, as Volta taught. From profound study of the two orders of phenomena, it deduces a system of procedure for the cure of very many maladies by electricity. Consequently, an exposition of the relations between electricity and life must begin with examining the electricity that exists naturally, in the same way that heat does, in animals, and then go on to explain the action of the fluid on the organism, whether in a healthy or morbid state. Such a description will complete what has been written in the *Revue* respecting the relations of life with light and heat—relations that we may to-day consider as forming the features of a new science.

I.

The most authentic witnesses to the existence of animal electricity are fish. The torpedo, the silurus, the gymnotus, the ray, and other fishes, develop spontaneously a more or less considerable quantity of electricity. This fluid, the production of which depends upon the animal's will, is identical with that of common electrical machines; it gives the like shocks and sparks at a certain tension. The apparatus for its formation consists of a series of small disks of a peculiar substance, kept apart by cells of laminated tissue. Fine nerve-end fibres are scattered over the surface of these disks, and the whole represents a sort of membranous pile, usually placed in the region of the head, sometimes toward the tail.

These fishes are the only animals provided with an apparatus specially devoted to the production of electricity; but all animals are electric, in this sense, that a certain quantity of that fluid is constantly forming within their organs. The existence of electricity peculiar to the nerves and muscles, and independent of their special modes of action, has been settled by numerous experiments, particularly by those of Nobili, Matteucci, and Du Bois-Reymond. To prove the currents of nervous electricity, it is sufficient to prepare a frog's muscle, and touch it at two different points with the two ends of a nerve-filament of the same animal. The muscle then undergoes contraction under the influence of the nervous current. Another experiment, as simple, proves the existence of the muscular current. In an animal living or just killed, a muscle is exposed and cuts made in it perpendicularly to the course of the fleshy fibres, and communication effected by the two wires of a very sensitive galvanoscope between the natural surface of the muscle and the surface made by incision. The needle of the instrument then betrays the passage of a current. This muscular electricity may be obtained in tolerable quantity by placing a number of slices of muscle together in the form of a pile. The positive pole of the system will be the natural surface of one of the terminal slices, and the negative pole the cut surface of the other. Such a battery acts upon galvanic instruments, and can even excite contractions in other muscles.

Independent of these nervous and muscular electric currents, other sources of this fluid exist in the animal economy. Currents are produced between the outer and inner surfaces of the skin, in the blood, in the secreting vessels, in fine, almost throughout the whole organism. The experiments, as delicate as original, to which Becquerel has for several years devoted all the activity of his green old age, authorize him now to assert the preponderance of electro-capillary phenomena in animal life. According to this accomplished physicist, two solutions of different nature, both conductors of electricity, separated by a membrane or a capillary space, compose an electro-chemic circuit; and, if we reflect on the anatomical elements of the various tissues, cells, tubes, globules, etc., in their connections with the fluids that moisten them, we find that they give rise to an infinite number of pairs constantly evolving electricity. The blood of the arteries with that of the veins forms a pair, having an electro-motive power of 0.57, that of a pair with nitric acid being 100. Becquerel explains, by the intervention of these currents, many physiological phenomena hitherto imperfectly understood. Granting the reality of such actions, yet it must be acknowledged that the general doctrine which combines them each with the other, and links the whole together with the various modes of action of the organism, is far from being clear and precise. We need to know how these currents are distributed and circulate, what lines and courses they follow. It is now time for experimental physiology to attack these difficult problems, the solution of which is absolutely necessary for accurate knowledge of vital determinations, that is, for the computation and the estimate of those various factors which are terms in all the equations of organic movement.

Vegetables, too, develop electricity. Pouillet has clearly demonstrated that vegetation throws it off. Other physicists, particularly Becquerel, have proved the existence of currents in the fruits, stems, roots, and leaves of plants. Becquerel took a branch of young poplar full of sap, introduced a platinum wire into the wood and another into the bark, and brought the two ends of the conductors together in a galvanoscope—the needle at once showed the passage of a current. Buff has lately made experiments, taking care not to injure the organs. Two vessels containing mercury received platinum wires; over the mercury stood water containing the vegetables to be examined as to their electric condition. Taking the leaves and roots, Buff proved a current passing through the plant from the roots to the leaves; in a branch severed from the stem the current passed toward the leaves, too. To sum up, the existence of vital electricity is incontestable, though we do not yet precisely understand the conditions of this internal excitement, and know nothing of its true relations with the unity of physico-chemical operations in the living organism.

The latter are, at all events, exceedingly complex. There is in us, and in every organized being, an infinite world of the most various actions going on. The forces penetrating us are as manifold as the materials we are moulded from. In every point of our bodies, and at every moment of our existence, all the energies of Nature meet and unite. Yet, such order rules in the course of these wonderful workings, that harmonious blended action, instead of bewildering confusion, characterizes beings endowed with life. Every thing in them commands and answers, with balance and counterpoise. Buffon long ago felt and expressed this. "The animal," he said, "combines all the forces of Nature: his individuality is a centre to which every thing is referred, a point reflecting the whole universe, a world in little." A deep saying, coming from the great naturalist as the flash of an intuition of genius rather than the result of rigid investigation—words which the movement of science confirms with ever stronger proofs, while borrowing from them light for its path.

Having determined that living bodies are in themselves sources of the electric fluid, we next inquire into the nature of the effects produced in the animal organism by electricity under different forms. The atmosphere contains a variable quantity of positive electricity; the earth itself is always charged with negative electricity. It is not yet precisely known how this diffused and silent force originates. Physicists suppose that it proceeds from vegetation and the evaporation of water. Becquerel has quite lately set forth a number of reasons, more or less plausible, for the belief that the chief part of atmospheric electricity is derived from the sun, and diffused by it into space together with light. Whether this be true or not, while the sky is clear this fluid has no visible effect on human beings; but, whenever it accumulates in the clouds, and gives rise to storms, it produces effects that are the most manifest proofs of the influence exerted over life by electricity. Persons killed by lightning present a great variety of appearances. Sometimes one struck by lightning is killed outright on the spot, the body remaining standing or sitting; sometimes, on the contrary, it is thrown to a great distance. Sometimes the flash tears off and destroys the victim's dress, leaving the body untouched, and sometimes the reverse is the case. In some instances the destruction is frightful, the heart is torn apart and the bones crushed; in others the organs are observed entirely uninjured. In certain cases flaccidity of the limbs occurs, softening of the bones, collapse of the lungs; in others, contractions and rigidity are remarked. Sometimes the body of the person struck decomposes rapidly, but at times it resists decay. Lightning, which shatters trees, and overturns walls, seems not to produce mutilations in animals at all readily. When the stroke does not produce death, it creates at least serious disturbances—sometimes temporary, but oftener beyond remedy. Besides the burns and various eruptions noticed on the skin of those struck by lightning, they often suffer, very curiously, a complete loss of hair; they are affected with paralysis, dumbness, deafness, amaurosis, or imbecility. In brief, the destructive attacks of atmospheric electricity touch all the functions of the nervous system.

The action of electric fishes may be likened to that of lightning, in being independent of our intention. The shocks of the gymnotus are particularly formidable. Alexander Humboldt relates that, having put both his feet on one of these fish, just taken from the water, he experienced so violent a shock that he felt pains in all his joints the rest of the day. These shocks throw the strongest animals down, and it is necessary to avoid rivers frequented by the gymnotus, because, in attempting to ford them, horses or mules might be killed by the discharges. To capture these fish the Indians drive wild-horses into the water, stirring the eels up out of the mud by their trampling. The yellowish livid creatures press against the horses under their bellies, throw down the greater part, and kill some of them, but, exhausted in their turn, they are then easily taken with the aid of small harpoons. The savages employ them to cure paralysis. Faraday compares the shock of a gymnotus, which he had the opportunity to study, to that of a strong battery of fifteen jars. A live eel out of water, when touched by the hand, communicates a shock strong in proportion to the extent of surface in contact, and the stroke is felt up to the shoulder, and followed by a very unpleasant numbness. It may be transmitted through twenty persons in a chain, the first one touching the back, and the last the belly of the eel. The fishermen discover the presence of an eel in their nets by experiencing a shock in throwing pailfuls of water on, to wash them. Water is a good conductor, and this fish kills or benumbs the animals it feeds on by delivering a discharge through the water.

Other sources of electricity are known to exist, besides thunder-storms and fishes. Friction-machines, batteries, and induction instruments, yield three kinds of currents that act on vital functions, sometimes in a similar way, but oftener with marked differences, which have only recently been clearly distinguished. The action of static electricity, and that of electricity of induction, more sudden and violent, is particularly marked by mechanical effects so striking that they have long distracted experimenters from examining with due attention those effects of another sort, produced by the galvanic current. Yet the latter in reality affects the animal tissues in a deeper way, and its resulting phenomena deserve the liveliest interest from a theoretical point of view, as well as from their applied uses.

Dutrochet proved, by remarkable experiments, that, when a tube closed below by a membrane, and containing gum-water, is placed in a vessel containing pure water, the level of the gum-water rises little by little through the gradual introduction of pure water into the tube, while a certain quantity of the gum-water inside mingles with the pure water outside. In a word, a mutual exchange takes place between these two fluids, communicating by the membrane, and the current, passing from the thinner liquid toward the denser one, is ascertained to be more rapid than that moving in the opposite direction.

This experiment reveals one of the most important phenomena of life in plants and animals, noted by the word endosmosis. Now, Dutrochet had before observed that if the positive pole of a battery be inserted in the pure water, and the negative pole in the gum-water, the acts of endosmosis are effected more energetically. Qnimus and Legros discovered, further, that, if the contrary arrangement be adopted, that is, if the positive pole be placed in the gum-water, and the negative pole in the pure, the level of the liquid in the tube descends noticeably, instead of rising. Electricity, therefore, can reverse the usual laws of endosmosis. It exerts an influence not less distinct on all the other physico-chemical movements, taking place deep in the organs. In them it decomposes the salts, coagulates the albuminoid elements of the blood and the tissues, just as it does in the vessels of the laboratory. Take a very curious instance: In chemistry, on decomposing the iodide of potassium, iodine is freed, and betrays itself by the tinge of intense blue which it develops on contact with starch. Now, if an animal be injected with a solution of iodide of potassium, and then electrified, it is noticed, after a few minutes, that all the parts near the positive pole of the battery turn blue in presence of the starch, proving that they are impregnated with iodine. The iodide has been almost instantly decomposed, and the iodine carried by the current toward the positive pole.

It is not surprising, then, that the action of electricity influences the whole system of the nutritive operations. Onimus and Legros found that ascending continuous currents quicken the twofold movement of assimilation and disassimilation.[1] Animals electrified under certain conditions throw off a greater proportion of urea and carbonic acid, proving a higher energy of the vital fire. On the other hand, if young individuals, in course of development, are subjected to the action of the current, they grow tall and large more quickly than in ordinary circumstances, furnishing the proof of an increase in the quantity of substances assimilated. To show how far vital phenomena are stimulated by electricity, we will cite another experiment made by Robin and Legros on noctilucæ. These are microscopic animals, which, when existing in great numbers in sea-water, render it almost as white as milk, and at certain times phosphorescent. Now, a current directed into a vessel filled with such water suffices to bring out a trace of light marking all its course. Electricity stimulates the phosphorescence of all the noctilucæ met on its passage between the two poles.

Interrupted currents, or currents of induction, contract the blood-vessels and slacken the circulation in almost every case: if they are intense, they even effect its complete check by a strong contraction of the little arterial

---

[1] Electricity passes in a machine between two poles. It is ascertained that the current circulates from the positive pole toward the negative one. The current is called ascending when the positive pole is applied to the lower part and the negative to the upper part of the spine; it is called descending in the reverse case.

branches. Continuous currents do not act in this way; usually they quicken the circulation, while occasioning an enlargement of the vessels; at least, this has been established by Robin and Hiffelsheim, in the microscopic examination of the flow of blood under electric stimulus. Onimus and Legros afterward proved that these movements are governed by the following law: The descending current dilates the vessels; and the ascending current contracts them. A striking experiment proves the value of this law: A part of the skull of a vigorous dog is removed, so as to expose the brain. The positive pole of a pretty strong battery is then placed on the exposed brain, and the negative pole on the neck. The slender and superficial vessels of the brain contract visibly, and the organ itself seems to collapse. Arranging the poles in the contrary order, the reverse is remarked; the capillary vessels swell and distend, while the substance of the brain protrudes through the opening made in the walls of the skull. This experiment proves the possibility of increasing or lessening at will the intensity of circulation in the brain, as indeed in any other organ, by means of electric currents. Onimus lately made an equally interesting experiment. Many persons know that the famous physiologist Helmholtz introduced into medicine the use of a simple and convenient instrument called the ophthalmoscope, by means of which the bottom of the eye may be quite distinctly seen, that is to say, the net formed by the nerve-fibres, and the delicate vessels of the retina. Now, on examining this net, while the head is put under electric influence, the little blood-tubes are plainly seen to dilate and grow of a more lively crimson.

Let us now study the effect of the electric current on the functions of the motor system, and on sensibility. Aldini, a nephew of Galvani, undertook the first investigations of this kind upon human beings. Convinced that the proper study of the effects of electricity on the organs required the human body to be taken at the immediate instant after the extinction of life, he believed he would do well, as he relates himself, to take his place beside the scaffold, and under the axe of the law, to receive from the executioner's hand the blood-stained bodies which were the only really suitable subjects for his experiments. In January and February, 1802, he availed himself of the occasion of the beheading at Boulogne of two criminals, whom the government willingly gave up to his scientific inquiry. Subjected to electric action, these bodies presented so strange a sight as to terrify some of the assistants. The muscles of the face contracted in frightful grimaces. All the limbs were seized with violent convulsions. The bodies seemed to feel the first stir of resurrection, and an impulse to spring up. For several hours after decapitation, the vital centres of movement retained the power of answering to the electric excitement. At Glasgow, Ure made some equally noted experiments on the body of a criminal, which had remained on the gallows nearly an hour. One of the poles of a battery of 270 pairs having been connected with the spinal marrow, below the nape of the neck, and the other pole touching the heel, the leg, until then bent back, was forcibly thrown forward, almost oversetting one of the assistants, who had a strong hold on it. Placing one of the poles on the seventh rib, and the other on one of the nerves of the neck, the chest rose and fell, and the abdomen underwent the like motion, as in the act of breathing. On touching a nerve of the eyelid at the same time with the heel, the muscles of the face contracted, "rage, horror, despair, anguish, and fearful grins, combined in hideous expressions on the dead man's face." At the terrible sight one person fainted, and several were obliged to leave the room. Afterward, by exciting convulsive movements of the arms and fingers, the corpse was made to seem to point to one or another of the spectators.

Later researches have precisely fixed the conditions of this influence of electricity upon the muscles. Continuous currents, led directly to these organs, produce contractions at the moments of opening and of closing the circuits; but the shock produced on closing is always the strongest. While the continuous current is passing, the muscle remains persistently in a half-contracted state, as to the nature of which physiologists disagree. Influenced by excitements rapidly repeated and prolonged for a short time, the muscles assume a state of contraction and shortening, like that seen in tetanus. In this state, as Helmholtz and Marey have shown, the muscle suffers a repetition of very slight shocks. Contraction is the result of the fusion of these elementary vibrations, indistinguishable by the eye, but capable of recognition and measurement by certain contrivances. Currents of induction produce more powerful contractions, but not lasting ones, which are succeeded, if electrization is prolonged, by corpse-like rigidity. Muscular contraction effected in such a case is attended by a local rise in temperature, proportioned to the force and length of the electric action. This increase of heat reaches its maximum, which may in some cases be four degrees, during the four or five minutes following the cessation of the electric impulse, and is due to the muscular contraction, which always gives rise to disengagement of heat.

The effect upon the nerves is very complex, and betrayed by movements and sensations very variable in intensity. Onimus and Legros state in general its fundamental laws thus: In acting on the nerves of motion, we see that the direct or descending current works more energetically than the other, with the reverse result on the nerves of sensation. The excitability of those nerves of a mixed kind is lessened by the direct and increased by the inverse current. This is true as to battery-currents, but currents of induction behave differently. While the sensation called out by the first is almost insignificant, the others, besides the permanent muscular contraction, produce a pain lasting as long as the nerve retains its excitability. The spinal marrow is one of the most active parts of the system. In the form of a thick, whitish cord, lodged inside the vertebral column, it constitutes a real prolongation of the brain, of which, under some circumstances, it takes the place. The unconscious depository of a part of the force animating the limbs, by means of the nerves sent out from it, it transmits to them their direction and power to move, while the brain is unaware of its action. This takes place in what are called reflex motions, and these occur in beheaded animals, through the simple excitement, direct or indirect, of the spinal marrow. Experiments may be cited, showing the action of electricity on those phenomena which have their seat in the spinal marrow. If a frog is plunged into lukewarm water, at a temperature of $40°$, it loses respiration, feeling, and motion, and would die if kept in it a long time. When taken out of the water, and placed in this state under the action of the current, it contracts strongly when its vertebral column is electrified by an ascending charge; but no motion follows if the descending current is applied. On the other hand, if the latter is sent into a beheaded animal, stimulated to reflex motions, by the excitement of the spine, it tends, as experiment shows, to paralyze these motions. In general, this is the law discovered by Onimus and Legros—the ascending battery-current, directed on the spine, increases the excitability of that organ, and consequently its power of producing reflex phenomena; the descending current, on the contrary, acts in the reverse way.

When the brain of animals is directly electrified, the modifications in circulation already spoken of result, but no special phenomena are observed. The animal shows no pain, and makes no movement, experiencing a tendency toward sleep, a sort of calm and stupor. Some physicians have gone so far as to propose electrization of the brain as a means of developing and perfecting the mental powers. Nothing hitherto justifies the belief that such a course could have the slightest influence for good over the functions of thought. On the contrary, it is very certain that the electric agent must be applied only with extreme caution to the regions of the head, and that it very easily occasions mischief in them. A strong current might readily cause rupture of the vessels, and dangerous hæmorrhage in consequence.

Again, electricity stimulates all the organs of sense. Directed upon the retina, it excites it, producing sensations of glare and dazzling. When sent through the organ of hearing, it produces there a peculiar buzzing noise, and, if brought in contact with the tongue, it calls forth a very characteristic metallic and styptic sensation. And in the olfactory mucous membrane it creates a sneezing irritation, and also, it seems, an odor of ammonia.

The currents not only act on the cerebro-spinal nerves, and the muscles concerned in life, as related outwardly, but affect also the parts of the nervous and muscular systems devoted to the functions of nutritive life. Electricity by induction, applied to these muscles, causes contraction in them at the point of contact with the poles, while the part situated between the poles remains without motion. Continuous currents produce, at the instant of closing the circuit, a local contraction at the junction with the poles, and then the organ becomes quiet; if it is previously in action, motion ceases. In the case of the intestine, for instance, peristaltic movement is checked; and by means of electricity contractions of the uterus may be suspended in an animal, during parturition. In general, the fluid suppresses spasms of all the involuntary muscles.

All these facts relating to electric action upon the

muscles and nerves have been the occasion, particularly in Germany, of laborious investigations, with which are connected the names of Du Bois-Reymond, Pflüger, and Remak. The doctrines of these learned physiologists, regarding the molecular condition of the nerves in their various modes of electrization, are still very much disputed. It must be said that they are not supported by any experimental certainty, and perhaps the ideas developed by Matteucci supply better means for the general solution of these difficulties. This eminent experimenter opposed to the German theories about the electrotonic faculties of the nerves certain evident phenomena of electrolysis, that is, of chemical decompositions effected by the currents. He supposed that the modifications of excitement in the nerves, brought about by the passage of electricity, depended on the acids and the alkalies resulting from the separation of the salts contained in animal tissues. To this first class of phenomena may be added those electro-capillary currents lately observed by Becquerel. Here must be sought the deeper causes of that complicated and as yet obscure mechanism of the strife between electricity and life.

The effects of electricity on plants have been much less studied, experiments made on this subject being neither accurate nor numerous enough. We know that electricity causes contractions in the various species of mimosa, particularly in the sensitive-plant, etc. Becquerel has studied its action on the germination and development of vegetables. Electricity decomposes the salts contained in the seed, conveying the acid elements to the positive pole, and the alkaline ones to the negative. Now, the former injure vegetation, while the latter benefit it. Quite lately the same experimenter has made a series of researches upon the influence of electricity on vegetable colors. Employing strong discharges obtained from friction-machines, he has noticed very remarkable alterations of color, usually due to the rupture of the cells containing the coloring-matter of the petals. This matter, freed from its cellular covering, disappears on simply washing with water, and the flower becomes almost white. In leaves showing two surfaces of different shades, as the *Begonia discolor*, a kind of mutual exchange of colors between the two surfaces has been noticed.

II.

The physiological phenomena just spoken of are usually confounded in books with the facts of electric medical treatment, and it seems better to distinguish the two classes. The true method consists in first explaining the phenomena displayed in the healthy organism, as the only way of understanding afterward those that are peculiar to disorders. Electric treatment forms a group of methods to be classed among the most efficacious in medicine, provided they are applied by a practitioner well trained in the theory of his art. Indeed, the most thorough physiological knowledge is essential for the physician who would make the electric currents erviceable. Mere experimenting, even the most sagacious, must here be barren of good results—a fact of which it is well to remind those who impute to the method itself the failures it meets with in unskillful hands. It is true that, since the days of Galvani and Volta, physicians have used galvanism in the treatment of many diseases. Early in the century, galvanic medicine was much talked of, and supposed to be the universal panacea. Galvanic societies, journals, and treatises, undertook to spread its usefulness. The fashion lasted a certain time, and would perhaps have grown indifferent, when the discovery of induced electricity, due to Faraday, in 1832, called professional attention once more to the virtues of the electric fluid, and led to a new and interesting range of experiments. Yet it is likely that the true systems of electric medical treatment, after the extraordinary illusions of their earlier days had vanished, would at length have sunk into disuse, had they not escaped from the ruts of empiricism. With its usual boldness, it had at first gained them a high rank, which it had no power to maintain. It was experimental physiology, with its exact analysis of the mechanical effects of this fluid upon the springs of the organism, which made its application in the healing art sure, true, and solid, as it now is. In this, as in all things, blind art has been the impulse to scientific research, which in turn steadily enlightens and perfects art.

It is singular that induction currents have met with much better fortune than galvanic ones. The latter, the use of which introduced electric treatment, have gained real importance in physiology and medicine only within a few years, and after the reputation of induction currents was well established, thanks chiefly to the efforts of Duchenne. A German physiologist and anatomist, Remak, who died six years ago, was the first to urge the singular remedial virtues of the voltaic current. Remak, after devoting twenty years to the study of the most difficult questions in embryology and histology, undertook, in 1854, the systematic examination and ascertainment of the action of continuous currents on the vital economy. He soon gained remarkable dexterity in dealing with the electric agent, and detecting with the readiest insight the proper points for applying the battery-poles in each malady. Those who, with us, witnessed in 1864 his practice at the hospital, will remember it clearly. The methods of Duchenne were almost the only ones accepted in practice in France, till Remak came to prove to Paris physicians the powers of electrization by constant currents, in cases where Faraday's currents had been without effect. The teaching of the Berlin practitioner bore its fruits. A rising young physician, Hiffelsheim, was beginning to spread throughout Paris the use of the constant current as a healing agent, when death removed him in 1866, in the flower of his age. Another physician, who benefited by the lessons of Remak, Onimus, resumed the interrupted labors of Hiffelsheim, and is now busy in completing the system of the methods of electric medical practice, by subjecting them to an exact knowledge of electro-physiological laws. A few instances, from the mass of facts published on the subject, will serve to show how far the efficiency of these methods has actually been carried.

Experiment proves that, under certain conditions, the electric current contracts the vessels, and thus checks the flow of blood into the organs. Now, a great number of disorders are marked by too rapid a flow of blood, by what are known as congestions. Some forms of delirium and brain-excitement, as also many hallucinations of the different senses, are thus marked, and these are entirely cured by the application of the electric current to the head. No organ possesses a vascular system so delicate and complex as the brain's, nor is there any so sensitive to the action of causes that modify the circulation. For this reason, disorders seated in the brain are peculiarly amenable to electric treatment, and, when carefully applied, it is remedial in brain-fevers, mental delirium, headaches, and sleeplessness. Physicians who first employed the current were quite aware of this benign influence of the galvanic fluid over brain-disorders, and even had the idea of utilizing it in the treatment of insanity. Experiments in that direction have not been continued, but the facts published by Hiffelsheim justify the belief that they would not be barren. These facts testify to the benefits that electric currents (we mean only continuous ones) may some day yield in brain-diseases—a point worth the attention of physicians for the insane. Till lately it was thought that electricity was a powerful stimulant only, but what is true of interrupted currents is not true as to currents from the battery. Far from being always a stimulant, the latter may become in certain cases, as Hiffelsheim maintained, a sedative and calming agent. This control over circulation, joined with the electrolytic power of the galvanic current, allows its employment in the treatment of various kinds of congestions. A congested state of the lymphatic ganglia, the parotid glands, etc., may be relieved by this means, the current acting in such cases both on the contractility of the vessels and the composition of the humors.

In cases of paralysis, more than any others, electricity displays all its healing power. Paralysis occurs whenever the motor nerves are separated from the nervous centres by any injuring cause, or by any modification of texture impairing their sensitiveness. With a destroyed nerve, paralysis is incurable, but, in case of its disease only, its functions can almost always be restored by electric treatment. As there is always some degree of muscular atrophy in the case, electricity is directed upon the nerves and the muscles at once, and the battery and the induction current are usually employed together. As a rule, the first modifies the general nutrition, and restores nervous excitability, while the last stimulates the contractile power of the muscular fibres. The difference of action between the two kinds of currents is clear in certain paralyses in which the muscles show no contraction under induction currents, while under the influence of constant currents they contract better than the uninjured muscles. Experiments made some years ago in Robin's laboratory, on the bodies of criminals executed, proved that, after death, muscular contraction can still be produced by Volta's currents, though Faraday's current has no such effect.

When the motor nerves are in a state of morbid excitement, they compel either muscular contractions that are lasting, as tonic spasms, or intermittent ones. The different motor nerves most commonly excited are the facial nerves, the nervous branches of the forearm or the fingers, which are affected in " writer's cramp," [1] and the branches of the spinal nerve, whose irritation occasions tic-douloureux, chronic wryneck, etc. Now, electricity cures, or at least noticeably benefits, these different morbid states, and exerts the like influence over neuralgic and neuritic affections, wherever these disorders are not the symptoms of other deeper maladies. Currents restore the normal activity of nutrition in the diseased nerves, and the corresponding muscles; they act on rheumatism, too, in the most beneficial way, modifying the local circulation, quieting the pain, and stimulating reflex phenomena, which are followed by muscular contractions. Erb, Remak, Hiffelsheim, and Onimus, have proved beyond question this salutary action on swellings of the joints, either in acute or chronic cases.

The discoveries respecting the influence of electricity over the spinal marrow have been used with advantage in the treatment of such disorders as arise from unduly-excited activity in this organ, such as chorea, St. Vitus's dance, hysteria, and other nervous convulsions, more or less similar. We cite two instances of this sort published by Dr. Onimus, giving an idea of the mode of applying the current in such cases. A child, twelve years old, was seized with a frightful attack. Every five or six minutes it lost consciousness, rolled on the ground; its eyes turned upward, then grew so rigid that none of its limbs could be bent. The attack over, it regained its senses, but the least impression, at all vivid, sufficed to bring on a new attack. Ascending currents were first applied to the spinal marrow. The child was at once seized with a violent crisis.

---

[1] Writer's cramp consists of a kind of spasm of the finger-muscles, preventing their regular contraction in holding or guiding a pen or playing the piano, while the muscles of the hand and forearm preserve all their normal strength.

Descending currents were then used for fifteen days in succession, after which the little patient regained health. A young girl aged seventeen, in hysteric condition, presented very strange symptoms in the larynx, the velum of the palate, and the facial muscles, among others a sort of barking, followed by vehement sniffing and horrible grimaces. By placing the positive pole in the patient's mouth against the arch of the palate, and the negative pole on the nape of the neck, all these morbid affections were completely subdued. The disposition of the poles in the reverse order, on the other hand, aggravated them. After sixteen repetitions of electric treatment, the young girl was almost completely cured, retaining only a muscular twitch of little importance, compared with her former ailments. Several cases of tetanus also were treated with complete success by similar methods. This terrible disease, the most fearful of all surgical complications, is due to an acute inflammation of the spinal marrow. It is followed by such an alteration of the motor nerves, that all the muscles of the body experience general contraction, and a painful rigidity that by degrees attacks the vitally essential organs. When an attack of this kind reaches the muscles of the chest and heart, death occurs, through asphyxia. In such a case the continuous current restores the motor nerves to their normal state. Two other chronic diseases of the spine, the first being particularly serious—progressive muscular atrophy and locomotive ataxy—often yield to the rational use of electricity, or at least are checked in their progress, the natural issue of which is death. It is worth remarking that these two disorders were discovered and described by Duchenne, in the course of his researches into this method of treatment. Electricity served his purposes of diagnosis, as it serves in physiology as a means of study, taking in that science the place of a kind of reactive agent, and revealing functional differences that no other process could have detected. To it alone, according to the way in which it affects a nerve or a muscle, belongs the power, under certain circumstances, of determining the nature and even the degree of alteration in nervous or muscular elements.

Aldini said that galvanism afforded a powerful means of restoring vitality when suspended by any cause. Several physicians, at the beginning of this century, restored life by this means to dogs, after they had undergone all the processes of drowning, and seemed dead. Hallé and Sue proposed at that period to place galvanic machines in the different quarters of Paris, particularly near the Seine. This wise and useful plan has not yet been put into execution, though all experiments made since that time confirm the proof of the efficiency of electricity in cases of asphyxia and syncope, produced either by water or by poisonous gases. The galvanic current also restores respiration in cases of poisoning by ether or chloroform, even when recovery seems hopeless. Surgeons who understand this effect, remember it whenever chloroform seems dangerous to the patient under its influence.

Electricity is transformed into heat with great ease. If an intense current is passed through a very short metallic wire, it heats, reddens, and sometimes vaporizes it. This property has been taken advantage of by surgeons for the removal of various morbid excrescences. They introduce a metallic blade at the base of the tumors or polypi to be extirpated, and when this kind of electric knife becomes incandescent, under the influence of the galvanic current, they give it such a movement that the diseased part is separated by cauterization, as neatly as with a cutting instrument. This method, which avoids effusion of blood, and is attended by only slight pain, has yielded excellent results in the hands of Marshall, Middeldorpf, Sédillot, and Amussat. Besides this application, in which heat plays the chief part, electricity has been used to destroy tumors, by a kind of chemical disorganization of their tissue. Crusell, Ciniselli, and Nélaton, have made decisive experiments of this nature. Pétrequin, Broca, and others, suggest the same method to coagulate the blood contained in sacs, in aneurisms. If this novel surgery is not so widely known and used as it deserves to be, the reason is that the manipulation of electric instruments requires much practice and dexterity, and surgeons find the classic use of the scalpel more convenient.

This rapid historical view shows that the method of treatment by electricity is useful in very many diseases. Whether resorted to to modify the nutritive condition, to quicken or check circulation in the small vessels, to calm or excite the nerves, to relax or stimulate the muscles, to burn or detach tumors, electricity, if managed rationally, is destined to do distinguished service in the healing art. The range of treatment by heat is less considerable, yet of some extent. The examination of the medical value of treatment by light has scarcely begun, nor has much been done toward the study of weight or pressure, in their relations to medical science. At all events, there is now forming and gaining increased development, alongside of the medicinal use of bodies, a medicinal use of forces—besides the physic of drugs, a physic of powers. It is impossible to say at present which of the two will definitely prevail—more probably both will be called on to render valuable services to art.

The first *savants* who studied the action of galvanic electricity on dead bodies, and saw them recover motion, and even an appearance of sensation, supposed they had touched the secret of life, likening to the vital principle that other force which seems to warm again the frozen organs, and restore their springs. Slight reflection on the facts collected in the foregoing pages reveals the thorough illusiveness of such a hope. Not only is electricity far from being the whole of life, but it cannot even be regarded as one of the elements of life, or be compared, for instance, with nerve-force. In fact, the experiments of Helmholtz have proved conclusively that such a comparison contradicts the truth. What is the peculiar sign of the vital forces and of vital unity, or the definite expression of their simultaneous action in one organism, is, precisely, organization. But electricity has no causal relation with organization proper. That is the work of some higher activity. That power in action, whatever it be, takes to itself all the forces of Nature, but it links them, coördinates them, and, fixing them into special conditions, compels their service to the purposes of life. Gravitation, heat, light, electricity, all these forces are maintained within living beings—only they are there disguised under a new phenomenal unity, just as the oxygen, hydrogen, carbon, nitrogen, and phosphorus, that make up a nerve-cell, vanish in it into a new unity of substance, without ceasing to exist in it as distinct chemical elements. The inorganic powers of Nature are as essential to life as lines and colors are in the composition of the painter's picture. What would the picture be without the painter's soul and labor? The picture is his peculiar work: the physico-chemical forces are the lines and colors of that homogeneous and harmonious composition, which is life. In it they would want meaning or power, if they did not in it, by the operation of a mysterious artist, undergo a transformation which raises them to a dignity not theirs before, and assigns their place in the supreme harmony. Thus, in the infinite solidarity of things, there is, as Leibnitz dreamed, a constant uprising of the lower toward the higher, a steady progress toward the best, a ceaseless aspiration toward a fuller and more conscious existence, an immortal growth toward perfection.

ODORS AND LIFE.

DESCARTES, Leibnitz, and all the great minds of the seventeenth century, believed that phenomena are such interdependent parts of one whole, that they require to be explained by each other, and consequently that a very close mutual connection should be maintained among the sciences. In their view, this was the condition of rapid advance and intelligent development. The experimental method, constant to systematic obstinacy in erecting so many barriers between the different sections of natural philosophy, has greatly hindered the completeness of whatever knowledge we possess as the result of mutual interaction among all truths. At this day, such barriers are tending to vanish of their own accord, and the science of man in his relations to external media begins to show the outlines of its plan and harmony. We have before this sketched several of its chapters, and we will endeavor now to write another, on the subject of odors.

I.

The seat of smell, or the olfactory sense, is the pituitary membrane lining the inner wall of the nostrils. It is a mucous surface, laid in irregular wrinkles, and receiving the spreading, slender, terminal filaments of a certain number of nerves. This membrane, like all other mucous ones, constantly secretes a fluid designed to lubricate it.

By the aid of the muscles covering the lower part of the nostrils, the apparatus of smelling can be dilated or contracted, precisely like that of sight. This understood, the mechanism of olfaction is quite simple. It consists in the contact of odorous particles with the olfactory nerve. These particles are conveyed by the air to the inside of the nasal cavities, and there strike upon the sensitive fibres. If the access of air is prevented, or if the nerve is altered, no sensation is produced. Experiments in physiology, in fact, have settled that the olfactory nerves (or those of the first pair) are assigned exclusively to the perception of odors. Loss of the sense of smell occurs whenever the nerves are destroyed or injured by any process, or even whenever they are merely compressed. On the other hand, it is a matter of common observation that impeding the passage of air into the nostrils is quite as effectual a way of making any sort of olfactory sensation impossible. Let us add that the region most sensitive to odors is that of the upper part of the nasal cavities. There are, as we shall notice in proceeding, considerable differences as regards the degree of sensitiveness in this sense of smell, comparing one man with another. But it is a still more singular fact that sometimes, without apparent cause, the sense is utterly wanting. In other cases it is unaffected by the action of certain odors only, an analogous infirmity to that which students of the eye call *daltonism*, and which consists in the perception of certain colors only. We find in scientific annals the case of a priest who was insensible to all odors except that of a manure-heap, or that of decayed cabbage; and another, of a person to whom vanilla was entirely without scent. Blumenbach speaks too of an Englishman, with all his senses very acute, who perceived no perfume in mignonette.

Olfaction is sometimes voluntary, sometimes involuntary. In the former case, by an act which is called scenting something, and is resorted to for the sake of a keener sensation, we first close the mouth, and then sometimes draw in a full breath, sometimes a succession of short, quick inspirations. Then the muscular apparatus edging the opening of the nostrils comes into play, to contract that orifice, and point it downward, so as to increase the intensity of the current of inhaled air. When, on the contrary, we wish to smell as little as possible, the organ becomes passive. We effect strong expirations by the nose to drive out the air that produces scent, and inhalation, instead of being performed by the nostrils, instinctively takes place through the mouth.

Scents and the sense of smell have an important share in the phenomena of gustation, that is, there is a close connection between the perception of odors and that of tastes. Physiological analysis has clearly brought out the fact that most of the tastes we perceive proceed from the combination of olfactory sensations with a small number of gustatory sensations. In reality, there are but four primitive and radical tastes—sweet, sour, salt, and bitter. A very simple experiment will convince us of this fact. If we keep the nostrils closed when tasting a certain number of sapid substances, so as to neutralize the sense of smell, the taste perceived is invariably reduced to one of the four simple savors we have just named. Then, whenever the pituitary membrane is out of order, the taste of food is no longer the same; the tongue distinguishes nothing but sweet, sour, salt, or bitter.

It is time now to begin the study of the physiological and chemical conditions of smell, and for this we must first inquire how odorous substances behave with regard to the medium which separates them from our organs. Prévost, in an essay published in 1799 on the means of making emanations from odorous bodies perceptible to sight, was the first to bring to view the fact that certain odorous substances, solid or fluid, placed on moistened glass, or in a saucerful of water, instantly act on those molecules of the liquid which they touch, and repel them more or less, producing a vacuum. He judged that this method might serve to make odors sensible to sight, and enable us to distinguish odorous from inodorous bodies. These movements of odorous bodies on the surfaces of liquids, of which camphor particularly gives so curious an instance, have lately been studied with the greatest care by a French physiologist, with a view to establishing a theory of odors. With this purpose Liégeois has examined most of the odoriferous substances, and has ascertained that almost all of them perform various motions of circulation and displacement on the surface of water, resembling those noted with camphor. Some act precisely as camphor does. Among these are benzoic acid, succinic acid, the rind of bitter oranges, etc. With others, motion soon stops, for they are quickly surrounded by an oily film which keeps them confined. Some must be reduced to powder before the phenomenon takes place. As regards odorous liquids, it occurred to Liégeois to saturate very light and spongy seeds, themselves odorless, with them, and he then found, on throwing the seeds on water, that circulatory and displacing movements took place, as with other substances. He concluded, from a series of experiments methodically tried, that the motions in question must be attributed, not to a release of gas, acting in the manner of a recoil, but simply to the separation and rapid diffusion, within the water, of the odorous particles. The volatility of substances cannot be admitted to have any part in explaining the phenomenon. It depends wholly on the affinity of fluids for the odorous particles, and also for those of fatty matter. Liégeois found, for instance, that a drop of oil put on the surface of water, without sensibly lessening in size, emits an enormous quantity of microscopic droplets, which are diffused through the mass of the water. Aromatic essences produce a like effect. Though insoluble in water, they have a powerful tendency to disperse themselves throughout it, and water that receives a very small quantity of the odoriferous principle, in the shape of extremely fine powder, has enough to gain their perfume completely. Liégeois's experiments give proof of the most diligent labors and of praiseworthy sagacity. Science has accepted them with satisfaction, and, after employing them usefully, will preserve the memory of their author, taken away in the flower of his age, at the outset of a noble career as a physiologist and surgeon.

It seemed, to quote his words, as though in these experiments we were assisting at the formation of the odorous molecules. Those delicate atoms emitted from odorous substances and diffused through the atmosphere, are in fact the very same that impinge on our pituitary membrane, and give us the sensation of odors. Moreover, facts long ago observed display this revealing action, so to call it, of water upon odors. At morning, when the verdure is moist and the flowers covered with sparkling pearls of dew, a fresher and balmier fragrance exhales from every plant. It is the same after a light shower. Vegetation gains heightened tints, at the same time that it diffuses more fragrant waves of perfume. We remark an effect of the same kind in the physiological phenomenon of taste. The saliva serves as an excellent vehicle for diffusing the odorous principles; then the movements of the tongue, spreading that fluid over the whole extent of the cavity of the mouth, and thus enlarging the evaporating surface, are clearly of a kind to aid the dispersion of the odorous principles, which, as we have seen, take a considerable part in the perception of tastes.

Now, in the phenomena of smell, air acts in the place of water. It seizes the odorous particles and brings them into contact with the pituitary membrane. It is the vehicle, the solvent, of those extremely subtile atoms which, acting on the delicate fibres of the nerve, produce in it a special movement, which translates itself into the most varied sensations. Oxygen, and the existence in that gas of a certain proportion of odorous molecules, are the two essential conditions of this phenomenon.

Such is, at least, the result of earlier experiments, and of those performed of late years by Nicklès. A curious fact, well worthy of attention, is the remarkable diffusibility and degree of subdivision exhibited by some odorous substances. Ambergris just thrown up on the shore spreads a fragrance to a great distance, which guides the seekers after that precious substance. Springs of petroleum-oil are scented at a very considerable distance. Bartholin affirms that the odor of rosemary at sea renders the shores of Spain distinguishable long before they are in sight. So, too, every one knows that a single grain of musk perfumes a room for a whole year, without sensibly losing weight. Haller relates that he has kept papers for forty years perfumed by a grain of amber, and that they still retained the fragrance at the end of that time. He remarks that every inch of their surface had been impregnated by $\frac{1}{2691064000}$ of one grain of amber, and that they had perfumed for 11,600 days a film of air at least a foot in thickness. Evidently the material quantity of the odorous principle contained in a given volume of such air is so minute as to elude imagination. We can readily conceive how philosophers cite such instances to give a notion of the divisibility of matter.

In fact, we are now considering matter emitted by odorous bodies. This shows that they do not act as centres of agitation, occasioning vibrations which pass in waves to our organs, to exert on them a purely dynamic influence. This giving off of odorous matter, with the necessary aid of oxygen in the atmosphere, proves, too, that odors are in no respect comparable to light or heat, which one may regard in an abstract way, in the immaterial and ethereal space which is the region of their motion, as proper forces, and acting from a distance. Odors, to be perceived, must be taken up by oxygen, and borne by it to the organ of smell. In a word, odor is the odoriferous particle itself, while light is not the light-giving body.

Does oxygen exert a chemical influence on those atoms of which it robs odorous substances? We do not know, neither do we know of what kind is the action which occurs on the contact of odor with the olfactory nerve, whether the phenomenon is a mere mechanical agitation, or whether some chemical decomposition takes place in the case. At any rate, it is allowable to reason from the observed facts that smell and taste are two senses peculiarly distinct from the others, as well with respect to the object of sensation as to the ideas which the mind derives from the sensation itself. Sight, touch, and hearing, in a manner physical senses, furnish us the ideas of external forms, harmonies, and motions. They introduce us to the conception of the beautiful, and are true fellow-laborers with the intellect. Taste and smell are rather chemic senses, as Nicklès calls them. They come into action only upon contact, and awake in us only such sensations as life and mind gain no profit from. While the former are the spring of the highest functions, the latter are of use only for the performance of acts of nutrition.

The learned and capable author [1] of a book on odors, published within a few years, fancies, however, that he can establish a kind of æsthetics of odors, more or less resembling that of tones. He has investigated olfactory harmonies, hoping to find in them the elements of a sort of music. "Odors," he says, "seem to affect the olfactory nerves in

---

[1] Piesse, on "Odors, Perfumes, and Cosmetics."

certain definite degrees, as sounds act on the auditory nerves. There is, so to speak, an octave of smells, as there is an octave of tones; some perfumes accord, like the notes of an instrument. Thus almond, vanilla, heliotrope, and clematis, harmonize perfectly, each of them producing almost the same impression in a different degree. On the other hand, we have citron, lemon, orange-peel, and verbena, forming a similarly associated octave of odors, in a higher key. The analogy is completed by those odors which we call half-scents, such as the rose, with rose-geranium for its semitone; 'petit-grain' and neroli, followed by orange-flower. With the aid of flowers already known, by mixing them in fixed proportions, we can obtain the perfume of almost all flowers." In accordance with these fancies, Piesse has formed gamuts of odors, parallel with musical gamuts, and exhibiting concords of scents at the same time with those that produce discords. As a painter blends his tints, the perfumer should blend his fragrances; and Piesse maintains he can only gain that object by following the laws of harmony and contrast in odors. This theory is certainly quite ingenious, and deserves attention, but it is open to serious objections. If the harmony of colors and of sounds exists, it is because optics and acoustics are exact sciences, and harmony in this case is reduced to numerical relations, determined in a positive way. These relations, as concerns odors, can have no other basis than a capricious and relative sensibility. They are thus incapable of being reduced to form, *a fortiori* of being translated into fixed precepts.

To complete these details, it remains to say something of the delusions of the sense of smell; for this sense, like the others, has its aberrations and hallucinations. The delusions of smell are hardly ever isolated; they accompany those of hearing, sight, taste, and touch, and are also less frequent than the latter. Insane people, who are affected by them, complain of being haunted by fetid emanations, or congratulate themselves on inhaling the most delicious perfumes. Lelut mentions the case of a woman, an inmate of la Salpêtrière, who fancied that she constantly perceived a frightful stench proceeding from the decay of bodies she imagined buried in the courts of that institution. Impressions of the kind are usually very annoying. Brierre de Boismont relates the account of a woman affected by disorder of all her senses. Whenever she saw a well-dressed lady passing, she smelt the odor of musk; which was intolerable to her. If it were a man, she was distressingly affected by the smell of tobacco, though she was quite aware that those scents existed only in her imagination. Capellini mentions that a woman, who declared that she could not bear the smell of a rose, was quite ill when one of her friends came in wearing one, though the unlucky flower was only artificial.

Such facts might be multiplied; but, as they are all alike, it is not worth while to mention more of them. The latest observations made in insane-asylums, among others, those of M. Prévost, at la Salpêtrière, have shown also that these delusions and perversions of the sense of smell are more common than had hitherto been supposed among such invalids, and that if they usually pass unnoticed, it arises from the fact that nothing spontaneously denotes their existence.

The intensity and delicacy of the sense of smell vary in mankind among different individuals, and particularly among different races of men. While some persons are almost devoid of the sense of smell, others, whose history is related in the annals of science, have displayed a refinement and range in the distinction of odors truly wonderful. Woodward, for instance, mentions a woman who foretold storms several hours before their coming, by the help of the sulphurous odor, due probably to ozone, which she perceived in the atmosphere. The scientific journals of the day relate the account of a young American girl, a deaf-mute, who recognized, by their odor alone, the plants of the fields which she collected. Numerous instances, moreover, prove that in savage races this sense is very greatly more developed than among civilized men. It is a traveler's story, that some tribes of Indians can pursue their enemies and animals of the chase by mere scent.

But it is among the other mammals that we find the sense of smell displayed in its highest degree of power and perfection. Among ruminants, some pachyderms, and particularly among carnivorous mammals, the olfactory membrane attains the keenest sensitiveness. Buffon has described these animals with extreme exactness, in saying that they smell farther than they see, and that they possess in their scent an eye which sees objects not only where they are, but even where they have been. The peculiarity of of scent in the dog is too well known to need more than an allusion.

If we can hardly give faith to those ancient historians who relate that vultures were attracted from Asia to the fields of Pharsalia by the smell of the corpses heaped together there after a famous battle, yet we must accept the assertions of naturalists so well qualified to observe as, for instance, Alexander von Humboldt. The latter relates that in Peru, and other countries of South America, when it is intended to take condors, a horse or cow is killed, and that in a short time the smell of the dead animal attracts a great number of these birds, though none had before that been seen in the country. Other more extraordinary facts are told by travelers. These must usually be received only with the greatest caution, because in most cases the sense of smell gains credit for what is due to the sense of sight, which, with these birds, is very keen and far-reaching. Yet, making allowance for exaggeration, it must be admitted that these animals have a very highly-developed sense of smell. Scarpa, who has made admirable researches on this subject, found that they refuse food which is saturated with odorous substances, and, as an odd instance, that a duck would not swallow perfumed bread till after it had washed it in a pond. The waders, which have the largest olfactory nerves, are also those birds that display the greatest keenness of scent. Reptiles have very large olfactory lobes, leading us to believe that they discern odors readily, but at present we know little of the impressions they are sensitive to in this respect. Fish also have an olfactory membrane. Fishermen have always remarked that they may be attracted or driven off by throwing certain odorous substances into the water. Sharks, and other voracious fish, collect in crowds and follow from very far about a body thrown into the sea. It is even said that, when blacks and whites are bathing together in latitudes where these fish abound, they particularly single out and pursue the more strongly odorous blacks. Nor are the crustacea indifferent to emanations which act on the olfactory nerve. The method used for attracting and taking crabs is familiar.

Regarding the lower animals, we have only still more uncertain information, except as to insects. Entomologists maintain that scent is very delicate in most insects, and rely on plausible conjectures on this subject, but they do not as yet know what the seat of the sense of smell in insects is. When meat is exposed to the air, in a few moments flies make their appearance in a place where none had before been seen. If refuse matter or bodies of animals are left on the ground, insects flock to them at once, feeding on such substances, and depositing their eggs in them. Scent alone seems to guide them, exclusively of sight even, for, if the object of their desire is hidden, they easily manage to find it. A curious fact as to the scent of insects is furnished by those kinds that prefer decaying substances. A beautiful arum is found in our woods, the cuckoo-pintle, whose white flower diffuses a disgusting odor. Now, the inside of this flower is often filled with flies, snails, and plant-lice, seeking the putrid source of this fetid smell. We may see the little creatures, in quest of their food or of a fit place to lay their eggs, move about in all directions, and quit most unwillingly the flower whose scent has misled them.

II.

Having thus learned what physiologists think of the sense of smell and the conditions of the perception of odors, let us see what naturalists and chemists have ascertained respecting the latter as viewed in themselves, what place they give to odorous bodies, and what character they attribute to them all. The three kingdoms possess odors. Among mineral substances, few solids, but quite a number of liquids and gases, are endowed with more or less powerful scents, in most cases not very pleasant ones, and usually characteristic. Those odors belong to simple substances, such as chlorine, bromine, and iodine; to acids, as hydrochloric and hydrocyanic acid; to carburets of hydrogen, as those of petroleum; to alkaline substances, ammonia, for instance, etc. The odors observable among minerals may almost all be referred either to hydrocarbonic or hydrosulphuric gases, or to various solid and liquid acids produced by the decomposition of fats, or to peculiar principles secreted by glands, such as musk, ambergris, civet, and the like. Vegetables present quite another variety of odors, from the faintest to the rankest, from the most delicious to the most disgusting. Absolutely scentless plants are very rare, and many, that seem to be so while they are fresh, gain, on drying, a very decided perfume.

The odor of plants is due to principles very unequally distributed throughout their different organs; some solid, as resins and balsams; others which are liquid, and known by the name of essences or essential oils. In most cases the essence is concentrated in the flower, as occurs with the rose and the violet. In other plants, as in bent-grass and Florence iris, only the root is fragrant. In cedar and sandal-wood, it is the wood that is so; in mint and patchouli, the leaves; in the Tonquin bean, the seed; in cinnamon, the bark, which is the seat of the odorous principle. Some plants have several quite distinct fragrances. Thus the orange has three: that of the leaves and fruit, which gives the essence known by the name of "petit-grain;" that of the flowers, which furnishes neroli; and, again, the rind of the fruit, from which essence of Portugal is extracted. A great number of vegetable odors belong exclusively to tropical plants, but the flora of Europe furnishes a large proportion of them, and almost all the essences used in perfumery are of European origin. England cultivates lavender and peppermint largely. At Nîmes, gardeners are particularly attentive to rosemary, thyme, petit-grain, and lavender. Nice has the violet for its specialty. Cannes extracts all the essences of the rose, the tuberose, cassia (the yellow acacia), jasmine, and neroli. Sicily produces lemon and orange; Italy, bergamot and the iris.

What, now, is the chemical nature of the odorous principles in plants? The chemistry of to-day reduces almost all of them to three categories of well-ascertained substances: hydrocarburets, aldehydes, and ethers. We will endeavor to give a clear account of the constitution of these three kinds of substances, and to mark their place in the register of science. The hydrocarburets are simple combinations of carbon and hydrogen, as, for instance, the petroleum-oils. They represent the simple compounds of organic chemistry. As to aldehydes and ethers, their composition is rather more complex; besides carbon and hydrogen, they contain oxygen. Every one knows what chemists mean by an alcohol; it is a definite combination of hydrogen, carbon, and oxygen, neither acid nor alkaline, which may be regarded as the result of the union of a hydrocarburet with the elements of water. Common alcohol, or spirits of wine, is the type of the most important series of alcohols, that of the mono-atomic alcohols. Chemists represent it by the formula C^2H^6O, to indicate that a molecule of it arises from the union of two atoms of carbon with six atoms of hydrogen and one of oxygen. Independently of the alcohols, which are of great number and varying complexity, organic chemistry recognizes another class of bodies, of which vinegar is the type, and which receive the name of organic acids, to mark their resemblance to mineral acids, such as oil of vitriol or aquafortis. Now, every alcohol, on losing a certain amount of hydrogen, gives rise to a new body, which is called an aldehyde; and every alcohol, on combining with an acid, produces what is called an ether. These rapid details allow us to understand precisely the chemical character of the essences or essential oils which plants elaborate within their delicate tissue. Except a small number among them which contain sulphur, as the essences of the family of crucifers, they all present the same qualitative composition—carbon and hydrogen, with or without oxygen. Between one and another of them merely the proportion of these three composing elements varies, by regular gradations, but so as always to correspond either to a hydrocarburet, or to an aldehyde, or to an ether. In this case, as in almost the whole of organic chemistry, every thing is in the quantity of the composing elements. The quality is of so little importance to Nature, that, while following always the same laws, and constantly using the same materials, she can, by merely changing the ponderable relations of the latter, produce, by myriads of various combinations, myriads of substances which have no resemblance to each other. The strange powers of the elements and the mysterious forces concealed in matter make themselves known to us in a still more remarkable phenomenon, to which the name of *isomery* is given. Two bodies, thoroughly unlike as regards their properties, may present absolutely the same chemical composition with respect to quality and quantity of elements. "But in what do they differ?" it may be asked. They differ in the arrangement of their molecules. Coal and the diamond are identical in substance. Common phosphorus and amorphous phosphorus are one and the same in substance. Now, the odorous principles of plants offer some exceedingly curious cases of isomery. Thus the essence of turpentine, the essence of lemon, that of bergamot, of neroli, of juniper, of savin, of lavender, of cubebs, of pepper, and of gillyflower, are isomeric bodies, that is, they all have the same chemical composition. Subjected to analysis, all these products yield identical substances in identical proportions, that is, for each molecule of essence, ten atoms of carbon, and sixteen atoms of oxygen, as denoted by their common formula, $C^{10}H^{16}$. We see how these facts as to isomery prove that the qualities of bodies depend far more on the arrangement and the inner movements of their minute particles, never to be reached by our search, than on the nature of their matter itself; and they show, too, how far we still are from having penetrated to the first conditions of the action and forces of substances. Among odoriferous essences placed by chemists in the class of aldehydes may be named those of mint, rue, bitter-almonds, anise, cummin, fennel, cinnamon, etc. The rest are ranged in the great series of ethers, which vary widely in complexity, notwithstanding the simple uniformity of their primary elements.

Such is the chemical nature of most of the odorous principles of vegetable origin. But chemistry has not stopped short with ascertaining the inmost composition of these substances; it has succeeded in reproducing quite a number of them artificially, and the compounds thus manufactured, wholly from elements, in laboratories, are absolutely identical with the products extracted from plants. The speculations of theory on the arrangements of atoms, sometimes condemned as useless, do not merely aid in giving us a clearer comprehension of natural laws, which is something of itself, but they do more, as real instances prove: they often give us the key to brilliant and valuable inventions. Piria, an Italian chemist, who was employed in Paris in 1838, was the first who imitated by art a natural aromatic principle. By means of reactions suggested by theory, he prepared a salicilic aldehyde, which turned out to be the essence of meadow-sweet, so delicate and subtile in its odor. A few years later, in 1843, Cahours discovered methylsalicilic ether, and showed that it is identical with the essence of wintergreen. A year after, Wertheim composed essence of mustard, while believing himself to be making only allylsulphocyanic ether. These discoveries produced a sensation. Nowadays the chemist possesses the means of creating many other natural essences. Common camphor, essence of bitter-almonds, that of cummin and of cinnamon, which are aldehydes, as we have seen, may be prepared without camphor-leaves or almonds, without cummin or cinnamon. Besides these ethers and aldehydes whose identity with essences of vegetable origin has been proved, there exist, among the new bodies known to organic chemistry, a certain number of products formed by the union of common alcohol or amylic alcohol with different acids, that is to say, of ethers, which have aromatic odors more or less resembling those of some fruits, but as to which it cannot yet be affirmed that the odors are due to the same principles in both cases. However this may be, perfumers and confectioners, more industrous and wide-awake than chemists, immediately made good use of these properties. Artificial aromatic oils made their first appearance at the World's Fair of London in 1851. There was there exhibited a pear-oil, diffusing a pleasant smell like that of a jargonel, and employed to give an aroma to bonbons. This product is nothing else than a solution of amylacetic ether in alcohol. Apple-oil was exhibited beside the pear-oil, having the fragrance of the best rennets, and produced by dissolving amylvaleric ether in alcohol. The commonest essence was that of pineapple, which is nothing else than ordinary butyric ether. There was observed, too, an essence of cognac, or grape-oil, used to impart to poor brandies the highly-prized aroma of cognac. The product which was then, and still is, the most important article of manufacture, is the essence of "mirbane," which very closely resembles in its odor that of bitter-almonds, and which commerce very often substitutes for the latter. Essence of mirbane is nothing else than nitrobenzine, which results from the action of nitric acid on benzine. Benzine, in turn, is met with among the products of distillation of tar, which also yield the substances used in preparing those beautiful colors called aniline. Besides the essences we have just mentioned, which are gaining an increasing importance in the manufacturing arts, artificial essences of quinces are also prepared, and essences of strawberries, of rum, etc. All these preparations serve, it must be admitted, to give an aroma to the cordials, confectioneries, and sweetmeats, which are so largely sold nowadays. In other words, the products of industry are constantly and in a greater degree taking the place of those of Nature. In all these cases, these instances of composition of odorous principles are among the finest triumphs of organic chemistry. The creative power of the chemist is ever widening its range. After the labors of Piria, Wertheim, and Cahours, came those of Berthelot, who has imitated the fatty matters of the animal economy. We are at this moment in progress toward the artificial manufacture of sugar. If we succeed in that, nothing more will remain but to effect the composition of albuminous substances, in order to give us the complete mastery of the processes which Nature follows in her elaboration of immediate principles. That gift of making its object a reality, which is the peculiar privilege of chemistry, is also one of the strongest arguments to bring in proof of the absoluteness of those laws which we ascertain respecting the system of forces external to us.

Linnæus, whose mind was remarkably analytical and classifying, not only arranged vegetables and animals in order, but also classified diseases, and even odors. He refers the latter to seven classes: aromatic odors, such as that of laurel-leaves; fragrant, like those of lilies and jasmine; ambrosial, such as amber, musk, etc.; garlicky, like that of garlic; fetid odors, like those of the goat, the orage, and others; disgusting odors, as those of many plants of the solaneæ order; and, last of all, nauseous odors. The terms of Linnæus have generally become current in language, but we understand, of course, that their value is merely conventional. As we have said before, there is no standard for the comparison of odors. We can only describe them by making comparisons between them, according to the degrees of resemblance existing between the impressions with which they affect our olfactory membrane. They have no qualities capable of being rigorously defined. This is the reason why it is impossible to give them any natural classification.

III.

The sensations produced by smells are perceived and judged of in a great variety of ways, though with less difference than prevails as to tastes. "I have seen a man," says Montaigne, "fly from the smell of apples quicker than from a cannonade." The instance he alludes to in this passage is that of Quercet, Francis I.'s secretary, who rose from table and took flight whenever he saw apples upon it. History tells us that Louis XIV. could not bear perfumes. Grétry was greatly annoyed by the odor of roses; that of a hare caused Mdlle. Contat to faint. Odors which disgust us, like that of asafœtida and of the valerian-root, are on the contrary highly enjoyed by the Orientals, who use these substances for condiments. Among other singular instances related by Cloquet on this subject, we will mention that of a young girl who took the greatest delight in inhaling the scent of old books, and that of a lawyer to whom the exhalations of a dunghill yielded the most agreeable sensations. So that it is out of our power to fix general rules with respect to the influence of odors on our organs, and the character of the sensations which they effect in us; still, from a purely physiological point of view, it is certain that some of them exercise a uniform influence. Chardin and other travelers mention that, when musk-hunters take from the animal the pouch containing musk, they must have the nose and mouth covered by a cloth doubled in several folds, if they would escape violent hæmorrhage.

The smell of the lily, the narcissus, the tuberose, the violet, the rose, the elder, etc., when it reaches a certain point of concentration, usually exerts an injurious influence on the system. It occasions more or less severe headaches, fainting-fits, and sometimes even more serious disorders. Some odors which have an agreeable perfume in a state of considerable diffusion, gain when concentrated a noxious and sometimes dangerous smell. This is particularly true of civet, patchouli, and the essences of neroli and thyme. Scientific records mention several cases of death occasioned by the poisonous action of some odorous emanations. It has been remarked that plants of the family of labiates, such as sage, rosemary, etc., offer in this respect no sort of risk, and seem rather to possess wholesome properties. Yet it is of consequence at this point to distinguish between the action of the odor which is in a manner purely dynamic, the intoxication from the essence, and the effect of carbonic acid thrown off by plants. These three influences have often been confounded by authors who have recorded accidents occurring after the more or less prolonged inhalation of odoriferous air.

This variable action of odors on the nervous system, sometimes wholesome, sometimes noxious, explains the part they have always played in the various circumstances of life among mankind. It would need a volume to relate the religious, political, economic, and gallant history of odors and perfumes. We must be content here with noticing its chief lessons, as far as they are connected with the physiological theory which is the basis of this study. For there is unquestionably something instinctive at the bottom of these general and uniform customs, which exhibit the affinity of man for odors. Doubtless we must recognize in this rather a refinement of sensuality than a natural craving; but the same result has occurred in this case as in the instance of beverages, of music, etc. Habit has become in some sort a second nature; the senses have acquired a taste for that especial intoxication which beguiles them, and disguises painful realities for them.

It is in religion, in the first place, that we observe the use of perfumes. Nothing holy or lofty was conceived of in which their influence was not present. Perfumes won the gods to give ear to the vows addressed to them in temples, where burning incense diffused its fragrant clouds. From the highest antiquity we find that the priests of different religions availed themselves of the use of odoriferous substances. Five times a day the disciples of Zoroaster laid perfumes upon the altar where the sacred flame glowed. Moses, in Exodus, recorded the composition of two perfumes used in rituals. The Greeks assigned a leading place to odors in their ingenious fictions of theology. They believed that the gods always declare their presence by an ambrosial fragrance, as Virgil tells us, in speaking of Venus;[1] and Moschus, describing Jupiter transformed to a bull. The use of perfumes in religious ceremonies had for its purpose the excitement of a sort of intoxication in the priests and priestesses, and also to disguise the smell of blood and of decaying matters, the offal of the sacrifices. The Christian religion borrowed from paganism the use of perfumes in the rites of worship. There was even a period at which the Church of Rome owned estates in the East devoted exclusively to plantations of trees yielding balsamic resins.

Besides these uses, odors were, in old times, still oftener employed in private life. Nothing surprises us more, in reading the ancient authors, than their relations on this subject. Among the Jews, the use of perfumes was restrained within proper limits, by the regulations of the Mosaic laws, which consecrated them to worship. But, with the Greeks, it reached an extraordinary height and refinement. They kept their robes in perfumed chests. They burned aromatic substances during their banquets; they scented their wines; they covered their heads with fragrant essences at their festivals. At Athens, the perfumers had shops which were places for public resort. Apollonius, a scholar of Theophilus, left a treatise on perfumes which proves that, even as regards the extraction of essences, the Greeks had attained astonishing perfection. Neither Solon's laws nor Socrates's rebukes could check the progress of that passion. The Romans inherited it from Greece, and enlarged the stock of Eastern perfumes by those of Italy and Gaul. They used them profusely to give

---

[1] " Then, as the goddess turned, a rosy glow
  Flushed all her neck, and from her head the locks
  Ambrosial breathed celestial fragrance round."

fragrance to their baths, their rooms, their beds, and their drinks. They poured them on the heads of guests. The awning shielding the amphitheatre was saturated with scented water which dripped, like a fragrant rain, on the spectators' heads. The very Roman eagles were anointed with the richest perfumes before battle. At the funeral of his wife Poppæa, Nero burned on the pyre more incense than Arabia yielded in a whole year. It is related, too, that Plancius Plancus, proscribed by the triumvirs, was betrayed by the perfumes he had used, and thus discovered to the soldiers sent to pursue him. Besides the odors extracted from mint, marjoram, and the violet, which were the most common, the ancients made much use of the roses of Pæstum, and various aromatic substances, such as spikenard, megalium, cinnamon, opobalsamum, etc.

It is singular to notice that the use of perfumes, brought from Rome with Grecian manners, was in its turn conveyed to France and Northern Europe with Latin manners, and chiefly by the Romish religion. It is from religious rites, indeed, that it passed into ceremonies of state, and thence into private life. Among the presents sent by Haroun-al-Raschid to Charlemagne were many perfumes. In the middle ages, among princes and men of highest rank, they washed their hands with rose-water, before and after eating; some even had fountains from which aromatized waters flowed. At this period, too, it was the custom to carry the dead to their burial-place with uncovered face, and to place little pots full of perfumes in the coffin. The French monarchy always showed an unrestrained passion for enjoyments of this nature, which seemed created as a necessary attendant upon all others. Marshal Richelieu so extravagantly indulged his passion for perfumes under every form, that he lost the perception of them, and lived habitually in an atmosphere so loaded with scents, that it made his visitors ill. Madame Tallien, coming from a bath of juice of strawberries and raspberries, used to be gently rubbed with sponges saturated with perfumed milk. Napoleon I. every morning poured eau-de-Cologne, with his own hands, over his head and shoulders.

IV.

Above all these questions which we have just skimmed, there rises another, of a graver and more mysterious kind, one which occurs at the end of all studies that treat of sensation, and with regard to which some reflections will not be out of place here. To what, outside of us, do those sensations which we experience within us correspond? What relation is there between the real world and that image of the world shadowed in our soul? In the special case we are concerned with, what is it in these substances which is the cause why they affect our sense of smell? It seems certain, in the first place, that odor in itself, so far as it is odor, is a mere figment of our mind. Contemporaneous physiology proves that excitement of the nerves of sensation is followed, in each one, by the sensation that corresponds with each. When we electrify the eye, we call up in it an appearance of light; when we electrify the tongue, we produce in it a sensation of taste; when we electrify the inside of the ear, we provoke in it the effect of a sound. So, too, a similar excitement, electric or otherwise, of the olfactory nerves, creates in our mind the sensation of smell, even though no odorous molecule takes part in the phenomenon. Sensation, therefore, seems to depend chiefly on the nature of the sensitive nerve. The external world seems to contribute to it only by setting in motion the nerve-fibres. Even this condition of an impulse infringing from without is not indispensable, since in sleep, and in madness, we experience sensations of smell which, by the testimony of our other senses, answer to no external agent. Still, we believe that we can distinguish cases of hallucination from cases of true perception; still, we maintain that there are, outside of ourselves, distinct causes of our distinct sensations. No skepticism has prevailed, nor will prevail, against this testimony of the most powerful evidence which exists in our inmost being. How can we account for this apparent contradiction? In reality, there is no contradiction. Observe, indeed, that even if the most indifferent causes can effect in us one and the same sensation, and thus delude us as to the outer world, our soul is never cheated. It knows perfectly well how to refer this one sensation to the dissimilar objective causes which have effected it; in other words, the causes which are alike, and are confused in one in the purely physiological act of sensation, divide and grow distinct in the psychological act by which the soul recognizes them, and conceives them as different. If we had, to give us knowledge, only the dull and ignorant passivity of our senses, there would be no separate reality for us; but the wise activity of the soul cannot merely assert the reality of outward objects, for a reason similar to that which makes it assert its own existence—it can, still further, argue from its various modes of affection to a corresponding variety of external forces. It moves in harmony with the world, rather than in harmony with the senses. In presence of the latter, it is like a good prince, who would be nothing without his subjects, but who regulates and civilizes them, by giving them laws, and ruling their morals. Thus, and this is the conclusion at which we aim, it is in the soul, regarded as the focus of all those rays refracted through the senses, as the central light outshining all others, that we must set the power and the right to discern what the senses do not discern, and to pierce to a depth forever beyond their reach. We shall never know what relation there is between the outward world and those images of it which we perceive, but the soul can hold the unshaken belief that the various points of those images correspond to points in the outward world situated in a like order, and that the forces which affect it are, in their essence, of the same nature as those forces of which, in its inmost depths, it feels itself the lord.

MEDICAMENTS AND LIFE.

To indulge doubts as to the healing art, is not to incur the reproach of ignorance. That sort of skepticism is the more warranted because many physicians freely admit that they have no very confident faith in the certainty of their art, and assert its illusions and its inefficiency complacently enough, even when they do not go so far as to deny the possibility of ever constructing a completely scientific system of remedial methods. The truth is, that medicine may be summed up as the application of certain sciences. Whenever these sciences make advances, that art should do so also, and in as clearly unquestionable a manner. The future development of the healing art will consist in preserving the balance between the progress of anatomy, physiology, pathology, and therapeutics, on the one hand, and that of practical medicine on the other, and in keeping the latter steadily subordinate to the former. Anatomy teaches how the organs are made; physiology, how they perform their functions in a healthy state; pathology, how they discharge them in a diseased state; therapeutics, how they behave in regard to media, that is to say, the modifying agencies of every kind with which they may be brought in contact. These four sciences, as definite and systematic as are all the other branches of natural philosophy, are the arsenals whence the physician takes his weapons for the contest he wages with disease. It is his part to make advantageous use of them, and to gain benefit, by quick perception, practised skill, and watchful diligence, from the inexhaustible resources of science. It is his to seize upon slight hints, and, with intuitive judgment, to refer the confused and irregular group of symptoms to the well-ascertained mechanism which only can explain them. He will perform this task the more easily and the more successfully, the more complete his knowledge is of the scientific truths which are its sole basis. Now these truths, at the present day, are in a condition of more rapid advance and enlargement than they have ever known hitherto.

I.

At the outset, the practice of physicians was confounded with that of the priesthood. Temples were also hospitals; but we know nothing certain as to the methods used in them to relieve or heal the sick, any more than as to the circumstances under which the discovery of the earliest remedies was made. The only certain point is that the latter were plants. Hippocrates used hellebore, bastard-saffron seeds, poison-carrot root, as purgatives. He prescribed oxymel and hydromel, and practised friction and bleeding. In reality, he used few drugs; his modes of cure were borrowed from dietetics and hygiene, of which he established the wholesome rules. The immortal practitioner of Cos believed that diseases tend toward a cure of their own accord. He admitted that there is such a thing as healing Nature, the effort of which the physician should aid by a suitable regimen. Asclepiades, of Bithynia, a scholar of Hippocrates, seems to be the first who understood the narcotic virtues of the poppy. In brief, the doctors of the schools of Cos and Cnidos had very few remedies at their disposal; but the tolerably rapid advance of natural history soon disclosed medicinal qualities in many substances derived from the organic kingdoms. Those works in which Aristotle and Theophrastus have summed up the condition of the botanical and zoological knowledge of their day, became the guide of experiments in healing, under the influence of which the first books relating to substances having medicinal qualities were written, among others the treatises of Scribonius, Largus, and of Dioscorides. That of Scribonius bears the title, "On the Composition of Medicines." It is dedicated to a freedman of the Emperor Claudius. The author had collected its materials in the different campaigns in which he had been attached as army physician to the Roman legions. Dioscorides also, who lived under Nero, was connected with the army in the capacity of a doctor, and collected in the countries he traversed a great number of substances taken from the three natural kingdoms. Returning to Rome, he made a selection of those which seemed to him to possess some efficacy in medicine, and described them in the Greek language in an important book, which gives us the most exact idea of the materia medica of the ancients, and which continued to be a classic until the sixteenth century. This book had the same vogue as those of Aristotle had; but we shall find that this kind of submissiveness to an ancient master has not stood in the way of progress.

Galen, the most learned and systematic among ancient physicians, gives a new form and impulse to therapeutics. Coming a little later than Dioscorides, he aimed to point out the best use that could be made of the weapons collected in the arsenal of pharmacy by the latter. The doctor of Pergamus had faith in the need of prescribing many remedies as firm as the conviction of Hippocrates that Nature should be permitted to act almost by herself in diseases. He substituted for the expectant methods the use of an abundance of drugs, and suggested the invention of those complicated mixtures known under the name of electuaries. Galenism is the origin of polypharmacy. It was supposed, under the control of those notions to which this doctor gave system and definiteness, that, while each substance retained its peculiar virtue in the general mixture, the compound enjoyed the properties of all the ingredients used in its preparation, and thus formed a sovereign panacea against an infinite number of ills. The most renowned of these compounds is the *theriacum*, which Borden calls the masterpiece of quackery, devoting to it a page full of wit. At first made up by Mithridates, it gained its perfect finish from the hands of Andromachus, Nero's physician. This theriacum comprised a hundred various elements, animal, vegetable, and mineral, some of them very odd, such as earth from Lemnos, and vipers' flesh. This opiated electuary was destined to occupy for a long time an important place in pharmacopoeias. It was compounded with great ceremony, and its qualities were so prized that rich men always kept a supply of it by them.

From Galen's time on, medicine is closely connected with scholastic philosophy. The later we come down, the more completely is it mixed up with theosophy and sorcery. The microcosm was held to be nothing but a copy of the macrocosm; men firmly believed that there is a close bond between the human body and the stars, and the doctor was bid to consult the latter before prescribing a remedy. A practitioner of the day, when asked if barley-gruel is fit for persons attacked by fever, answered that the draught could not do them any good, because it is a substance, while fever is an accident. This is the kind of advantage that medicine seems to have gained from that connection. While wrapped in the swaddling-clothes of this mysticism for nearly a thousand years, a travail was going on of the most amazing kind—some would say of the most injurious, but they are wrong. That subtile dialectic of the schools is the tie which binds Plato and Aristotle to modern philosophy, and gives continuous life to the tradition of speculative thought. That passionate pursuit of the philosophers' stone is the region in which the seeds of the future are slowly germinating. That phantom of the elixir of life is the step to a vast number of experimental attempts, from which the healing art gains profit in spite of them. In the general belief that every thing remains unmoving and wrapped in darkness, it will be found that, as early as the fifteenth century, the schools of Arabia and Salerno on the one hand, and the alchemists on the other, added a multitude of precious substances to the stores of the materia medica, such as several salts of antimony, sal-saturni, liver of sulphur, ether, ammonia, red precipitate, nitric, sulphuric, and muriatic acid, alcohol, etc.

Thus, when Paracelsus drew the attention of Europe to himself at the opening of the sixteenth century, the time was favorable to the design of that renowned physician. Paracelsus is the chief promoter of chemical therapeutics, and has thus exerted very great influence upon the destiny of medicine. He first put forward chemistry as the true method of preparing medicines, attacked the abuse of the complicated and often inert mixtures of Galen's polypharmacy, and brought to view the need of isolating the quintessences, the active principles of simples. He restored the almost forgotten opium to credit. He preached the use of powerful substances taken from the mineral kingdom, and showed the efficacy in medicine of the salts of mercury, of iron, arsenic, antimony, tin, gold, etc. His fortunate cures were as famous as his irregular life was. Paracelsus retained the forms of diction in use among his contemporaries, and even carried them to excess. His works abound in the mystical phrases of theosophy and the cabala, but he was at bottom a man of thoroughly emancipated mind, whose boasting may be pardoned in recollection of the opposition he met, and whose seeming madness we excuse when we remember the correctness of his fundamental ideas.

The seventeenth century, which was the grandest age of progress in the sciences and of literary greatness, saw therapeutics made richer by heroic remedies; emetics, quinine, and ipecacuanha. The use of these drugs was introduced under peculiar circumstances, which are connected with the most curious episodes in the history of medicine. Several compounds of antimony had been in use before the seventeenth century, as we have seen, but the most valuable of all, emetic or stibiated tartar, was prepared for the first time about 1630. The discovery and use of this new antimonial compound revived old discussions; among physicians and in the faculty it occasioned long-continued debates, very passionate and sometimes extremely comic. While Eusebius Renaudot published, in 1653, his "Antimony Vindicated, and Antimony Triumphant," James Perreau retorted, in 1654, by his "Kill-Joy for the Triumphant Antimony of Eusebius Renaudot." Perreau asserted that a monk, intending to purge the brothers of his convent, only made out to poison the whole of them, whence the name of antimony (*antimoine*). The quarrel grew far angrier, when one of the most bitter, but also one of the most reactionary, spirits of the time, the famous Gui Patin, contributed his sarcasms to those of the abusers of emetics. He would speak of stibiated tartar only by the name of stygian tartar, declaring it as deadly as the waters of the Styx, from which it seemed to him to issue. Yet Louis XIV. benefited by it, his doctors having ventured to prescribe a pretty strong dose of it for him in an illness he had at Calais. This was a severe blow to the enemies of antimony.

The name of the great king is also connected with the introduction of two other important remedies in therapeutics, quinine and ipecac. Quinine is produced naturally and abundantly in the forests of the Cordilleras. Probably its virtues as a febrifuge had been put to service for a long time by the natives of those countries when the corregidor of Loxa, in 1638, administered it for the first time to the Countess del Cinchon, the Spanish vice-queen in Peru. This lady was attacked by a very obstinate tertian ague, which the medicine easily conquered. As soon as this wonderful cure was known in the city, the townspeople of Lima sent a deputation to the viceroy, entreating him to give the new drug to the public. A large quantity of quinine was brought from Loxa and Cuença, which the vice-queen personally distributed among the inhabitants, and which was thenceforth called the countess's powder. A century later, in 1738, La Condamine gave the first complete description of the tree which furnishes quinine. His work served Linnæus as a basis for determining the characteristics of the genus, which he called cinchona, in memory of the Countess del Cinchon. In 1640, Del Cinchon went back to Spain, and his physician, Juan del Vego, brought with him a large cargo of the febrifuge bark, which he sold for a high price. The Spanish Jesuits soon made it the subject of profitable commerce, and in that way it entered into the European pharmacopœia. Yet its employment was not at first very general. In 1679 an English doctor, named Talbot, prescribed a secret remedy for the son of Louis XIV., who suffered from stubborn attacks of intermittent fever. The dauphin rapidly recovered his health, bought Talbot's secret for forty-eight thousand livres, and granted that physician a life annuity. Moreover, the remedy, which was merely a tincture of wine of quinine, was made public by the monarch's direction. As was the case with tartar-emetic, Peruvian bark gave rise in the schools to long discussions, in which, a singular fact, political and religious passions interfered; but quinine triumphed over all opposition, and, thanks to the efforts of Sydenham, Morton, and Torti, all practitioners were soon agreed in acknowledging its beneficial qualities.

Ipecacuanha was brought to France, and there used for the first time, in 1672, by a doctor named Legras, on his return from Brazil. He did not succeed in bringing into repute the powerful purgative and vomitive properties of that root. A few years later, another physician, of much greater enterprise, Adrian Helvetius, resolved to build his fortune on this drug. He posted placards in the streets of Paris, announcing an unfailing specific for the dysentery. By a lucky coincidence for him, several gentlemen of the court, and the dauphin himself, Louis XIV.'s son, were at the time suffering from that disease. The king, told by Colbert of Helvetius's secret, directed one of his physicians to enter into arrangements with the owner of the specific. The drug was first tried in the wards of l'Hôtel-Dieu. As soon as its efficacy was well established, they paid Helvetius one thousand louis d'or, with the added advantage of those medical honors to which they proposed later to raise him. Ipecac was spread very rapidly throughout France and the rest of Europe. Leibnitz himself thought it not beneath him to speak warmly in its praise. It must be observed, too, that all the great metaphysicians busied themselves with medicine. Descartes, Malebranche, and Berkeley, were not only practised in that science, but also devoted to it a part of their progressive meditations, and even their experiments. Under their influence, studies in medicine attained new exactness and activity. The methods and systems of physics and chemistry were introduced into biology; the composition of the forces, and the structure of the organs of the system, were studied. Philosophy, entering into medicine, imparted to it ardor in research and the passion for light. Let us not forget that the speculations of the seventeenth century are the real starting-point of that magnificent labor of expansion in the sciences of which this era and the following one present the spectacle.

The eighteenth century obediently followed in the sciences the impulse given by the preceding age. At that period Borden, with his Béarnese fire and his sparkling genius for medicine, made the use of mineral waters popular, particularly that of the sulphur and thermal springs of the Pyrenees, perhaps the most powerful of all. He recommended them for drinking, and made them famous by the talent with which he cleverly displayed their effects. Great Italian physicians studied the action of quinine very closely. Dating from the seventeenth century, opium gained an extraordinary popularity. The famous Sydenham, describing the epidemic dysentery of the years from 1669 to 1672, exclaims, after describing the preparation of the laudanum which has kept his name: "I cannot refrain from congratulating the human race that the Omnipotent has made it the gift of this remedy, which is apt for a greater number of cases than any other is, and excels all others in efficacy. Without it, the healing art would cease to be." Yet the effects of this remedy called forth long and passionate disputes, with which the name of Brown is connected. This doctor, who lectured at Edinburgh in the middle of the eighteenth century, there taught a theory of the effects of opium, which so carried his scholars away that they set up a statue to him, with these words carved on the pedestal: "Opium, assuredly, does not soothe." Brown indeed vehemently denied the sedative virtues of poppy-juice. He classed it among the stimulants, and, to prove himself in the right, swallowed enormous doses of it at his lectures whenever his fluency flagged. In that same school at Edinburgh, Cullen too was a professor, one of the great physicians of the eighteenth century. To him we owe the discovery of the chief property of digitalis, which is to check the movements of the heart, and consequently lessen the rapidity of the pulse. Before this, Withering and Charles Darwin had recognized its diuretic properties and its efficacy in dropsy, but Cullen justly claims the honor of having clearly proved the important fact that digitalis is "the opium of the heart."

The rapid advance of chemistry at this period could not fail to have an effect on that of therapeutics. For one thing, it had given origin to new systems as to diseases, and gained admirable drugs for practitioners. It is in the eighteenth century that the use of the purgative salts of magnesia began; that the discovery was made, by Goulard, of the acetate of lead, and the powerful astringent properties by which it is marked; and that the use of the salts of bismuth was recommended by Odier. At the same period Van Swieten made the solution of corrosive sublimate famous which has kept his name, and by which he replaced the inconvenient mercurial preparations in use before his time. These useful acquisitions, doubtless, encouraged the development of the art, but they did not much enlighten science in especial, and the time was drawing near when the question must necessarily be asked, how and why these drugs act. Hardly a thought had been given to that point before Bichat appeared.

Bichat, after having reconstructed anatomy and physiology, and then pathology, was ambitious to reform therapeutics also. Struck by the disorder and want of exactness of that science, he believed that it might be brought nearer perfection by the methodical study of the action of medicinal substances, not upon diseases, which are complicated phenomena, but upon the tissues. With this purpose he undertook at l'Hôtel-Dieu, at which he had just been appointed physician—he was then thirty years old—a series of exact experiments with regard to the effect of remedies. More than forty pupils began to assist him in this undertaking, and in each one of the course of lectures he was making on these substances he gave an account of the results obtained; but Fate did not allow him to go far in this untried path, for he died on the 3d of Thermidor, of the year X., aged hardly thirty-two. Thus the labors that might have impressed a new tendency upon therapeutics at the very beginning of the century, were checked by the death of the great man who had conceived the idea of them, and who would surely have successfully pursued their difficult execution. In truth, this surprising genius was too much in advance of his time. Among the physicians who came immediately after him, either no one saw the importance or else no one felt himself strong enough to attempt the realization of Bichat's design. Science had yet to await for more than fifty years those investigations which destroyed empiricism, and established therapeutics firmly and definitely. It is to Claude Bernard, in great part, that we owe this reform.

II.

Empiricism is so tenacious of life, tradition so mighty, that when Bernard undertook his first labors in scientific therapeutics, and explained its principles, twenty years ago, he had to struggle against the opposition of the most distinguished doctors. These physicians—among whom we may name Trousseau, with a mind of marvelous suppleness and brilliancy, gifted with the brightest artist-faculties, which for him took the place of those of the sage—persistently maintained that the action of remedies cannot be reduced to fixed laws, and that vital operations elude any exact ascertainment. Claude Bernard has disproved these unphilosophic assertions. He has unfolded, in many essays, the methods which permit a rigorous solution of the problems of therapeutics, and he has joined example with precept in his investigations as to curare, oxide of carbon, ether, nicotine, the alkaloids of opium, etc. His methods are the application of the rules of Cartesianism itself. "We must analyze," in his own words, "complicated actions, and reduce them to simpler actions, more easily determined. . . . Only experiments on animals enable us sufficiently to make those physiological analyses which will throw light and clearness upon the effects of medicinal substances as they are noted in man. In fact, we find that every thing we observe in man is repeated in animals, and *vice versa*, only with such peculiarities as the difference in their organisms accounts for; but the nature of physiological actions is fundamentally the same. It could not be otherwise, for, unless this were so, there could never be either any science of physiology or any science of medicine." The most famous of modern surgeons, Sédillot, has demonstrated, for his part, that surgical therapeutics can have no other basis than the unchangeableness of vital phenomena in their relation of cause and effect. He has made it plain that the art must be founded on the unity and generality of science, instead of leaving it at the mercy of individual fancy.[1] We now see in the clearest manner, thanks to the efforts of these two *savants*, how the study of those manifold resources which the physician has recourse to for the treatment of diseases may be advantageously pursued.

[1] "The unchangeableness of phenomena in their relation of cause and effect," says Sédillot, "is a law without which no science, no observation, no order, could be possible. Man, notwithstanding the very great complexity of the causes of his physiological manifestations, is no exception to it. What has occurred once, in given circumstances, will be constantly represented under like circumstances, and a change in etiological conditions is the only reason for modifications in function. This fundamental starting-point is indispensable for the physician, whose mind doubts and whose judgment is uncertain if he is not convinced of the constancy of facts submitted to his researches. No doubt the analysis he engages in is difficult; but, whatever its complexity, the most clearsighted, attentive, and persevering observer will make discoveries in it every day, with the hope of still adding to their number, and of introducing light and certainty where all was only darkness and confusion."— *Contributions to Surgery* (*Preface*).

Governed by these ideas, Bernard has studied the various active principles contained in opium, as regards their comparative influence over the animal functions, and has ascertained that they exhibit properties not merely differing from, but opposed to, each other. He has made more than two hundred experiments with morphine, narceine, codeine, narcotine, papaverine, and thebaine. These examinations have proved that, among these six principles, only three produce sleep; these are, morphine, narceine, and codeine. The three others have no soporific effect; they possess a power, either stimulating or toxic, which rather tends to thwart or to modify the narcotic effect of the former three. In the scale of their power to produce sleep, narceine holds the first grade, morphine the second, and codeine the third. As stimulants, thebaine has more power than narcotine, and the latter more than codeine. And last, as to their toxic quality, Bernard arranges them in the following order, begining with the most poisonous: thebaine, codeine, papaverine, narceine, morphine, narcotine. We see that the author of these investigations has not been content with merely describing the differences in their action which mark the alkaloids of opium, but that he has also measured the degree of intensity with which each one of them displays the kind of physiological or therapeutic activity peculiar to it.

These studies have been taken up again quite lately, by Rabuteau. This experimenter has examined the action of the alkaloids of opium on sensibility and on the intestine, and has made trial of them in a methodical way on the human subject, at the hospitals of la Charité and la Pitié. The order in which the various principles of opium may be classed, with regard to their activity, is not the same in the case of man as it is with animals. Thus Rabuteau found that morphine, which has relatively but little toxic power over the latter, is in the highest degree effective upon man in that manner. Narceine puts animals to sleep more readily than morphine, while the reverse is the case with us; yet the former, though less powerful than the latter as to the soothing of pain and the production of sleep, seems to be preferred with good reason in therapeutics. Narceine, in a dose of twenty-five centigrammes, induces a calm and refreshing sleep, followed by an awakening after which none of the troubles are experienced which follow the administration of morphine, such as weariness and nausea. It should be preferred also as a remedy for pain, since, in neutralizing pain in patients, it produces in them a most desirable condition of comfort; nothing is better for neuralgia, for instance. Narceine and morphine have, moreover, a property which explains the well-known effects of opium in intestinal discharges.

These labors present another proof of the benefit therapeutics gains from chemistry, and of the fixed connection there is between the improvement of one and the advance of the other. So long as opium was a mystery for chemists, it was one for doctors too. The moment the substance of that complex drug was decomposed into a certain number of well-defined principles, and the nature of their blending was ascertained exactly, that moment it became possible to decompose not merely the substance, but the physiological force of opium, and to reduce it to a small number of distinct potencies. Now, thanks to the labors of Bernard and Rabuteau, physicians can arrive at an understanding of the mode in which ancient therapeutics felt its way as to the use of opiates, and they are able for the future to act with precision on this or that function, by prescribing this or that pure alkaloid whose properties are known.

By uniting with the influence of narceine or morphine that of chloroform, we produce new and very curious phenomena. Bernard had already observed that insensibility produced by chloroform is prolonged in animals when they have taken opium. Nussbaum, having made a subcutaneous injection of acetate of morphine with a patient under operation, and who was put under the action of chloroform, noticed that the subject did not wake as usual, but slept on quietly for twelve hours. During this sleep he was insensible to pain. Goujin and Labbé have confirmed this fact, and made use of it in their practice, and have found that, by uniting weak doses of chloroform and of a salt of morphine, we may effect complete insensibility for several hours, without sleep necessarily attending it. Rabuteau also performed the following experiment: A dog to which five centigrammes of narceine had been administered, and which was then put to sleep by chloroform, had no feeling on awaking. It walked about in the laboratory, recognized a voice calling it, but had wholly lost the use of its sensitive nervous system. It could be pinched, or pricked, or its toes stepped on, without the least show of suffering. This singular condition, in an animal completely awake, lasted some hours; the next day sensibility had returned.

From chloroform to chloral the transition is natural. Chloral, which was discovered in 1832 by Dumas and Liebig, differs from common alcohol in having an excess of chloride, and less of hydrogen.[1] For nearly forty years this substance remained unused; its physiological qualities were not suspected. At length, in 1868, a German chemist, Liebreich, remembering that chloral may be reduced by alkalies into chloroform and formic acid, asked himself whether such a decomposition might not occur in the living organism as well as in a laboratory crucible. He tries the experiment, and Nature replies by an emphatic yes. Chloral is decomposed in the system on con-

---

[1] This substance may be regarded as tri-chlorated aldehyde. Chemists represent it under the formula C^2HCl^3O.

tact with the alkalies of the blood; it produces chloroform in it, but so very slowly that the sleep induced may last for some hours. This sleep, less deep and more quiet than that obtained by chloroform, has the additional advantage that it may be prolonged without any inconvenience by new doses of the anæsthetic compound. The success of chloral has been rapid. From 1832 to 1868, a few kilogrammes of it had been prepared for the demands of science; at present the Berlin manufactories, of themselves, furnish to commerce a hundred kilogrammes daily. This popularity is well founded, and will last, and the more so because chloral is not merely the same thing for medicine that chloroform is for surgery. It singularly lessens the excito-motor power of the spinal marrow, and may thus claim to be of remarkable utility in the treatment of several complaints; but is especially applied every day in calming violent and stubborn pain, like that of inflammatory rheumatisms.

The poppy contains several alkaloids which differ in their effects respectively. Various plants present the like complexity as regards therapeutics; others, on the contrary, like hemlock and belladonna, contain only a single alkaloid. Cicutine, the extract of hemlock, and atropine, obtained from belladonna, have very lately been the subject of interesting examinations. Martin, Damouret, and Pelvet, who have studied hemlock, have confirmed by experiment the precision of those historic details which have come down to us as to the symptoms experienced by Socrates, after he had swallowed the deadly draught.[1] Atropine has opened a new path in the treatment of disorders of the eye, thanks to the singular property it has of dilat-

---

[1] "When they brought him the poison, Socrates asked what he had to do. 'Nothing,' answered the jailer, 'but to walk about after swallowing it, till you feel a heaviness in the legs.' He drank, and walked about, and, as soon as he felt his legs weaken, he lay down on his back. At the

ing the pupil of the eye when dropped into that organ, or introduced through the usual passages. An extremely minute quantity of this active principle is enough to produce this phenomenon almost instantly, the importance of which Harley was the first to indicate. The exact knowledge of the effects of atropine, which, moreover, acts upon the whole nervous system, furnishes an explanation of the strange circumstances, among others the remarkable madness, of which ancient authors speak when describing some cases of poisoning by belladonna.

There exists a substance which exerts over the apparatus of sight an influence directly opposed to that of atropine; this is the Calabar bean, the properties of which were discovered in 1863 by a skillful physician of Edinburgh, Mr. Fraser. This seed, or rather the alkaloid contained in it, and which was isolated in 1865 by a French chemist, Vée, occasions so powerful a contraction and narrowing of the pupil of the eye, that the orifice almost completely vanishes. This constriction of the pupil reaches its highest point about an hour after the active principle has been administered, and persists for about three hours, and then slowly disappears. This action upon the muscles governing the movements of the pupil depends on the excitement of a particular nerve. Atropine paralyzes this nerve, thus occasioning dilatation of the pupil. There is thus an opposition between the active principle of the Calabar bean and that of atropine, and experience shows that the effects

same time, the man who had brought him the poison touched him, and after a little while examined his feet and legs; then, pressing one of his feet strongly, he asked him if he felt it; Socrates answered, 'No.' Afterward he again pressed the lower part of his legs, and, thus advancing upward, he showed us that the body was growing cold, and becoming rigid. He still continued feeling, and said, 'Whenever it reaches the heart he will die.' Already almost all the parts near the lower abdomen were chilled. Socrates then uttered a few words, then went into a convulsion, and died."—PLATO.

of one neutralize those of the other. Physicians professing the treatment of the eye are beginning to take advantage of these properties.

We find that every alkaloid, apart from a general action on the system, has also a more special one upon a certain part of the system, or a certain organ. Now, digitalis is a poison, or a remedy in heart-disease. Since Cullen's time, although he had so clearly indicated the true uses of that medicine, it was but little employed, except as a diuretic. Only of late years Traube, professor at Berlin, and Hirtz, professor at Strasbourg, have again taken up the study of this vegetable product, and again brought into view, by clinical experiments and results, the importance of the effect it produces upon the circulation and heat of the system. Thanks to the power it possesses of making the heart's pulsations slower, and consequently checking the movements of the blood, this agent is of service in all diseases, particularly those of a febrile kind, in which the activity of internal heat needs to be lessened. Digitalis owes these properties to a substance which till very lately there had been no means of isolating entirely. We were able only to obtain from it a formless substance, yellowish and complex, and varying in force of action. Within a few months a skillful chemist, Nativelle, has succeeded in extracting from it a principle quite definite in composition, in fine needles of crystals, white and extremely bitter, and which is true digitalis. The Academy of Medicine awarded an extraordinary prize to the author of this discovery. Digitaline, prepared by the new method, is so powerful that, in a dose of a quarter of a thousandth of a gramme only, with the human subject, it affects the movements of the heart, and in one of five thousandths of a gramme would produce death! On the other hand, its effect is so certain and so characteristic that, when digitaline exists in a mixture in quantity so minute that it can be discovered in it only by chemical reactions, there is an unfailing way of distinguishing it by observing the action of the mixture on the heart of a frog. This device was resorted to a few years ago, in a celebrated case of poisoning by digitaline. Physicians have also lately been using another alkaloid, veratrine, which, like the former, exerts a powerful action upon the muscular fibres, especially on those of the heart, and is serviceable in inflammations of the internal organs, particularly in inflammation of the chest.

Something may properly be said here of the *Eucalyptus globulus*, which has been so much talked of for several years. The eucalyptus, lately brought by Ramel from Australia to Southern Europe, where it is readily acclimated, is a gigantic tree of the family of *Myrtaceæ*. It contains a volatile oil, imparting peculiar properties to the leaves and bark, which have been employed with advantage of late in therapeutics—thanks to the efforts of several French doctors, particularly those of Grinbert. The essence of eucalyptus impairs the reflex sensibility of the spinal cord, and thus quiets cough and relieves oppression in very many pulmonary complaints. By the effect it produces on the mucosities it deserves a place in the first rank of remedies used in the treatment of catarrh. Prosper Mérimée, who spent the last years of his life at Cannes, constantly smoked eucalyptus cigarettes there, and seemed to derive great relief from them. Besides this essence, this Australian tree contains a bitter principle very efficient in intermittent morbid conditions, particularly malarial fevers. Indeed, in South America, Spain, Corsica, Algeria, and Roumania, the infusion of eucalyptus begins to enjoy a certain fashion as a febrifuge, and it is the more eagerly resorted to in those regions because it often subdues cases that have resisted the action of quinine. A fortunate wholesomeness, too, is the privilege of countries in which this tree is very common. The balsamic exhalations which it throws off constantly sweeten and cleanse the air. Travelers and physicians who have closely studied its physiological properties are persuaded that it might be introduced with advantage for giving salubrity to marshy countries where fever is endemic, by not merely altering the air, but also drying up the soil, and preventing the development in it of the aquatic vegetation from which miasma proceeds.

These new medicaments of which we have spoken are all of them organic compounds, that is to say, they are obtained more or less directly from vegetable or animal substances. Therapeutics also makes use of quite a number of mineral medical preparations. There are few among the latter whose introduction into practice is of recent date. Yet one of them that has come into use only within a few years has lately taken a very important place in the treatment of nervous disorders—we mean bromide of potassium. This salt, as to which physiologists had remarked its calming action on the nerves and vessels, has lately been adopted by practitioners as a remedy for nervous affections, and particularly for epilepsy. Given in a dose of several grammes a day, it exerts the most striking sedative action upon that fearful nervous malady; if it does not cure it completely, it at least effects a long intermission between the attacks, and always quiets the shocks, the convulsions, and irritability of patients. Observations made on a great scale seven or eight years ago, in England and France, leave no doubt as to the reality of this result. Another mineral preparation in medicine, employed for a long time, arsenical acid, has become, through recent labors of Magitot, one of the most certain agents used in dental treatment; it possesses the singular property of inducing reproduction of the ivory in teeth.

The facts we have here cited prove productive activity in the study of scientific therapeutics of late years, and form the best answer that can be given to doubts on the subject of medicine. We may believe, without indulging illusions, that this advance will not pause. We desire no better proof of it than the genuine ardor with which these researches are now followed in all countries. To use Rabuteau's words, we are no longer satisfied to know that a medicine cures, we wish to know also how it works a cure.[1] This sort of curiosity has seized upon almost all physicians; and even those who appear not to think that therapeutics deserves the name of a science, willingly make efforts to gain a better knowledge of the mechanism of action by medicinal substances.

Is there a relation between the chemical nature of bodies and the degree of their poisoning and curative power? We can now answer this question affirmatively. Certain observations, by way of experiment and conjecture, had long ago been made upon this point. Thus, we knew that the salts of heavy metals are more active than those of light ones; that the salts of lead and of mercury have poisonous properties, while the salts of soda and of magnesia are relatively harmless; but this was a mere comparison, without exactitude. Rabuteau has stated with precision the general relation between the physiological potency of mineral compounds and their chemical character. The power of the soluble metallic salts is in direct ratio to the atomic weight of the metal contained in the salt. The atomic weights of metals being in inverse ratio to their specific heats, Rabuteau's law may be otherwise expressed under this form: The metals are more active in proportion as their specific heat is weaker. The law is the same as to metalloids of the oxygen family; it

---

[1] "Elements of Therapeutics and Pharmacology," 1873 (preface). This remarkable work is the first treatise published on scientific therapeutics. It groups together with uncommon merit the latest labors respecting the action and usefulness of medicinal substances.

is inverse for those which are related to chlorine, and for those of the arsenical class. This untiring investigator, in order to establish these laws, undertook experiments six years ago, which have been steadily followed up till very lately; and the Academy of Sciences has recognized their discovery by a brilliant reward. Their practical interest may easily be estimated. When a physician, in future, has need to choose between different salts, all that will be required will be to consult a table of atomic weights in order to learn at once their respective activities, and consequently to fix upon the proper dose of them. When a physiologist wishes to test the action of a metallic compound, he will be able to foretell its relative intensity, and thus to guide his use of it in experiment. When the effect of salts of thallium was tried upon animals some years ago, this being one of the metals just revealed by spectrum analysis, it was noted with much surprise that these salts, so extremely similar in other respects to those of soda and of potassa, were yet powerfully poisonous. This is because the atomic weight of thallium is very high; its poisoning potency is thus in exact agreement with Rabuteau's law.

The improvement of the healing art is thus allied in the closest way with the advance of our knowledge as to the true action of toxic and medicinal substances. To enlarge this knowledge, we must follow Bernard's example and methods in the examination of effects produced upon animal tissues. It is of moment, too, as Dumas recommends, to test the action of all those new substances which organic chemistry has been for some time producing, several of which undoubtedly carry in them medicinal qualities. The study of these effects is very refined, and those *savants* who undertake it will need to handle with equal skill the instruments of physics, of physiology, and of chemistry. The point is not simply to analyze the manifest symptoms arising from disorder of the organs, to distinguish the parts affected, and to decide on the kind of change they have undergone; it is indispensable, besides, to investigate the alterations occurring in the direct composition of the secretions and excretions, as well as the passages and modes by which the active substances are eliminated; and, moreover, to measure the variations of temperature, pressure, muscular energy, etc., by which the therapeutic action becomes evident. To carry out successfully so complicated an examination, we use the common implements of vivisection, recording contrivances, most of which were devised by Marey, chemical reacting agents, microscopes, spectroscopes, and polarizers. In a word, all the sciences yield their tribute to the physiologist who seeks in his turn to furnish the physician with therapeutic precepts that may be confidently applied.

Such are, in respect to physiology, the just hopes of therapeutics. It may fairly indulge no less promising ones with regard to chemistry. The latter, which has already rendered so many and so great services to the healing art, will render it the last and the most desirable of all, by the artificial creation of those active principles which we are as yet still compelled to extract from vegetables. The preparation of the alkaloids by the aid of plants is so tedious and costly, and may be impeded in certain contingencies in a way so injurious to the interests of public health, that chemists should exert themselves to make those operations of a rude art unnecessary for the future. The knowledge of the inner structure of molecules is complete enough, the power of methods of synthesis is perfect enough, to allow such an attempt to be undertaken without rashness. In the vessels of a laboratory, vegetable acids, essences, and fats, are reproduced complete; pungent perfumes and brilliant colors are prepared from them by delicate chemical reactions; why might not chemists discover the secret of the formation of those subtile principles, beneficent or terrible according to their various natures, which sometimes restore endangered health, and sometimes quench the flame of life? It is true that attempts hitherto made in that direction have not been crowned with success; at least medicine has gained no advantage from them. It was while following out experiments on the means of obtaining quinine artificially, and while studying toluidine with this view, that Perkin, in 1856, discovered, instead of the precious medicine he was in search of, a red compound which became the source of aniline colors. This check, of so singular a kind, should not discourage investigators; permanent fame is reserved for him who shall succeed where Perkin failed.

We may be allowed to suppose, too, as A. W. Hoffmann lately took occasion to say, that the same thing will take place in future in therapeutics that has occurred in the art of dyeing. At this day no one endeavors, as used to be done, to obtain different shades by the mechanical mixture of several coloring-matters. One principle is taken, and, according to the color desired, is subjected to a determinate chemical transformation; one and the same molecule, modified in its inner structure by suitable reagents, becomes in succession red, blue, green, violet. One who watches attentively the influence of chemistry upon all manufactures, cannot doubt the realization of similar progress in other directions; he will trust that therapeutics will some day succeed in modifying, as it may choose, the properties of medicinal principles, not, as now, by means of mixtures in the druggist's glass, but with the help of fixed and regulated metamorphoses, effected in the very inmost structure of the molecule of the active principle. Late experiments by Messrs. Crum-Brown and Fraser have made a brilliant beginning in researches of this kind.

Therapeutics has been aided, and may be more and more benefited, by the labors of physicists. The employment of electricity, heat, cold, magnetism, and light, in the treatment of diseases, is yet in its earliest stages, though momentous results have even now been gained. We shall need to study with careful exactness the action of these various forces on the human system. Are not these very forces closely linked to the cosmic medium in which we live, a medium swayed by the general conditions of celestial mechanism? This is saying that the advance of medical art is not independent of progress in investigations upon the relations of the organism with agents which seem to touch it but slightly, and from afar.

Thus, history displays to our view all the sciences in constant mutual reaction, and completing their improvement by the reciprocation of profound influences. It is thus that they sustain each other inseparably in communion, and that the blended power of the whole gives at length, to the healing art as well as to industries of every other kind, increasing vigor and certainty. Such is the virtue of meditations and systematic experiments undertaken without any concern for the useful; but precisely because this manifold and painstaking evolution is performed unconsciously, to those who are its workmen, under the influence of a small number of general ideas of which philosophy is the perpetual source, it results that the sciences, enriched by philosophy, minister in their turn to its advance and perfection.[1]

---

[1] This essay may properly be completed by noting the labors which have lately led Rabuteau to suggest and recommend the protochloride of iron as that salt of iron which is most readily absorbed, and best adapted to the treatment of the many diseases in which preparations of iron are required.

ANIMAL GRAFTS AND REGENERATIONS.

SCIENTIFIC examinations followed out by the method of experiment are usually of a kind which either aids in completing theoretical conceptions as to the world, or else serves to stimulate useful applications in the region of industry and the arts. They sometimes join both these advantageous objects. The subject—an entirely new one—of animal grafting and regeneration presents this twofold interest in a very high degree. It sheds light on physiological theories, and supplies medical practice with novel resources; but it possesses another character of marked singularity in this respect, that the positive results it yields contribute at once to confirm the boldest conjectures of philosophic genius in past times, and to authorize the most daring hopes indulged by naturalists who have faith in man's omnipotence in times to come. It is our design to give a succinct demonstration of this truth.

I.

At the opening of the eighteenth century, hardly any other instance was known of the case of reproduction of organs in animals except that of the lizard's tail, which grows again after having been cut off. At least, *savants* knew no others, or rather they denied and classed with fables the declarations of fishermen regarding the regeneration of the limbs of crawfish, lobsters, etc. Réaumur determined, in 1712, to get at the truth as to these stories, and undertook experiments. "Having an opportunity," he says, "to examine the shores of the ocean, which are crowded with a vast number of crabs, a creature something of the nature of crawfish, I could not escape the suspicion that philosophers were wrong in this matter, and common people right." Réaumur took lobsters and crabs, removed one or several of their limbs, and shut up the creatures so mutilated in reservoirs communicating with sea-water. At the end of a few months he was astonished to find that new legs had taken the place of those that had been removed. He repeated his experiments with crawfish also, and described, with the precision which has given him renown, the mechanical method of these new growths.

Thirty years later, Abraham Trembley, while walking near a lake at the Hague, remarked in it certain fine green filaments, provided with appendages, and looking like vegetables. To learn whether he was really dealing with plants, he cut one of them into several bits. The separated parts soon reproduced each a complete whole, and these individual wholes moved, changed their place, and seized insects with their arms to carry them into their digestive cavities. They were fresh-water polyps, true animals. Trembley learned that, when one of these polyps was cut in two, the head reproduced the tail, and the tail the head. He cut two of them lengthwise, and joined them in a graft; instead of a polyp with eight arms, he had one with sixteen. A short time afterward Charles Bonnet repeated Trembley's experiments on the reproduction of the polyp, and tried others on a fresh-water worm called the naiad. He remarked that this worm, like the polyp, grows again those of its parts that are removed. He made like trials with the earthworm, and proved to his great astonishment that this highly-complex animal, which has so many rings, with delicate locomotive organs attached to each ring, which has, too, digestive and generative systems, etc., possessed a like power of reproduction. If considerable parts of its body, either in the region of the head or that of the tail, are removed, these fragments grow again in a very short time. Bonnet saw a worm shoot out twelve heads in succession in this manner. At almost the same period, Spallanzani went even further than the famous Geneva naturalist. He cut off the horns and even part of the head of the shell-snail, and saw them grow out again. He cut off the feet and tail of the water-salamander, and remarked their restoration in the same way. This last fact, more extraordinary than all the former ones, occasioned general surprise. In fact, the feet and the tail of the salamander contain bones, nerves, muscles, the reproduction of which seemed impossible. Certainly, the tail removed from the land-lizard had been observed to grow again, but without bony vertebræ. On the contrary, the salamander's tail grew anew with its complete bony frame, and of its original size. The untiring Italian experimenter also showed that the legs and tails of salamanders may be amputated several times, and the same organ reproduced many times over, with the same vitality.

These memorable experiments of Réaumur, Trembley, Bonnet, and Spallanzani, on the regeneration of animals, of which Leibnitz had long before conjectured the results, made a deep impression on Buffon's mind. He not only perceived in them very curious facts of natural history, but he also believed, as Bonnet did, that they gave force to certain ideas of a very high order. He discovered in them a wonderful demonstration of that conception of Leibnitz, that animated beings are made up of an infinite number of small parts, more or less resembling each other, that is, that life does not dwell in the whole, but in each single one of its unseen elements; or, in other words, to use a phrase of Bordeu's, that the general life is nothing else than the sum of a great number of special lives. That was a splendid period in the history of the sciences, at which observation, proving the intuitions of genius true, exhibited by instances so astonishing the composition of the organized individual to be such that every one of the living molecules that make it up has in itself a principle of activity and of individual development. Whatever corrections need to be applied to the way in which Buffon and Bonnet, after Leibnitz, have unfolded that doctrine, it remains, in its essential tenor, the starting-point of a rich evolution for biology, and the true expression of what is real.

The experiments just mentioned have been often repeated and ingeniously varied by naturalists. Little freshwater worms, to which the name of *planarii* has been given, have been a subject of study to several *savants*, among others to Draparnaud, Moquin-Tandon, and De Dugés. The latter cut in two a number of single specimens of the largest kind, either across or lengthwise, and he observed each fragment build itself anew, in twelve or fifteen days in winter, and four or five in summer, the head producing a sucker and a tail, and the tail a head and a sucker, and the piece in the middle sometimes keeping its sucker, sometimes losing it and again forming it, together with a head and a tail. Immediately upon the cutting, the outside bulges up like a cushion, while the centre shows the pulp exposed, and on this centre part the first outlines of the renewed portions make their appearance. A single one divided thus gives birth to several new ones, the size of which, at first proportional to the dimensions of the fragment, very quickly grows up to that of the original whole. More lately, Vulpian cut off the tail of a young frog, still inclosed in the egg, and put it in water. This rudiment of a tail maintained its life there, and developed regularly, passing through all the phases of its embryonic existence. Having reached the condition of perfect organization, its life ceased. Not long ago, Philippeaux noted the entire restoration of the spleen in animals from which that organ had been removed.

Charles Legros, who has undertaken of late years many interesting experiments upon regenerations, has discovered that time takes an important part in these phenomena. The tail of a lizard grows out again rapidly as to its outward shape; in two or three months the severed organ reappears with its usual length and thickness; but the interior is unlike that of regular tails, containing, as it does, nerves, muscles, and vessels, but no vertebræ. This texture remains unaltered for a long time, and naturalists had inferred from this that the bones of the lizard's tail are not reproduced. Legros has watched the advance of development in this organ for several years continuously, and has noted the appearance of vertebræ at the end of two years. This *savant* experimented with green lizards. The restored tail continued gray for a long time, and did not assume the color of the rest of the body before the beginning of the third year. In another case Legros cut off the tail of a dormouse at the beginning of winter. The wound shaped itself into a sort of pad, which lengthened, became covered with hair, and attained nearly the same length as the original tail, which it surpassed in thickness. Unluckily, the animal's hibernation was not perfect; it frequently awoke, and at the end of three months it died. There had been no opportunity for a complete restoration of the inner parts of the organ.

To these recent observations must be added those made quite lately on the crawfish by Chantran. This skillful and patient observer remarked that in the case of the crawfish the antennæ grow out during the time that intervenes between one shedding of the shell and the next, that is, in an interval varying, according to the creature's age, from six weeks to six months. The claws and the tail-plates are also reproduced, but much more slowly. The restoration is longer in proportion as the animal is older. With crawfish under a year old, all the severed limbs grow again in about seventy days. In the case of full-grown males, their complete restoration requires from eighteen months to two years, and with females from three to four years. Chantran discovered, moreover, last year, a strange phenomenon of quite another kind. He proved by experiment that crawfishes' eyes are reproduced after removal, and that sometimes, in place of an eye taken out, two grow again.

This is what experiment has confirmed regarding the reproduction of limbs and organs in animals. We must now examine in what way the tissues are restored. All the tissues that have been destroyed in the full-grown subject—the skin, nerves, muscles, bones—are capable of being regenerated, and they are regenerated, by going through a series of phases identical with those of their embryonic development, of their generation properly so called. The force which has brought them to birth is the same force which effects their new birth. In every case, the elements of the new tissue are produced exactly like those of the old, and these phenomena, in no wise unusual or exceptional, bear witness once again to the unity and simplicity of physiological mechanical action.

The epidermis is reproduced with the greatest ease. It grows again as the hair and the nails do. It is the same tissue with them. The crystalline humor of the eye, which may be considered like the substance of the epidermis, also grows again after it has been removed. At least this is the result of the very numerous experiments performed by Milliot on dogs and rabbits. That physiologist constantly observed that, after effecting with one of these animals the removal of that biconvex lens which is one of the chief organs of the system of sight, it was restored after a few months. The disease known by the name of cataract consists in the loss of its transparency by the crystalline humor, and in its becoming opaque, so that the rays of light no longer pass through it. The only remedy for this disorder in the eye is the operation called that for cataract, which consists in removing the crystalline lens. The eye thus operated on does not regain its original clearness of sight, but it can perceive light and outward objects much better than with its crystalline lens impenetrable to rays of light. The crystalline humor removed in such a case from the human subject is not renovated; but, by pursuing investigations of the kind which Milliot has begun, we may hope to discover the conditions of such a reproduction, which would be priceless to surgery. Restoration of the skin is noticed in all ordinary scars. The tissue of scars is made up of the usual anatomical elements composing the derma, that is, chiefly of laminated or elastic fibres. The vessels that are torn or broken, the severed tendons, in like manner, repair with the greatest ease those losses of substance they have suffered. In a word, in all these organs there is a tendency, observed by surgeons of every age, toward regeneration, a plastic and radiant force which makes itself known by an unceasing elaboration of *blastema*, within which new anatomical elements grow forth to supply the void of those removed.

Regeneration of nerves was remarked for the first time by Michaelis, Cruikshank, Monro, and Haighton, in the latter part of the last century. In 1801, Bichat expressed a perfect theory of it, with admirable clearness. Upon interruption of the continuity of a nerve, the severed part can reproduce itself after a certain time. When, for instance, a segment a centimetre long is cut out from the sciatic nerve, there is at first remarked a change in the nerve-substance of the ends produced by cutting; then, six weeks or two months after the operation, we see a grayish bunch proceeding from the point of one of the ends, which directs itself toward and soon rejoins the opposite end. This bunch is made up of laminated tissue and nerve-tubes more slender than the original tubes; but by slow degrees it enlarges, grows whiter, its fibres become complete, and, after a lapse of from four to six months, we have a nerve-cord of new formation. Such a cord is reproduced even when a part of the nerve six centimetres in length has been removed. During the time of restoration of the nerve-substance we remark the gradual reëstablishment of its sensor, or motor, or mixed functions. Vulpian and Philippeaux, who have studied this subject particularly, have ascertained that nerves absolutely severed from the nerve-centres can, after a period of change, thus regain their normal structure and properties. But the most instructive experiment made by these physiologists consists in joining together the ends of two nerves having quite different functions, as for instance the motor nerve of the tongue and the pneumogastric nerve, and in establishing anatomical connection and physiological communion between two nerve-cords which, in their usual state, have no mutual relation.

In 1867, Legros discovered the reproduction of cartilage, which till then had been regarded as impossible. He made his investigation upon dogs and rabbits, in whose cartilaginous tissues he had made free incisions, and at the end of about two months he noted a thorough renovation of that tissue. This is the same physiologist who first proved the reproduction of smooth muscular tissue, that is, tissue which is the organ of involuntary movement, such as that of the intestine. To exhaust the list of the organic tissues, it remained to be seen whether the muscular fibres in the living animal can restore, by means of like fibres, the losses of substance they have undergone. The following year Dubreuil was able to answer that question in the affirmative. He cut certain muscles of Guinea-pigs through the middle, and, on examining the organ some months afterward, he observed complete reunion between the separated parts, and ascertained that the solution of continuity was filled up by a fresh growth of muscular tissue. Thus all the tissues of the animal system can be reproduced in the grown-up subject, and these regenerations are uniformly identical operations with those which have as their result the first formation and the development of the very same tissues in the embryo or in the young animal.

In the practice of the surgical art the knowledge of these facts of reproduction has been the occasion of more or less remarkable inventions and operative methods, some of which are as yet under investigation. Those which relate to the renovation of bony tissue have interested the public peculiarly of late years. It has always been known that, when a bone is broken, the solution of continuity in it is filled up, after a certain time, by a portion of bone of fresh formation, a true bony scar, a callus. It was not before the middle of the last century that a French physiologist, Duhamel, and after him a Neapolitan physician settled at Paris, Troja, investigating the phenomenon of callus closely, discovered its physiological mechanism. They believed they could observe that the chief agent in the elaboration of bone is a thin fibrous sheath applied and adhering closely all around the bones, the membrane called the periosteum.[1] Their experiments were neither numerous nor striking enough to disclose to surgeons the advantage that might be gained from the knowledge of the bone-making property peculiar to the periosteum. The attention of practitioners did not begin to be drawn to this point until later, toward 1830, by the labors of a professor at

---

[1] The bones may be regarded as formed of three concentric layers, each inner one sheathed in another—the inmost one the marrow, next the bony substance properly so called, which is covered by the periosteum.

Wurzburg, Bernhard Heine. He removed more or less extensive portions of bone from living animals. In some cases he effected the removal of half of the bones he operated on. The parts destroyed were reproduced after a few months, and the limbs were restored to their original condition.

Still more famous than Heine's are the patient and skillful labors of Flourens. The varied experiments of this learned physiologist clearly established the truth of the first observation of Duhamel. In the words of Flourens, "Since it is the periosteum which produces the bone, I must of course be able to get bone wherever I can have periosteum, that is to say, wherever I can succeed in carrying or introducing periosteum, I shall be able to increase the number of an animal's bones; if I choose, I shall succeed in giving it bones which naturally it did not have." Among other experiments made to prove the truth of this proposition, Flourens conceived the idea of piercing a bone and inserting in it a little silver tube. The periosteum engaged in this tube became thicker there, swelled, and produced a cartilage which soon became bone. A skillful surgeon of Lyons, Ollier, cut out long ribbons of periosteum in an animal, leaving them still adhering to the bone by a little strip, and then twisted them round the neighboring muscles. After a certain time, this ossified periosteum had produced bones of circular shape, in spirals, in figures of eight, etc., according to the manner of twisting the periosteal strips about the parts near them.

In all these experiments, periosteum was used provided with the very delicate layer which adheres to it, and separates it from the bone. Now, Robin has proved that in the adult this layer is formed of bony cells, and of cartilaginous substance when a bone in course of development is operated on. It is in this that the bone-making power dwells, and, when the periosteum is stripped of this, it becomes unfit for ossification. Robin and Dubreuil have also proved that bony tissue may be formed without any cartilage existing beforehand, without any intervention of membrane, and may proceed directly from a bone deprived of membrane. These discoveries, without taking from the periosteum the evident share which it has in producing renovations of bone, give a conception of its mechanical action which differs from that which physiologists had admitted. They prove that really, in experiments of the kind tried by Duhamel, Heine, Flourens, it is bone which produces bone, as the severed nerve produces nerve. The cartilaginous or bony layer adhering to the periosteum is in fact nothing else than bone in process of formation; and whenever, whether by means of the periosteum or by means of an irritation, the reproduction of a certain quantity of bone is procured, it is because, in the first place, conditions fit for the production of cartilage have been brought about. These remarks will allow us to understand and to give a rapid estimate of the value of surgical methods founded on the knowledge of these facts.

Diseases of the bones are numerous. Independently of those cases in which they are directly injured by projectiles, they are liable to inflammations, tumors, and decay of every kind. These diseases are slow, in proportion to the slowness of vital elaborations in those organs, but they are not the less destructive, and they always end by bringing about a more or less considerable corruption of the substance of the bones. It is then necessary that the matters given off by the diseased bone should be cleared away: the mortified portions must be got rid of. The limb very soon swells, and becomes painful. Pieces make their way through the skin, suppurations are set up, and, if art does not interfere, the patient is led by exhaustion to a miserable death. To this concourse of evils surgery opposes difficult operations. It cuts deep openings, it loosens the tissues, it gives an outlet to whatever must pass away, it modifies the diseased surfaces; but there are cases in which neither Nature nor art can avail further, and in which the bone is so far gone that amputation becomes the only chance of safety for the patient. In these desperate situations surgeons have recourse to methods which allow them to effect a regeneration of the bone destroyed by the working of disease. The most useful of these methods, due to Sédillot, is that of scooping out.

The operation of scooping, as it is practised since the beautiful experiments of Sédillot, is very simple in itself. The skin, flesh, and periosteum, are cut through, down to the injured or diseased bone, and, when that is once laid bare, it is attacked with the gouge, chisel, and mallet. It is cut out and shaved away so as to remove the entire diseased portion, and to spare all that has suffered no alteration. Thus reduced to its sound parts and layers, the excavated bone by slow degrees repairs its losses. The destroyed substance is renewed, a new bony tissue fills the vacancies shaped by the operator's gouge, and after a few months the organ, which has never lost its form, is again restored to the conditions of common vitality. Sometimes, no doubt, the scene, in which, to borrow Hippocrates's thought, the surgeon himself, in the midst of another's agony, endures his own tortures, becomes complicated in an unforeseen way, and dangerous risks make it more tragic still; but art consists precisely in foreseeing and subduing these, and it is in this that the superior practitioner is eminent above another.

While Sédillot teaches and proves that it is necessary, in the interest of the reproduction of bone and the restoration of the limb, to get rid only of the diseased part of the endangered bone, and to preserve its sound layer clinging to the periosteum, some surgeons maintain rather that every thing should be removed, except the periosteum, that is to say, that the bone should be withdrawn from it, almost as one draws the finger out of a glove. They maintain that, this membrane being the exclusive agent in the production of the bones, they themselves may be cut away completely, and that they must be reproduced entirely, so long as the membrane is preserved.

Two distinguished practitioners, Larghi, of Verceil, and after him Ollier, of Lyons, have advocated that mode of operating which has received the name of sub-periosteal resection. The propriety of such a method of operating, after having been the occasion of doubts among surgeons who were in the way of examining it directly, is at this time unanimously condemned. The reasons against it are decisive. Indeed, how can it be admitted that the mere periosteum, that is to say, a soft sheath, without support or firmness, exposed by a cruel operation, more or less impaired by dissection, should effect the reproduction of a bone with its proper shape and size, when it is so difficult at any rate to effect the consolidation of a simple fracture without shortening? Would not this sheath, lost in the midst of the muscular mass, be in danger of inflammations of every kind, and exposed especially to the influence of many mechanical causes which will be apt to distort it, and consequently to cause the production of an irregular bone, shortened, and useless for serviceable action? Such are the fears and objections which impressed surgeons, and dissuaded them from sub-periosteal resections. These operations have in some cases allowed the renovation of the removed bone, but under such conditions that the limb has lost all strength and mobility, and has not escaped endless and fatal suppuration. The question in surgery is not merely as to reproducing bones, they must also be renovated with sufficient regularity of shape and sufficient firmness of structure to insure full use of the limbs. Now, such a result can only be gained by preserving the regularity and fixed consistency of the surfaces, sheaths, or moulds, in which the cells of the new bones are to deposit and grow together. The method of cutting out assures the existence of such a firm and unchanging mould by keeping a sheath of bone in the best conditions to procure a new growth of bony tissue, while that of sub-periosteal resections expects the regeneration of the organ out of a periosteum unsupported, injured, weakened, and bent under the influence of muscular contraction. Sédillot, who has the finest feeling for ancient medical art, and understands it thoroughly, has not left us in ignorance that Celsus had already, a little less than a thousand years ago, proposed cutting out of the bones; but the teaching of Celsus had not been accepted in practice. The famous French surgeon rescued these precepts from oblivion, proved their usefulness and importance by new arguments, explained the causes that warrant them, and their success, and has thus restored to the skillful and enlightened practice of the art one of the most precious means of relief for the formidable injuries and diseases of the bones.

II.

Life is a searching and expanding force which strives to seize upon all that comes within the range of its activity. We have just seen that it fills up the voids produced by the removal of certain organic parts; we are now about to see that it wins, by inverse operation, certain parts which it adds to living beings; for grafts are nothing less than living fragments pieced on to an organism already complete. In the vegetable graft, the grafted part does not make an integral portion of the single whole to which it has been transplanted. It does not live with the same life. It develops itself after a kind of parasitic fashion at the expense of the other, like misletoe on the oak; and, whether the grafted fragment be or be not of the same species as the tree to which it is united, it remains always physiologically distinct from it. The case is not the same with animals.

Animal grafting consists, in a general way, in fixing upon some point in an individual a part taken from another point in the same individual, or from a different subject, and in effecting the connection of the grafted part with the organism which serves for its support, in such a way that it may become completely incorporated with the latter, and may live with the same life, and follow the same physiological course. We may thus transfer from one animal to another either fragments of tissue, or whole organs in their completeness, or simple anatomical elements. The cells of the choroid of the eye, placed beneath the skin of an animal, preserve their vitality in that new region, and there even become the starting-point for a more or less extensive formation of similar cells. Transfusion of blood is nothing but the introduction of red globules borrowed from one organism into a different organism. This operation succeeds, even when the blood passes from one individual to another of quite a different species. Thus the blood of a mammal may be introduced into the veins of a frog, and those globules be found in the latter after some time, still living, and easily distinguishable as those of the superior being. We can without difficulty graft upon a cock's comb either spurs taken from the same bird, or teeth from a mammal; but such facts have hitherto had no interest other than that of curiosity, and need not detain us.

We have seen that bones may readily be reproduced by means of the periosteum. This property has suggested to some experimenters the idea of transplanting fragments of periosteum into different parts, so as to learn whether they would there occasion a formation of bone. Ollier, among others, has shown that the periosteal membrane, quite separated from the bone and grafted at some remote point, produces upon its deeper side a new bone. He effected a like reproduction by grafting not the whole periosteum, but merely the cells which compose the rudimentary layer adhering to that membrane, and which are the true producers of the elaboration of bone. Goujon has brought about the production of bone by grafting marrow. The insertion of a few medullary cells beneath a dog's skin, for instance, caused the development of a small bone at the spot in a few months. Surgeons at one time hoped to gain some advantage from these facts in the artificial renovation of the bony parts. Some of them affirm that they have even made new noses; but it is now clearly proved that noses procured by grafting with periosteum or with marrow have an insuperable tendency to be reabsorbed, and to disappear after a longer or shorter time, on account of the unfavorable conditions, with regard to nutrition, in which they exist. With no vascular or nerve connections, they are like foreign bodies in the place where they are developed.

We may class with the grafting of bones those experiments, still in course of execution, in which Magitot and Legros are engaged, relating to the grafting of teeth. The teeth grow out of a little sac called the dental follicle, in which are distinguished the organ of the ivory, or bulb, and the organ devoted to the growth of the enamel. By grafting upon a full-grown dog a complete follicle taken from a dog just born, these experimenters have noted the regular development of the germ and the production of a complete tooth. The organ of the enamel, grafted by itself, did not retain life; the germ of the ivory, on the contrary, occasioned a formation of regular ivory. Again, when the follicle, grafted in its entirety, was injured during the experiment, whether by accident or purposely, the appearance of a sort of bony tumor was noticed. These extremely interesting investigations allow us to hope that we may be able at some time to produce, in clearly-defined conditions, the physiological replacement of teeth removed. It is proper to remark, indeed, that in this case a grafting is made of a whole complete organ, with a structure and vascular arrangements which may make its development certain, while the transplantation of a fragment of periosteum or of marrow has the effect of isolating and encysting it.

The most exact and curious experiments that have been made in animal grafting, of late years, are due to Paul Bert. This learned physiologist has shown that, if the tail of a young rat be cut off and inserted, after flaying it, under the animal's skin, in any part of the body, it adheres to the place and continues to develop there. The organ gains in size almost as rapidly as in its normal conditions. Bert has also practised animal layering. He flays the point of a rat's tail, inserts the end in a hole made beneath the animal's skin, near the head, for instance, and joins the edges of the two wounds by stitches at points. The parts placed in contact quickly unite, and the tail, thus endowed with the shape of a handle, keeps its vitality. If it is then cut at any point, it is found that the fragment grafted in at the head preserves its physiological properties. The vessels are formed again in it, the nerves renew their life, and sensibility returns by degrees. The rat is thus furnished with a sort of trunk as much alive as its other organs. The return of sensibility in this trunk proves not only the connection of the nerve-threads of such an appendix with those of the back, but also the possibility of the propagation of sensor nerve-action in an opposite direction to that it previously followed, that is to say, the power of the nerves to carry impressions in a centripetal course as well as in a centrifugal one.

Siamese grafting has been effected by Bert under exceedingly interesting conditions. Strips of skin are separated by cutting along the opposite sides of two animals, and by means of these ribbons pressed face to face, and stitched together, the two subjects are sewed into union.

After a few days the connection has grown complete, and we have such a pair as the Siamese twins. Bert kept two white rats thus banded together for more than two months; but they lived on such bad terms that at the end of that time it was necessary to separate them. By poisoning one of two animals of such a brace, the other is poisoned also, thus proving that there is complete mutual circulation of blood. Bert effected like graftings between the white rat and the Norway rat, and between the white rat and the Barbary rat. He attempted to perform them between animals of different species—between a rat and a Guinea-pig, between a rat and a cat—but the success was never complete; only the beginning of adherence was obtained. Still this failure seems to depend less on the incompatibility of the tissues themselves than on the difficulty of keeping animals so little disposed to live harmoniously together in the necessary state of quiet. Once more, Balbian succeeded in uniting two fragments of tails taken from two different young bull-heads, so as to obtain a physiological adhesion for a certain length of time.

If the interest attached to such experiments is rather philosophic than practical, a point to be considered hereafter, this is not the case with those which obtain as results what are called epidermic grafts. These indeed have had the privilege of attracting the highest degree of attention from physiologists, and particularly from surgeons. We owe to a Swiss surgeon, Reverdin, formerly an *interne* of the Paris hospitals, the discovery and the first application of these. Whenever, after a surgical operation, a burn or a wound, the skin over a certain extent of surface is destroyed, the void produced is filled up only very slowly by means of a growth of scar-tissue. In spite of the use of the most judicious methods of dressing, the exposed surface is never restored but with difficulty. In seeking a remedy for this grave inconvenience, Reverdin conceived the idea of applying over such wounds a shred of healthy skin, taken from the injured subject himself or from some other person. The first attempts were undertaken in 1869, in the Paris hospitals, and were crowned with full success. Numerous experiments were at once made. Gosselin, Guyon, Ollier, Duplay, Hergott, and others, in France, obtained very satisfactory results. English, Russian, and German practitioners did not hesitate to contribute their share of confirmatory observations, and we may be allowed to say that at this day epidermic grafting has taken a definite place in surgical practice. This does not prevent the admission that it presents difficulties of more than one kind. This application of shreds of foreign substance to the denuded surface of a wound requires extreme delicacy of attention on the part of the surgeon who proposes to effect it. In the first place, an attempt to cover the entire wound by one single grafting would not succeed; several slips of very small dimensions must be applied, the progress of cicatrization must be watched day by day, the strips that fail to adhere replaced, etc. Usually the graft is complete at the end of twenty-four hours. At that time the transferred part forms one body with the wound, by the intervention of cells produced in the interspace between them. It thus follows that cicatrization is completed very rapidly. The scar is firmer and more pliant than the ordinary ones, and does not exhibit, as they do, any disposition to contract.[1]

The name given to this process, "epidermic graft," is not quite precise. In reality, the strips used in such a case are not composed of epidermis alone; to procure them, the epidermis is detached in connection with the thin

---

[1] Grafts on men have been made not only of human skin but of skin borrowed from animals also. Dubreuil has lately performed some curious experiments on this subject. He has grafted Guinea-pig's skin upon a man.

cellular layer (Malpighi's layer) on which it directly rests, and this condition is essential, because the Malpighi cells seem to be the seat of that formative elaboration which effects the adhesion of the graft. Since Reverdin's experiments, some surgeons have attempted to transfer the whole complete skin, instead of the epidermis. Ollier has tried to graft large cutaneous strips, comprising the whole thickness of the skin. The chances of success by this process seem to be much slighter, and nothing as yet encourages us to regard cutaneous grafting, properly so called, as a fortunate operation.

III.

These grafts, in which we see an organized portion, severed for a time from the individual whole to which it belongs, retain the springs of life and regain its functions when it is transplanted to another individual even of a different species; these regenerations, in which we see destroyed organs grow again with their original forms and their properties, living fragments reproducing a whole complete being—are facts of a kind to yield us, if suitably examined, valuable knowledge as to the essence of vitality itself. They prove that it does not depend on an indivisible spirit animating the body (*mens agitat molem*), but on an activity distributed among the minute particles that make it up, consubstantial with these particles, and as variable in its characteristics as they themselves are in their structure; in other words, the total life of the individual is but the sum, the resultant, of the lives peculiar to each anatomical element, the harmonious union of the simultaneous working of myriads of monads—the monads of Leibnitz—gifted with life in different degrees, from the bony cell, almost inert and mineral, to the nerve-cell in which a strong and fine fire burns unceasingly.

Every one of these living corpuscles is a complete whole,

having at bottom the same forces, the same tendencies, the same aspirations as the more or less complex systems to which it gives birth by a thousand associations and various interweavings. "Nature's machines," says Leibnitz, "are machines throughout, however small the part in them one may take; or, rather, the least part is in its turn an infinite world, and one even that expresses, after its fashion, all that there is in the rest of the universe. This surpasses our conception, yet we know that it must be so, and all that infinitely infinite variety is established in all its parts by a sublime constructive wisdom more than infinite." [1]

But what is in itself the vital force peculiar to these tiny machines, the force that we observe maintaining itself in the several parts of the organism, and restoring the voids produced in the tissues? what is the fundamental character, the mark of life? It is nutrition, that is to say, the fact, as plain as it is inexplicable, of the continuous molecular renewal of organized substance. It is in the understanding of the phenomena of nutrition, the "trophic" phenomena, that the whole future of biology lies. We shall never grasp the secret of the deepest and most essential vital actions, until we shall comprehend the equations of the statics and dynamics of those fleeting systems, restlessly passing through cycles of change, which compose the anatomical elements.

Whatever future the knowledge of trophic phenomena will bring with it, the conception of life won for us by natural philosophy opens from this time forward a new path for investigations. It suggests the thought of examining into the variations of physiological determinism, that is, of studying the boundaries within which life moves, or, in other words, the profound modifications of which organisms are susceptible, whether from the point of view of the specific

[1] "Letter to Bossuet," Unedited Works, published by Foucher de Careil, vol. i., p. 276.

type, or from that of their internal modes of action. The plan of such an undertaking is the boldest of all those that imagination and human knowledge dream of, in the region of scientific activity. Yet Claude Bernard, whom no one suspects of unfaithfulness to the method of experiment, does not hesitate to regard it as allowable. He is convinced that, by acting on the phenomena of evolution, we might be able to alter the configuration and to transform the arrangements of the organs. "Observation tells us," he says, "that by cosmic influences, and especially by means that modify nutrition, we act upon organisms in various ways, and we create individual varieties possessing special properties, and making, in some sort, new beings. . . . There is no reason why these modifying agencies, working on the living organism under certain conditions, may not produce changes such as would create new species: for we must conceive of species as being in themselves the result of persistence for an indefinite time in their same conditions of being and of nutrition, in consequence of an earlier organic tendency which was communicated to them by their ancestors. By modifying the internal media of nutrition and evolution, by taking hold of organized matter in some sort at its springing state, we may hope to change its course of evolution, and consequently its final organic expression." [1]

These remarks of the famous physiologist, to which, perhaps enough attention has not been given, are, however, in the highest degree worthy of attracting notice from those *savants* engaged in the problem of the transformation of species. Certainly Darwinism is something more than a bold hypothesis. The partisans of his teaching assert that living species have been in former times transformed, but thus far they have produced no instance of such a transformation taking place in the past, and the doubt is allowable whether they will ever be able to give retrospective proofs

---

[1] "Report on the Progress of Physiology," pp. 3 and 113.

of it. The fact is, that species heretofore have been subjected only to the action of Nature's spontaneous influences, and of the arts of zootechny; but that which forces of this kind were powerless to effect yesterday might very well be accomplished to-morrow by the powers which the physiologist now has at his disposal. By directing action to the eggs, as Claude Bernard suggests, that is, to the living germs, we gain a far more powerful and solid grasp on the remote plans of life. The embryo, that faint and indefinite sketch of the future being, that microcosm in which the silent forces of vitality slowly possess themselves of a soft pulp, sensitive to the slightest disturbances, is not forced to unfold itself in accordance with any unbending law: Robin has demonstrated this.[1] It might then be possible to occasion, in the embryo of an animal, modifications compatible with life, to maintain these in the animal once formed, to repeat and multiply them gradually upon the products of following generations, so as to fix them definitely by means of heredity. Some experiments made in this direction, among others those of Dareste, Brown-Séquard, Trécul, etc., are highly promising; but the subject, we easily see, requires the diligent coöperative labor of many lives of men. It is in this way that the philosopher will be able to disturb the mechanism of things, and invert the course of natural transmutations. He will impose his own will on the forces of the universe. Whenever he is shattered by them, they know nothing of it; when he subdues them, it is with absolute knowledge of what he is doing.

These corpuscles themselves, these ultimate monads in which life dwells, may we not regard them in their turn as being susceptible to the action of inward modifications, and capable of displaying new properties? It is very interesting to remark that the same anatomical element shows

[1] *See* his remarkable work on the "Appropriation of Organic Parts," 1869.

the same composition in all living species, at the lowest degrees as well as at the heights of the zoological scale; that is to say, that living molecules, whatever be the variety of the different systems they form by association, are at bottom always the same. On what do this unity and constancy of composition in the elements out of which organic tissues are woven, depend? On the fact that they all live in the same medium, and all positively absorb exactly the same nutritive materials. We might believe that the organization exerts an act of choice among the mass of the bodies that surround it, that it has a particular affinity for certain principles, and a repugnance to assimilating others. Very certainly, some substances, a very small number of them, are absolutely incompatible with life, at least such as we conceive it; but this does not prove that organisms are endowed with the power to exert distinct selection among the total chemical ingredients of the air, earth, and water. The first germs, and the animals born of them, took naturally and spontaneously what they found around them, and grew by degrees accustomed to it. The clay out of which a mysterious hand has fashioned them is a complicated combination of every thing that exists in the medium in which they float. That which was chance in their original constitution became the law of their ultimate constitution. Those immediate principles, thus more or less readily assimilated during the rudimentary periods, became adapted, under the sway of heredity, to conditions most favorable to life; harmony gradually arose between matter and form; and the nature of the functions followed upon that of the organs. At least nothing authorizes us to assert the contrary, and every thing leads to the belief that, if the materials of the earthly medium had been otherwise proportioned, the composition of living organs would not be the same that we know. We thus see that the question is no other than a completely rational one, whether we might not undertake to modify directly the existing composition of anatomical elements.

This latter conception, which sets the bounds of physiological determinism at a far greater distance than the former does, is also capable of verification by experiments. Just as we act upon phenomena of evolution, we may, by processes of methodical and persistent boldness, disturb the order of the operations of nutrition. The method we have followed in our own researches on this subject consists in suppressing certain essential principles of nutrition, and substituting for them new immediate principles, more or less similar. But the immediate principles that are nutritious are found mingled with the substances of food in the conditions most favorable to assimilation. The mineral salts in them are intimately combined with azote matters. In order, then, to replace these mineral salts of common food with others, phosphate of lime, for instance, with phosphates of a different kind, it is necessary not merely to disengage the food as much as possible from the salts that we wish to reject, but also to associate with it in the closest manner the new salts which we intend to fix in the system; that is to say, we must introduce them into it under the form fittest for assimilation, and most capable of overcoming the natural resistance of the organism. It is also clear that it is best to experiment on young animals, in which the action of assimilation is most intense. Under such conditions, and by such processes, we reach the end of modifying the order and kind of the immediate principles in organized substance. Personal experiments permit us at least to assert this, as far as it regards the bony tissue, and thus far we have seen nothing that compels us to doubt our power of producing at length, by gradual transformations, following upon certain contrivances of nutrition, organisms of a new and harmonious equilibrium, from the point of view of the system of immediate principles. In any case, investigations of this kind have a very great interest. They give us the means of determining the relations between the molecular weights of immediate principles, and their nutritive coefficients. On the other hand, by introducing at a given time a certain assimilable principle into the organism, and marking the time that elapses between the moment of its entrance and that of its issue, we have a process for measuring the speed of nutritive movement.[1]

We do not dwell any longer on these experiments. It is enough for us to have traced succinctly their general direction in agreement with the movement going on in the rest of physiology. No doubt, such labors are tedious and difficult. Besides knowledge and patience, we need, to attack them, faith and imagination; but the labors of the present can only be fruitful on the condition of a clear vision of ideal truth, that glorious star in which the philosopher deserving that name will never cease with passionate striving to read the destinies of the spirit.

[1] *See* two memoirs published by me on this subject ("Comptes rendus of the Academy of Sciences," 1870, vol. lxxi., p. 372, and 1873, vol. lxxvi., p. 352).

FERMENTS, FERMENTATIONS, AND LIFE.

UNTIL very lately, all fermentations were supposed to be produced by the spontaneous decomposition of organic matter within a fermentable liquid. It was said that on contact with air this organic matter undergoes a special change which gives it the character of leaven, and this was regarded as an agent having the power of spreading decomposing movement. It is true, brewer's yeast had long been well known; the facts of its cellular composition and its organization were familiar; but no relation was recognized between this organized condition and those phenomena of fermentation produced by yeast in saccharine liquids, such as grape-juice or the wort of ale. In the first few years of this century Turpin, and afterward Cagniard-Latour, attempted in vain to prove that such a relation existed; it was always denied that any thing else could be observed in alcoholic fermentation than an operation resembling all those slow decompositions that were classed among fermentations. We have admitted, in our time, that alcoholic fermentation, instead of being an exception, is on the contrary the very type of the phenomena we are treating of; that the yeast-cells, far from being unimportant, take an essential part in it, and that in all fermentations whatever there occur low organizations, microscopic corpuscles, more or less analogous to those of yeast. At least this is the first result of investigations carried on in the past fifteen years by several men of science, among whom in the first rank Pasteur is to be cited.

Pasteur began the course of his labors in 1858, by the study of alcoholic fermentation. He placed it beyond a doubt that, in the case of grape-juice or beer-wort, as in that of any other saccharine liquid exposed to the air, the more or less rapid production of alcohol is always connected with the production of a microscopic fungus, consisting of rounded globules, a few thousandths of a millimetre in diameter. These globules, known under the name of brewer's yeast, multiply in the fermenting liquid at the expense of the organic matters it contains, and, by the exchanges of growth they give rise to, produce decomposition of the sugar into alcohol and carbonic, succinic, and glyceric acids. These are the four invariable products of alcoholic fermentation. Sugar is the food of the yeast-fungus; these products are its excretions. The laws of the inner mechanism that elaborates them are yet unknown. But every thing leads us to believe that the yeast-cells secrete a substance more or less resembling those that work out the phenomena of digestion in the higher animals. Alcoholic fermentation would thus be a kind of digestion of sugar within the globule.

Dumas, who signalized his entrance upon the career of studies in natural science half a century ago, by memorable discoveries in microscopic physiology, has lately returned to researches of the same kind, precisely, in respect to fermentations. In Pasteur's laboratory at the Normal School he has taken up investigations on this subject, the results of which, quite lately published, show that the distinguished *savant* in question has lost neither his cautious diligence in experimental processes, nor his lucid conception in the grasp of principles. He has attempted, among other things, to determine the decomposing force, the amount of activity, possessed by each cell of the alcoholic ferment. To ascertain this, he measured the quantity of sugar decomposed in a given time by a fixed weight of yeast, and he found—after first establishing that a cubic millimetre of yeast contains about 2,772,000 cells—that the power of a million of cells represents the force capable of decomposing four grains of sugar in an hour. If we attempted according to this estimate to express in figures the number of cells employed in producing the wine, beer, and cider, consumed every year, as Dumas says, even astronomers would shrink from the task.

This active property of decomposing sugar, and forming alcohol in consequence, does not belong to the cells of brewer's yeast exclusively. Several chemical agents possess the same power, and certain vegetable cells also are adapted to use it. When fruits are placed in a medium filled with oxygen, they absorb this gas, and occasion the release of carbonic acid; if, on the contrary, they are left in carbonic acid or any other inert gas, they effect the production of alcohol. The fruits remain firm and hard, without suffering any external change, but the sugar they contain is transformed in part into alcohol. How is this phenomenon to be explained? In common air, the cell of the fruit is fed by oxygen; if this gas is withheld, it is forced to borrow the materials of nutrition from the fluids that moisten it, that is, from the saccharine juice, and then the latter is decomposed. Pasteur has noted that a similar alcoholic fermentation takes place in other vegetable organs, in leaves, for instance, and in every case he has proved that the phenomenon is due to the cells of the vegetables alone, and not to yeast-globules. Far from throwing any doubt on the physiological doctrine of fermentation, these singular facts agree in lending it support, by giving it deeper and more general application.

We have seen that the fermentation of sugar yields alcohol. The latter, brought in contact with certain porous substances, as, for instance, platinum sponge, can absorb the oxygen of the air and transform itself, by oxidation, into acetic acid. A phenomenon of this kind occurs in wine when it sours, the alcohol contained in it being changed into acetic acid; only, the agent in the transformation is in this case a microscopic plant, made up of little elongated globules, some thousandths of a millimetre in diameter. These globules, these mycoderms, develop on the surface of wine exposed to the air, and form a scum which plays the part of storing away a certain stock of oxygen, afterward used to produce acetification in the liquid. This scum, which is called mother of vinegar, only acts while in communication with the air. As soon as it is below the surface, it loses its efficacy, and the production of acetic acid is checked. Thus the development of vinegar in the acetic fermentation is reduced to an oxidation of alcohol, in which microscopic cells are the vehicles of the oxygen.

When milk turns and sours, that phenomenon also is due to the formation of an acid—lactic acid. This substance proceeds from the decomposition of sugar contained in the milk, and this decomposition, again, is a fermentation. The microscopic being that effects it assumes several forms; sometimes it is made up of cells presenting much resemblance to the cells of yeast, sometimes it consists of straight and exceedingly fine rods. Milk also contains casein, which is the substance that composes cheese, and, when the fermentation of the sugar in milk is over, that of the casein begins; after lactic acid, butyric acid is produced. Examining with a microscope the casein transforming into butyric acid, we observe in it little rods, two thousandths of a millimetre in diameter, and of a length from two to five times as great; this is the butyric ferment, which, concurrently with other microscopic vegetable growths, determines in various cheeses the slow production of butyric acid and several analogous acids, equally strong in smell. To cite a last illustration, the decomposition of urine, giving rise to an abundant release of ammoniacal gases, is also the result of a fermentation; under the action of cells smaller than those of brewer's yeast, the contained urea changes to carbonate of ammonia, rendering the liquid highly alkaline and strongly odorous. In short, the fermentations we have just described, and many others of the same kind, participate in the nutrition and development of microscopic beings, of an average size not exceeding some thousandths of a millimetre, and presenting the form sometimes of spheroidal or of egg-shaped globules (as mycoderms, torulaceæ), sometimes of straight, bent, or curving rods (as vibrios and bacteria). These diminutive beings engender the ferment within the fermenting liquid itself, in the degree and rate of their propagation in it.

There is another class of fermentations in which the immediate presence of definitely-shaped corpuscles cannot be traced. Thus diastasic fermentation consists in the transformation of starch into sugar under the action of a formless yellowish matter, called "diastase." Amygdalic fermentation is that in which amygdaline becomes the essence of bitter-almonds, by the action of a like ferment, known as "synaptase." The former takes place in the vegetable embryo when the amylaceous matter of the seed is converted into a soluble sugar, which permeates the growing tissues of the plant. The latter occurs when bitter-almonds are crushed in water; on contact with the liquid, the mixture of these odorless kernels takes the characteristic smell of the essence of bitter-almonds, which results from the fermentation of amygdaline. We regard as fermentations, moreover, a certain number of similar phenomena which can be produced with the implements of a laboratory, and which are constantly taking place in living organisms, of which the cause is a zymotic substance. There exists, for instance, in the saliva a principle called ptyaline, which, like diastase, converts amylaceous matter into sugar. The gastric juice contains another principle, pepsin, which has the effect of liquefying albuminous substances, so that they may be prepared for absorption. The pancreatic fluid contains another principle which acts in a similar way. Digestion is thus reduced to a series of fermentations, as the ancient chemists had rightly conjectured in regard to it. These different phenomena, as well as those in which organisms take part, have the two general characteristics of fermentation; they occur only within certain limits of temperature, and the weight of the fermentable matter is always much greater than that of the ferment which suffices to decompose it.

To conclude, fermentations occasioned in certain media, by the act of development and nutrition of ascertained microscopic animal or vegetable existences, present a group of well-defined characteristics. They follow obediently all the variations that may occur in the physiological activity of the microscopic beings contained in the liquid. This does not go into fermentation all at once; it delays more or less, and molecular movement makes itself perceptible in it by degrees. The phenomenon is one of evolvement. This appears to be the characteristic of alcoholic, lactic, acetic, butyric, glyceric, and putrid fermentations—all of those, in short, which Pasteur has studied with so convincing accuracy. Is it the same with the conversion of amylaceous substances into sugar, under the influence of diastase or ptyaline, with the dissolving of proteic substances by pepsin, with the change of amygdaline into the essence of bitter-almonds, by contact with synaptase? Evidently not. These phenomena present another aspect; they show no stages of evolvement. Doubtless they require a certain time for their completion; but they take place all at once, and without any relation to the surrounding air.

These differences between the two kinds of fermentation clearly depend on this: that, in the former, the phenomenon is subjected to the conditions and vital progress of those organized corpuscles which elaborate the ferment within the substance of the fermentable liquids, while, in the latter, the phenomenon is brought about by a ferment already formed and prepared. But this latter ferment is no less of organic origin; it, too, arises from living beings, animal or vegetable. Whether it emanates, like diastase, from the young cells of the seed, or results, like pepsin, from work done in the digestive apparatus, it is the labor of life, just as much as if it had been completed by globules of yeast or bundles of bacteria. Thus the efficient sources of all fermentations are the same. All ferments are at bottom alike, whether procured directly for the fermentable liquid by microscopic bodies inhabiting it, or emanating from corpuscles that inhabit elsewhere. The true doctrine of fermentations consists in this point.

Henceforth, then, we may consider ferments as products of a fecundation taking place in cells, as secretions elaborated by those myriads of infinitely little corpuscles, some crowded, squeezed, condensed, into the palpable organs of animals and plants—others free and moving, disseminated, as we shall see, into vast, intangible space. The energy which distinguishes these microscopic animal and vegetable growths also belongs to the microscopic elements making up the living tissues in the higher animals. We must give to this property, hitherto considered as special, the high dignity of a fundamental and universal attribute of organized cells. We must detect, in the most complex conversions and processes of nutrition in superior beings, the same untiring and primitive force that marks the subtile action of invisible and insignificant monads.

No doubt, the corpuscles of different species—to which, in the last analysis, we reduce animals and plants of every kind and degree—are not identical. Each species has its own structure, its specific energy, its mode of nutrition, its fixed secretions—characteristics, moreover, which vary with circumstances and media. Yet we can point out more than one interesting similarity between certain ones of these species, which seem to discharge quite distinct functions, and hold very unlike stations, in the vast harmony of vital monads. The cells of fruits, when placed in certain conditions, behave, as has been seen, like the cells of brewer's yeast; they both decompose sugar and yield alcohol. We may trace resemblances not less close, as Blondeau and Pasteur have done, between acetic mycoderms and blood-globules. Both alike serve as carriers of oxygen—the first for the slow combustion of alcohol; the last, for the slow combustion of the albuminoid matters in animal tissues. It is even likely that there is a principle in mycoderms similar to hemoglobine in the blood-globule, and provided with a special affinity for oxygen. However this may be, comparisons of this kind open a new path for physiology. As that science is definitely summed up in the explanation of existences and processes in the microscopic elements of organs, it is plain that nothing can be more useful to it than the study of these one-celled organisms in which the phenomena are extremely simple, and life is reduced, in a manner, to its primitive factors. It becomes more and more evident that progress in the comprehension of the superior animals is bound, with the very closest ties, to advance in the comprehension of the mechanism of nutrition in the rudimentary units of life, in the smallest beings that it is given us to study.

II.

Now, whence come those organized microscopic corpuscles to which, as we have seen, very many of the alterations of organic matter must be attributed? Upon this great problem, opinions at this day are still very contradictory.

Neither patient observations, nor minute experiments, nor profound reasonings, have been wanting; yet some still believe that these little bodies grow, by spontaneous generation, within fermentable liquids, while others assert, and profess to have proved, that they come from germs contained in the air. Certainly, the former opinion involves nothing contradictory nor impossible. Those who reject it by begging the question, in the name of some unknown, mystical doctrine of life, do not even deserve to be listened to in the investigation. It might possibly have occurred that organized beings should be produced, complete at all points, in a medium deprived of organization; yet experiment proves that this does not occur. We must, then, accept the other opinion—the panspermist doctrine—that is to say, we must concede that the germs of microscopic animals and vegetables, with which so many fermentations and putrefactions are connected, exist in the air. This is one of the conclusions, and perhaps the most legitimate and most fertile one, of Pasteur's striking studies.

He deserves the glory of it precisely because he has not priority in it. In truth, the originator of this idea only had, and could only have, a dim intuition of it. He could measure neither its importance nor its consequences. The importance and the results of a great idea, whatever it may be, only become apparent when, after undergoing a certain evolution, it has gained the precision, certitude, and establishment, that nothing but long experience can confer upon it. A conception must have acquired some age in science to wear a fixed authority, and bestow fame on those who comprehend, and cause to be comprehended, all its grandeur and power. The circulation of the blood had long been seen by glimpses, in the schools of physiology, when Harvey gave it complete and vigorous demonstration. Gravitation had long invited research, and suggested presentiment, before Newton drew its perfect system. So, too, the panspermist theory, neglected and ignored since the time of its earliest authors—among whom Astier, in 1813, deserves particular mention—has only been definitely established in our time, through the experiments made by Pasteur. That famous chemist has improved a vague sketch into a finished and masterly drawing. These experiments, repeated and varied in a thousand ways, all refer to the investigation, by comparison, of what takes place in the same fermentable liquid, under the different conditions of exposure to common air, filled with dust, and of contact with purified air. For instance, Pasteur puts a certain quantity of a liquid, that readily undergoes change, into glass balls through which a current of air may be made to pass. Fermentation and the development of small organisms take place very soon in the balls through which common air circulates; but, if the air, before entering them, passes through a plug of cotton, no change in the liquid is observed. When the volume of air, thus filtered through cotton, is considerable, the plug is so filled with dust as to turn black. Now, this dust, in addition to a quantity of mineral particles, and fluff of many kinds, contains spores and germs of fermenting substance, as is proved by the fact that the smallest quantity of it, sprinkled in pure liquid, will produce fermentation in it. An experiment of another kind is this: Pasteur, by an ingenious arrangement, inserts and withdraws from a glass jar, filled with pure air, the juice from the inside of a single grape, so that, during the experiment, the juice communicates neither with the surface of the grape nor with the atmospheric air. The juice, thus obtained, shows no trace of fermentation, remaining unchanged as long as the jar is closed; but if it is opened, or if its contents are mixed with a few drops of water in which the surface of the grape has been washed, fermentation is set up in it at once. This is because the outside of grapes is always covered with yeast-germs, even when the bunches have been subjected to constant rains. In this case, plainly, fermentation is due to the germs suspended in the air, or deposited on the surface of the grapes and stems. Pasteur draws blood from an animal's veins by a similar process, and introduces it into a glass vessel in contact with pure air. The blood continues fresh for years. Pasteur asserts and proves by experiment that grape-juice, milk, blood, and all liquids that most readily undergo change in ordinary conditions, are incapable of fermentation in air which is pure, that is to say, deprived of the corpuscles it contained. They remain, when so placed, for an indefinite time, in a singularly sound state.

Pasteur had made still another set of experiments. He had obtained development of fermentation in liquids freed from albuminoid substances. It was supposed, before his researches, that the cells remarked in the fermentation of grape-juice proceed from the conversion of the albuminoid substances which this fluid contains in its natural state. Pasteur prepares a solution of sugar, tartrate of ammonia, and some other salts, and sprinkles a few yeast-globules in it. They swell, develop, and propagate in this artificial medium quite as well as in the grape-juice. So it was supposed that in the acid fermentation of milk the ferment is a product of the conversion of casein. Pasteur proves that supposition to be unfounded, by artificially producing the lactic ferment in a compounded liquid containing not a trace of casein. These very delicate experiments have not only increased the vogue of the panspermic theory, but they have been of great value also to vegetable physiology.

Many objections have been raised to these theories on the origin of ferments, to which Pasteur has almost always replied by unquestionable facts and solid reasonings, though he has sometimes done himself the injustice to be rough and contemptuous in discussion toward his opponents. Truth is strong enough to indulge charity for error. The gravest of these objections, it must be said, have applied to problems which do not concern the very foundation of the dispute between the panspermic system and its opposite. For instance, Trécul, the skillful and noted micrographer, Béchamp, and others, have proved that Pasteur mistakes with regard to the evolutions and transformations undergone by microscopic beings in fermenting media. Pasteur has certainly made more than one mistake on this subject, and there probably does exist between certain ferment-corpuscles a closer relationship than is supposed at the laboratory of the Normal School; but that does not in the least alter the fundamental character of the theory. Attention is also called to the fact that corpuscles with a determinate structure can be produced complete, without germs, in some liquids. No doubt, this is true, but only on condition that the liquids are living ones. No doubt, the cambium of vegetables, the blastema of animals, and generally all protoplasmic fluids, are fertile hatching-fields for the spontaneous development of the cells and fibres of living tissues. It is thus that the first elements of the embryo show themselves in the animal ovule. And in this respect the labors of Robin, Trécul, Onimus, Legros, and a great number of other observers, are decisive; but life is the property of these protoplasms; they depend upon an organized system. In the depths of the organism, and shielded from the air, they toil at the creation of microscopic corpuscles. Place them in contact with purified air, in Pasteur's glass globes, and then they would be barren.

The last objection Pasteur has to meet is, that, if the germs of all these microscopic vegetable and animal lives are in the atmosphere, they should be discovered and recognized there. But, in examining the dust of the air microscopically, we do not by any means detect all the rudiments of that infinitely minute flora and fauna whose existence is attested by the fermentation and putrefactions of organic matter. Pasteur has thus far met this argument only by the evidence of his experiments which prove that, in contact with purified air, neither fermentations nor putrefactions are possible. That is strictly sufficient, but we can go further. It is by no means a sure conclusion that these germs do not exist, because many of them are invisible under the lens. To begin with, we do note with certainty a certain number of species in atmospheric dust. It is therefore an admissible presumption that, if the remaining ones elude our eyes and our microscopes, that merely proves them to be smaller than the observed ones. But, perhaps, the problem ought to be viewed in a different way. We believe that these visible germs are the exceptions, that is, that they are beings already arrived at a certain degree of development, and that, in reality, all true germs are of dimensions forever beyond the reach of microscopic observation, even conceiving lenses to be immensely more powerful than they now are. The microscope barely brings within our range of vision points that measure at least a ten thousandth part of a millimetre. The primitive germs of life cannot even approach the hundred thousandth part of a millimetre. Physics and metaphysics both assure us that we must here give up the hope of measuring and estimating things according to the powers of our limited senses. An effort is needed to pursue with the mind's eye these perpetually-dwindling dimensions, still to go on though the imagination fails in the task, and to realize at last how far removed are the bounds of the microcosm. If the faculty of reaching out beyond the limits of our nature, which is one of the noblest prerogatives of our intelligence, does not desert us, we attain to the idea of the vital monads of Leibnitz, the organic molecules of Buffon, the comprehension of existence for primal organisms diffused throughout the world by myriads of myriads, and the conception of the infinitely minute within the infinitely minute.

Thus, just as the infinite universe through which the spheres roll is filled with invisible particles of a subtile matter to which physicists and astronomers give the name of ether, and which supplies the only key to cosmic phenomena, the finite universe in which organization unfolds itself is thronged with corpuscles no less invisible, forming what the illustrious Ehrenberg calls the milky-way of lower organisms, and no less essential for the explanation of the processes of which we have traced the general course. As there is an ether wanting in life, so there is an ether endowed with life—a vital ether. Both are above denial; they surpass our reason, yet reason cannot but demand them. They elude the close grasp of experiment, yet experiment does not permit them to be avoided; they are unseen, and without them there could be nothing seen. The mind clings to them with the stress of all its power to embrace, perhaps because it feels a secret, mysterious affinity with them, perhaps because it is in substance of the same essence with them.

III.

Our atmosphere, then, is the receptacle for myriads of germs of microscopic beings, which play an important part in the organized world. Penetrating agents of decay, baneful toilers for disease, they lie ever in wait for the chance to pierce the internal machinery of animals and plants, and create slight or grave disturbances within it. Life often resists or escapes them, but nothing can contest with them its deserted vesture. The corpse is their natural aliment, and death their chosen laboratory. There these lowest of created things work out their lofty destiny in the eternal drama of renewal of organic existences.

When the thin pellicle covering sweet fruits is torn at any point, an opening is made for atmospheric germs. Fermenting cells pierce the interior of the fruit, and produce within it fermentation of the sugar, that is to say, the formation of a little alcohol; and this in its turn is susceptible of the passage into acetic fermentation, giving the pulp an acid taste. At last the pulp itself is destroyed by various fungous growths. When a fruit decays and takes a more or less unpleasant flavor, this depends on the intervention of ferment-cells of atmospheric origin, and on the production of acid or alcoholic substances. An able micrographist, Engel, who has lately studied these phenomena minutely, discovers that the yeast-cells which thus produce alcoholic fermentation in the juices of fruits present some slight differences in various fruits, neither do they have the same morphological character as those of grape-must or beer-wort. Varieties occur in these cases, corresponding to the different media in which the nutrition of the little fungus takes place.

The microscopic fungi of the atmosphere play as interesting a part in the alteration of wines. These grow acid, change, become filmy or oily, or take on besides a decided bitterness. All these sicknesses depend on the development of different little plants recognized and described by Pasteur; and this scientist, not stopping at the solution of the nature of these disorders, has sought the means of preventing them. Resting on some former observations by D'Appert, he conceived the idea of subjecting wines to the action of a very high degree of heat, so as to destroy the yeast-germs. There was no possibility of doubt as to the destruction of these germs and the prevention of any further change, but it might well be asked whether the delicacy and bouquet of certain wines would not be endangered by the effects of heating. Long-continued experiments prove not only that heating is an excellent method of preventing sickness in wines, but also that, instead of impairing their exquisite qualities, it ripens and strengthens them. The recorded minutes of tastings officially performed during the past year by several members of the syndical wine commission, at the suggestion of Pasteur, contain decisive testimony on this point. Fine Burgundy wines, heated in bottle seven years ago to temperatures varying between 131° and 149°, appeared, at the end of that time, superior to the same wines not so treated. Persons who spoke with some authority, Pasteur says, declared that heating would in time deprive the wine of its color. The contrary is the case, when the air is excluded during the process; the color grows livelier by heating. It was said that heating would in time alter the bouquet of fine wines, giving them dryness and too great age. On the contrary, the bouquet seems to be heightened with the lapse of time, more positively than with wines not heated. In the case of chambertin and volnay, particularly, the tasters noticed this fact. Pasteur was led by these studies to investigate the cause of the aging of wines, and he discovered that the phenomenon was due to slow oxidation. Wine kept in glass tubes completely filled and closely sealed does not age. By increasing and regulating the aëration of wine, and particularly combining it with heating, he succeeded in manufacturing in one month excellent old wine. In short, oxygen and heat, acting on wine in certain proportions, promote instead of hindering the development of those volatile principles to which the liquid owes its perfume and part of its flavor; but this discovery is additional to those he was in search of. What Pasteur did chiefly look for and did find, in giving exact and methodical rules for heating wines, is a process, applicable on a great scale, for preventing the diseases from which the common vineyard products so often suffer, and that fortunate application is a result from his researches on fermentation generally. In the same way, in consequence of the examinations he undertook as to the share of microscopic organisms in the diseases of silk-worms, he was led to prescribe a practical way of hindering the development of these organisms, and thus preventing the malady.

When we inject into the subcutaneous cellular tissue of a living animal a putrefied or septic liquid, that is, one containing those thread-like corpuscles known by the name of vibrios and bacteria, it sometimes happens that the animal experiences no inconvenience. Dogs particularly resist with vigor the poisonous influence of such a fluid, but the case is different with other species, and notably with rabbits. The system becomes the seat of grave phenomena, almost always mortal, of which the general group composes the affection known by the term *septicæmia*. The microscopic organisms in such a case poison the animal, not only by the mere fact of their presence in the blood, but besides and especially because they develop and propagate in it with astonishing rapidity, in the same way that yeast reproduces itself in barley-wort. But the most singular thing in these pathological fermentations is the fact noted some years ago for the first time by Coze and Feltz, and the study of which Davaine took up last year. Davaine demonstrates, by experiments made on rabbits and Guinea-pigs, that one drop of blood, from an animal affected with septicæmia, has the power of imparting the infection to another animal inoculated with it, that a drop taken from the second can transmit the disease to a third, and so on. Still more, very wonderfully, the poisoning power of the blood of these animals increases with the degree of advance in the series of inoculations. The culture of the virus heightens its maleficent properties. This gradual increase of the virulent force is such that, if we take a drop of blood from an animal representing the twenty-fifth term in a series of successive inoculations, and so dilute this drop with water that a drop of the dilution corresponds to one trillionth of the original drop, we get a liquid of which the smallest quantity still displays mortal activity. These experiments of Davaine, which exhibit the degree of venom as increasing in an inverse ratio to the apparent quantity of the poison, have been repeated and confirmed by several eminent physiologists, among others by Bouley, and have produced a sensation which still continues in the schools of physiology and medicine. Apart from the inherent difficulty of forming a notion as to the influence of those infinitesimal doses, they seemed to yield an argument of a kind to support the assertions of homœopathy. If the difficulty is real, though it may be got over, the argument, we take leave to say, is worthless. Let us look at the difficulty first. This drop which is still mortal, though representing only an infinitely small fraction of the original quantity of poisonous matter to which it is distantly related, permits no corpuscle to be detected. That is true, yet it contains the germs of them, and germs such in number, size, and reproductive power, that nothing prevents them from breeding again indefinitely, in spite of all efforts tried to get rid of them. The discussions that have just occurred in the Academy of Medicine on this grave subject, almost at the same time that the question of ferments was under debate in the Academy of Sciences, leave no doubt as to the reality of this progressive breeding of virulent germs by culture. But is this any argument for the homœopathists? None whatever. They attribute curative effects to extremely small doses of certain inorganic substances most evidently inert, which can in no way reproduce themselves. If the virulent elements occasion disturbances so profound in animal organisms, it is not by reason of their extreme minuteness, but it is because they multiply with prodigious rapidity in the depths of the tissues and humors, where they labor in a manner opposed to the harmonious life of the body

However this may be, the vibrios and bacteria have an undeniable share in the production of human maladies. They are found in the blood of persons attacked by infectious disorders, and, if in many cases their relation to these disorders is only that of concomitants, in others their relation of causality is very clearly ascertained. Thus Davaine's investigations prove that the maladies called carbuncular, so formidable in men and animals, are due to the excessive development of a species of bacteria in the blood. Typhoid fever also seems to acknowledge a cause of the same kind. Rabbits die from inoculation with blood taken from men attacked by this disease. Our knowledge upon this difficult subject, it must be owned, is very little advanced, in spite of the ardent labors devoted to its extension in the past few years. The illusions of the microscope and the exaggerations of a spirit of routine too often impair the value of studies undertaken in this direction. Without going so far as does the opinion of those who attribute all these disorders to microscopic corpuscles, and regard all morbid phenomena as fermentations, it may at any rate be admitted that these corpuscles, diffused throughout the air, take an important place among the eternal enemies of health. At all times surgeons and physicians have recognized the danger from penetration of common air into the interior of the organism, by the way of wounds or otherwise. We now understand the explanation of the danger. It is not the gases of the air that are dangerous; but the proto-organisms contained in that fluid must be charged with the fatal influence it exerts in traumatic cases, and putrid infection has no other origin. Thus the anxiety of practitioners now is to protect wounds from access by the germs in the air, by means either of impermeable coating or of antiseptic dressings containing alcohol or phenic acid, or by pneumatic closing up, or by filtration of the air itself through cotton. Under the influence of ideas distinctly introduced into science by the researches we have just reviewed, several practices in surgery have undergone great modifications.

After examining the alterations produced in the living, we have to consider those occasioned by fermentations in the dead. When life has retreated by slow degrees from all the parts of an organized being; when, after all partial deaths have occurred, total death has possessed the depths of the subject, and broken all the springs of its activity, the work of putrefaction begins. Its task is to unmake this body, to destroy its forms, and dissever its materials. The work to be done is to disorganize it, to reduce it into solids, liquids, and gases, fit to go back again into the vast reservoir whence new life is incessantly issuing. This is the task that heat, moisture, air, and germs, will undertake in unison. It is all performed with steady diligence. Nature knows no delays; as soon as the body is cold, the protecting coating that covers all its surface, the epithelium, decays in places, particularly in the moister parts. The agents of disorganization, vibrios and bacteria, or rather the germs of these thread-like corpuscles, penetrate through the skin, wind into the small ducts, invade the whole blood, and by degrees all the organs. Soon they swarm everywhere, almost as numerous as the chemical molecules in the midst of which they stir and circle. The albuminoid matters are decomposed into fetid gases, escaping into the air. The fixed salts, alkaline and earthy-alkaline, slowly release themselves from the organic matters with which they combined to form the tissues. The fats oxidize, and grow acrid; the moisture dries away. Every thing volatile vanishes, and, at the end of a certain time, nothing remains save the skeleton, but a formless mingling of mineral principles, a sort of humus, ready to manure the earth. Now, all these complex operations absolutely required the intervention of the infusoria of putrefaction. In pure air, deprived of living germs, they could not have been accomplished. To check putrid fermentations, to insure the conservation of animal or vegetable substances in a state of perfect integrity, only one means avails, but that is an infallible one—that of thoroughly precluding the access to them of the aërial germs of vibrios and bacteria. Whether we adopt D'Appert's method and begin by subjecting these substances to the action of high temperature, preserving them after that in hermetically-closed vessels; or whether, as we have seen very lately practised by Boussingault, we introduce them into an extremely cold medium; or whether we saturate them with such salts as have antiseptic properties, in every case they are protected from putrefaction by paralyzing the effects of the lower organisms. The corruption of animals is not more possible than the fermentation of grape-juice, barley-wort, milk etc., when it is made impossible for the germs to act. This is another fact demonstrated by Pasteur.

We have just used the term antiseptic, that is, capable of destroying germs, and preventing the action of ferments. The interest connected with such substances is easily understood. In truth, they are at the present time the chief objective point of therapeutic researches. At the same time that chemists and physiologists are engaged with persevering zeal in studying the functions of microscopic corpuscles in living Nature, physicians, perceiving their manifold and baneful activity in the production of disease, are seeking the means of reaching and destroying them. Every one knows those principles, like phenic acid, which are extracted from pitch, and are also found in smoke, to which they impart antiseptic properties that have been utilized from time immemorial. Other substances have been lately discovered, not less remarkable for their energetic resistance to fermentation and virus. Among the number are the alkaline sulphites and hyposulphites, which have been the object of very interesting examination on the part of an Italian physician, Polli; the borates and silicates of potassa and soda, to which Dumas invited the attention of physiologists a year ago; the acetate of potassa, and others. Hitherto the physiological virtues of active principles have been studied only with respect to the higher order of animals: Dumas pointed out the great interest there would be in examining the influence they exert over the lower organisms charged with the elaboration of ferments, and over ferments themselves. Such researches not only contribute to a better knowledge of the mechanism itself according to which these principles affect the system of vital phenomena, but they also gain the most useful indications for the healing art. Indeed, beginning with the moment at which Dumas and other chemists made known the result of their examinations on this subject, coincident also in time with the experiments of Davaine on septicæmia, a vast number of attempts were entered upon, in hospitals and in laboratories, to discover to what extent these anti-fermenting substances hinder morbid fermentations. These attempts are still proceeding; we cannot foretell their success, but we are authorized even now to say that they will not be barren of advantage to the healing art. In this, as in all other departments of scientific activity, we see abstract studies result in useful discoveries.[1]

As a general statement of the subject, all this immense work of fermentations, putrefactions, and corruptions of organic matter, is effected in the world by a small number of species of microscopic cells and filaments, by fungi and spores of the lowest order, of which the germs fill our atmosphere. This is one of the most certain acquisitions of modern science, one of the most important from the point of view of natural philosophy, one of the most productive for those arts that are concerned in improving the

---

[1] Since these lines were written, silicate of soda, experimented on by Rabuteau and myself, has taken a fixed place in the treatment of several purulent and putrid disorders.

condition of mankind. We may now regard it as firmly established; but let us not forget that its establishment has cost two centuries of investigations and labors. Leeuwenhoek, in the middle of the seventeeth century, was the first to reveal the microscopic world of the air, and to conjecture its momentous functions. What severe toil, what struggles and tedious trials, since the observations of the Dutch micrographer to the time of the experimental studies of our contemporary and compatriot, Pasteur!

GREAT EPIDEMICS—ASIATIC CHOLERA.

I.

On Monday, the 26th of March, 1832, epidemic cholera made its first appearance in Paris. Four persons, living in different parts of the city, were attacked during the day, and died in a few hours. On the 31st of March, thirty-five sections of the capital were found to be invaded, and the thirteen others the next day. The patients all presented the same group of symptoms. Already noted by physicians, who had studied the disease in neighboring countries, these symptoms soon became as well known to the practitioners of Paris and the rest of France as those of any other malady.

How did the cholera get into France? In the month of August, 1817, it raged with uncommon violence at Jessore, whence it soon spread over the whole province of Bengal, from the mouth of the Ganges to its junction with the Jumna. In 1819 it prevailed in the lower Indies, at Sumatra, and the Isle of France; in 1820 and 1821 it seized upon the whole of China, the archipelago of the Philippines, and Java. At the same time it crossed the gulf of Oman, extended along the shores of the Persian Gulf, and made its way into Persia. It ravaged the latter country for a long time before it penetrated into Europe. At last, in 1823, setting out from Recht, in the province of Ghilan, it passed along the coast of the Caspian Sea, and crossed the boundary of Russia. By the 22d of September of that year it had reached Astrakhan. It appeared there, however, for a short time only; but, in 1829, the cholera, which had raged without intermission in Northern Persia and Afghanistan, was brought to Orenburg, then to Tiflis, then to Astrakhan, and this time it prevailed over all Russia. By the 20th of September, 1830, it broke out at Moscow, where it continued a year. The plague then spread as far as Kiev, and throughout all the western provinces of Russia up to the frontiers of Poland. The armies at that time in the field in that country aided perceptibly in the spread of the disease, and the transmission of the epidemic by the movement of troops was distinctly observed there for the first time. In May and June, 1831, Moldavia and Galicia, and, in August, Prussia, were invaded; then came the turn of Hungary, Transylvania, and the Baltic coasts. The 27th of January, in 1832, the cholera was announced at Edinburgh, and on the 10th of February its presence was made known in London. From the English coasts the scourge threatened France and Holland. The 15th of March, 1832, it appeared at Calais, and on the 26th of March it was at Paris. The epidemic in the great city lasted six months; it gained its greatest intensity the 9th of April, on which day there were eight hundred and fourteen deaths, remained stationary for a few days, and then began to decrease; eighteen thousand four hundred people were carried off, out of a population of nine hundred and forty-five thousand inhabitants. From Paris the plague had radiated in all directions, and reached the rest of France by slow degrees. English emigrants had carried it on the other hand to America, Portugal, and Spain. It did not reach Italy before 1835. Switzerland and Greece were spared. The first invasion, as we see, was very slow; it took twenty years to reach all the world. The latter invasions will display more rapidity. Owing to the activity of transfers, the speed and frequency of communication, the germs of the cholera will be found to circulate after this with surprising celerity.

Between the years 1837 and 1847, Europe, freed from the cholera, cared very little about it; but physicians, who followed with a watchful eye the movement of diseases on the surface of the globe, still felt the fear of an earlier or later return of the Asiatic scourge. An epidemic which had ravaged the Burman Empire in 1842, and Afghanistan and Tartary next, had reached Persia toward the end of 1845. Thence it took its course in two different directions, from east to west by way of Bagdad and Mecca, and on the north toward Tauris and the Caucasian provinces. In the early part of 1847 the cholera broke out in the west of the Caucasus among the ranks of the Russian army then keeping the field in Circassia, and by slow degrees it reached the rest of Europe. Thus on the 5th of October, 1848, a vessel coming from Hamburg with sailors aboard affected with cholera landed at Sunderland; on the 24th of that month a part of Great Britain was infected; on the 20th of the same month, immediately after an English ship had come into port at Dunkirk, the disease made its appearance in the north of France; Lille, Calais, Fécamp, Dieppe, Rouen, Douai, in succession suffered the attack of the scourge. The 29th of January, in 1849, immediately after the arrival of a battalion of infantry-chasseurs coming from Douai, the first case of cholera was noted at St.-Denis. On the 7th of March the plague was at Paris.

Those two epidemics of which we have spoken were thus of direct Asiatic origin. The same thing could hardly be said of that which raged in Europe from 1852 to 1855; at least the track of no epidemic was followed marking a progress from east to west and from south to north. This visitation, after having prevailed without much violence in Bohemia about the end of 1851, displays itself with sudden and remarkable intensity, in the month of May, 1852, in the grand-duchy of Posen, whence it spreads at first toward the east in the direction of Russia, and then toward the west, approaching Germany. In 1853 we find it in Denmark, Sweden, and Norway, and then in England and France, where it reached its highest point of virulence in 1854. During this fatal year the scourge ravaged the whole of Europe. Those great movements of troops which were occurring at that period facilitated the diffusion of the poison, while at the same time the great multitudes collected together in Turkey and the Crimea formed a kind of secondary centre for the abundant increase of epidemic effluvia. The cholera of 1852 to 1855 entered Paris in November, 1853, declined in force there in January, 1854, revived in February, and raged violently in March and during the following months, leaving the capital in the month of August. Sixty-six departments, chiefly those of the northeast, received a visit from the plague. It must be observed that Switzerland, which had escaped the two former invasions, paid its tribute this time.

Hitherto these epidemics had made their entrance into Europe only by way of the land. That of 1865-'66 penetrated it by sea, through the ports, principally those of Marseilles and Constantinople. The cholera was introduced in 1866 into the Hedjaz by way of India and Java. It made terrible ravages there, and the pilgrims, mad with terror, hurried in crowds to Djeddah,[1] on the Red Sea, where they got the means, almost by force, of embarkation to the port of Suez. From the 17th of May to the 10th of June ten steamers brought into that city from twelve to fifteen thousand pilgrims, more or less ill, who thence scattered themselves over all Egypt. By the 2d of June, Egypt was invaded, and in less than three months over sixty thousand

---

[1] Djeddah is a port on the Red Sea, distant only two days' journey from Mecca; it is the point of embarkation for pilgrims returning by sea to Egypt, Asia Minor, etc.

victims were counted there. The panic that seized the inhabitants brought on a considerable emigration, which was directed to the great commercial towns of the Mediterranean coasts—Beyrout, Cyprus, Malta, Smyrna, Constantinople, Trieste, and Marseilles—whence the cholera could easily extend into the rest of Europe. In the former epidemics the disease, traveling by land, took years to pass over difficult routes. This time, brought over the sea by steam, it needed but a few months to become mistress of Europe.

To sum up, four great epidemics may be counted up to this time in France, those of 1832, 1849, 1854–'55, and, last, that of 1865, which continued more than two years. The invasion of 1832 attacks fifty-six departments, and destroys during the year from a hundred and ten to a hundred and twenty thousand victims; in 1849, the plague ravages fifty-seven departments, and causes from a hundred to a hundred and ten thousand deaths; the epidemic in 1854 gradually extends to seventy departments, and destroys over one hundred and fifty thousand people; that of 1865 begins in the month of June, rages for some time at Marseilles and Toulon, does not reach Paris till several months later, revives there during the following summer, lingers through the winter in the northwest of France, and only disappears completely at the end of 1867, after having ravaged less territory, and produced a smaller mortality, than the former epidemics did.[1]

If science has succeeded in tracing with some exactness the geographical advance of the symptoms of cholera, it has hitherto been powerless in fixing the real relations of that disease with the totality of conditions of climate, geology, society, etc. The many and diligent researches undertaken upon this subject have as yet yielded only ques-

---

[1] The mortality occasioned by this epidemic in France is not yet quite ascertained. In Paris alone more than six thousand fell victims to it.

tionable and contradictory results. In Europe, high regions have generally been spared, but the epidemic has raged violently on the plateaus of Mexico and the summits of the Himalayas. If localities overlying granite and other solid rocks have seemed to enjoy special immunity, as Pettenkofer has proved, cases are known, like that of Helsingfors in 1849, in which those parts of the town built on granite were decimated, while the marshy parts and those near the shore remained exempt. Some countries, such as Würtemberg, some cities, Lyons for instance, have hitherto escaped the attacks of the pestilence almost wholly, without any assignable reason. What is more indisputable is the fact that the collection of multitudes of people facilitates the development of the disease. Armies in the field, populous cities, make a sort of centre from which it radiates. Thus the war in Poland in 1831 seems to have been the cause of the rapid spread of the cholera in Europe. We know no instance of a rural population swept by the epidemic where there was not a town in the neighborhood which had first suffered from its effects. In the towns, the most closely-built and unwholesome quarters are attacked and affected more severely than the others. In a word, the cholera has a special affinity for large collections of human beings; in them it concentrates, and through them it spreads. Observed facts are decisive in this respect, and no argument could prevail against the accumulated evidence. The close study of epidemics shows that we must attribute the more or less rapid spread of cholera beyond the centre of its origin neither to winds nor to water-courses, nor to supposed miasmatic emanations, but it must be attributed to pilgrimages, fairs, movements of troops, and similar changes of place by masses of men. Single travelers in good health have, as may well be imagined, very few chances of carrying the disease with them from an infected country to a healthy one; but travelers in crowds, among whom there are always more or fewer sick ones to be found, necessarily transport the seeds of the plague. The Crimean War afforded many proofs of this; on that occasion it was our troops that imported the cholera into the East. The following fact is peculiarly instructive : the Bosquet division, affected with cholera, pitched camp at Baltchick the 9th of August, where a great part of our squadron, till then exempt, was anchored. At the end of ten days it was attacked, and in less than a week it counted more than eight hundred dead in an effective force of thirteen thousand sailors. If further instances were needed, we might mention also the introduction of the cholera in 1865 at Guadeloupe. The labors of Marshal de Calvi and of a skillful surgeon in our navy, Pellarin, prove that the cholera was brought into Pointe-à-Pitre by the ship Sainte-Marie, equipped at Bordeaux the 14th of September, 1865, cleared the same day for Matamoras, in Mexico, and touching at Pointe-à-Pitre the 20th of the following October.

On the whole, it is certain that the cholera travels from one country to another by the change of place of masses of human beings, which are true moving centres. It regularly follows the great channels of communication, frequented roads, navigable rivers, etc. Whether the question is as to pilgrims in India, caravans in upper Asia and Eastern Russia, armies crossing the Caucasus, or in our Crimean expedition, immigrants in America, or Moslem pilgrims to Mecca, the conditions of transmissibility of the epidemic are still the same, its propagation is always more rapid in proportion as the means of communication are more speedy.

How does a human being transport the cholera? The question is not completely settled. Some believe that the epidemic germs are planted in the organism itself, and there preserve their vitality. Others, as Pettenkofer, who has published remarkable essays on this subject, suppose that man, as an individual, has hardly any share in the propagation of the evil. This physician asserts that neither the living body, nor the corpse, nor the excretions of cholera-patients, have the power of retaining and increasing the unknown miasma which is the cause of the diffusion of disease. Pettenkofer holds even that the origin of the cholera is not to be looked for in some special physiological condition of the Indian population in the basin of the Ganges; that the pest must spring from certain circumstances of soil and climate; and, further, that it can only be diffused through the coöperation of certain telluric and atmospheric elements. It is, perhaps, going a little too far to maintain that neither man nor animal matters take any part in the production of the effluvia of cholera, and Pettenkofer's theory, ingenious as it may seem, is not likely to be generally adopted. The cholera sometimes is communicated by means of persons who are themselves free from it; this is the sole argument used by advocates of the non-transmissible nature of the disease; but it has little force, if it can be shown that the germs of cholera may have for their vehicle clothes, baggage, merchandise, etc. Now, this has been proved by several authors; among others, Grimaud de Caux. The latter even asserts that he has noticed, at the Marseilles post-office, cases of cholera transmitted by packets of letters.

Is the cholera contagious? It is beyond dispute that the cholera is brought into one country by collected masses of men who have contracted it in another country; but the transmission is not direct. A person positively affected with cholera does not transmit the malady to this or that person who in his turn communicates it to another, and so successively. The first patients who come into a healthy place infect the local atmosphere, and in that infected atmosphere the germs of the disease multiply which will carry off more or fewer victims; but they may be found among people who have kept themselves entirely apart from those affected, as well as among others who have been near them. Very few physicians die while attending such patients. It may perhaps be useful to recall our personal experience on this subject, and the observations we made during the epidemic of 1865, in connection with Legros and Goujon in the laboratory of Robin at the practice school of the medical faculty. Engaged for some months, and careless of any special precautions, in handling and examining in all ways the blood and excretions of cholera-patients, we suffered no injurious effects, no inconvenience even. Sédillot relates that during the campaign of Poland, in 1831, it happened to him more than once to sleep with impunity in sheets just taken from patients who had died of cholera. It is clear, therefore, that it is not transmitted by the contact of persons or objects affected. It is the air which within a more or less circumscribed space is the receiver of that subtile and unknown matter that the poison lurks in; we say the receiver, not the vehicle, for the cholera-germ which multiplies within that space has no spontaneous tendency to move away from it. Its movement further and its extension to a distance are occasioned by the constant migrations of mankind.

The very noticeable examinations of Tholozan have placed it beyond doubt that, independently of the four great epidemics, the cholera, since 1830, has hardly ceased at any time to exist in Europe in different degrees of intensity and under varying forms. Among us, as in India, it may be epidemic, endemic, or sporadic. It has been attempted, indeed, to mark a distinction between cholera which destroys a great number of people at one time and that which chooses only single victims;[1] but these two maladies offer no fundamental specific differences. The first, when it has

---

[1] The latter has been called "nostras cholera," in opposition to "Asiatic cholera."

finished its work, languishes, and seems to disappear, but it still continues to betray its presence here and there at longer or shorter intervals.

II.

We have seen that the first great epidemic observed in the Indies, before its appearance in Europe, occurred in 1817; at that date the cholera became a traveler, but it had long existed in Asia. The testimony of philology and archæology proves in the clearest way that it has been known there from early antiquity. Hindoo mythology relates that the two Aswyns, or sons of Surya, the sun, taught medicine to Indra, who composed the "Ayur-Veda," the most ancient medical book in India. Indra in turn taught the art to Dhawantrie, and he had for a scholar Susruta, contemporary with Rama, the hero of the Ramayana. Now, Susruta left a work which Dr. Wise, director of the medical service at Bengal, translated and abridged in 1845, and in which a distinct description of the cholera is found. It is not easy to give the true date for this composition; but Tholozan supposes there are good reasons for fixing it about the third century before the Christian era. Other Sanscrit works of the same date speak of a similar malady. The most curious illustration is an inscription copied at Vizzianuggur by Sanderson, upon a monolith, part of the ruins of an ancient temple. This inscription, which is ascribed to a pupil of Buddha, and seems to date from an age preceding the conquest of Alexander, reads as follows: "Blue lips, a shrunken face, hollow eyes, the belly knotted, the limbs cramped and crooked as if by effect of fire, are marks of the cholera, which comes down by malign conjurations of the priests to destroy heroes. The thickened breath clings to the warrior's face, his fingers are bent and twisted in different ways; he dies in contortions, the victim of the wrath of Siva." Many Hindoo and Persian works of a later date contain similar proofs. When the Portuguese, in 1498, and afterward the Dutch and the English, landed on the shores of India, they had frequent opportunities to observe epidemic cholera and it is not strange that a description of the disease could have been made by European doctors in the seventeenth century. We have still detailed accounts of the plagues that raged in the eighteenth century, of which that of Hurdwar is the most famous. In short, to whatever period we recur, we come upon one of the links of that long chronological chain of the cholera, which begins with the oldest books of Hindoo medicine.

The causes which have always aided the development of cholera in the Indies are active there at the present day. Almost every year the disease breaks out in places where pilgrims gather. Among these localities, of which some are also commercial towns, three particularly attract the crowd: they are Hurdwar, on the Ganges, in the north of Hindostan; Juggernath, on the coast of Orissa, at the northwest of the gulf of Bengal; and Conjeveram, in the south of Madras. Pilgrims arrive at these places in the warm season, after a journey of more than a hundred leagues, almost always made on foot, in a state of exhaustion and wretchedness of which we can hardly form an idea. Once in these holy places, their crowding together, their bad food, uncleanliness, and debauchery, bring them into such conditions that the germs of plague develop, and the epidemic kindles among them. This infected multitude then scatters abroad, and passes through the country in all directions, sowing miasma and contagion.

Thus these immense gatherings of people favor the extension of the cholera. Are they at the same time its originating causes? We cannot answer positively in either way. All possible suppositions have been indulged as to the origin of the cholera in India, but none of them really explains the difficulty. What is the cause that produces the birth of the miasma? Is it the crowding together of pilgrims under bad hygienic conditions? Is it the putrefaction of vegetable matters under a torrid sun, or the stagnant waters of the Ganges, loaded with corpses and filth, or is it a special state of the soil? We do not know. What is certain is, that pilgrimages aid in propagating the cholera, and that it in some way seeks out a pestilential atmosphere. Therefore the wish is reasonable that the British Government should control these pilgrimages, and give greater activity to the labors of canal-making and the sanitary measures it has undertaken to render the country healthy. When medical *savants* suggest going to attack the evil at its root and destroy it forever, and preach a crusade to India in which all civilized nations should join to cut off the heads of the hydra, as Hercules of old did those of the Lernean monster, we may applaud the spirit and generosity of the project, but must ask what means are to be found for its execution.

Persia, situated between India and Europe, is not a focus of cholera, but it is a country where the disease finds so suitable a region that it very often prevails in it. Only a few years ago the shah's kingdom presented a miserable spectacle in this respect. Dirt and offal were not removed; the bodies of animals, camels, oxen, horses, mules, were eaten by dogs, jackals, and birds of prey, in the towns or in their environs. A deeply-rooted religious belief in the country caused it to be regarded as a sacred duty to carry the dead far away and bury them in holy cemeteries. This transportation was performed under deplorable circumstances. The bodies, already in different stages of putrefaction, were merely wrapped in felt cloths, seldom inclosed in coffins of thin, ill-joined boards. In this state the bodies were carried on the backs of camels or mules, in all weathers, to distances averaging thirty or forty days' march. There were caravans of corpses, as there are caravans of pilgrims;

and travelers occasionally met some of them carrying one or two hundred dead bodies. It is needless to say how greatly these moving charnel-houses, by infecting the atmosphere, must have increased the energy of epidemic manifestations. The International Conference urged upon the Persian Government to prevent the extension of the cholera-poison throughout its own territory by all possible means. It insisted on effecting the suppression of customs and practices which could only keep up the unhealthy state of the country; it demanded the formation of councils of health commissioned to secure the carrying out of regulations admitted to be indispensable to protect Persia itself, and consequently to shield Europe against the attacks of the scourge. Similar wishes had already been many times expressed to the Shah of Persia by his physician, Tholozan. In 1867 a formal edict of the prince forbade everywhere transportation of bodies; at the same time other sanitary reforms were planned. The suggestions of the Conference, therefore, could not have been otherwise than generally well received by the government of Teheran; but, if it made no opposition itself, it has not been and it is not yet easy for it to overcome that of the inhabitants. Not in a day, especially among Eastern populations, can the suppression of ancient customs be brought about, when they are bound up with religious prejudices. The members of the Conference seem not to have always given sufficient heed to the difficulties of such an undertaking, and Tholozan urged with much wisdom the need of using caution and moderation. However that may be, Proust, physician of the Paris hospitals, who was charged in 1869 with a mission to Russia and Persia, for the study of preventive measures against cholera, could ascertain for himself the excellent inclination of the Persian administration. "Most of the measures which the French Government would urge to have put in practice," says Proust, "have already been begun upon by the government of the shah. A high council of health has been instituted; the chief physicians of Persia have been invited to seats in this council. They have considered the most important questions of public and private hygiene." Let us add that the Persian Government has determined, on Tholozan's suggestion, to order the breaking off of all intercourse, and the prevention of pilgrimages in case the invasion of cholera into neighboring countries is ascertained. In short, the situation is greatly improved as regards the internal hygiene of Persia, and it grows better every day, which is a great point gained. But a new question is now presented: how can the cholera be prevented from passing out of Asia into Europe? This is one of the gravest difficulties of sanitary police and international hygiene. Let us consider what has been done to solve it, and what degree of success, or rather what hope of succeeding at all, has been gained.

The cholera passes from Asia to Europe by land and by sea, that is, by the frontier between Russia and Persia, and by the Caspian Sea. It may also come across the Mediterranean, either from Asia Minor or from Egypt, and consequently there is occasion to prevent its introduction into those two countries by the boundary-lines separating them, whether from Persia or from Arabia. This simple geographical route shows the range and complication of the system it is proposed to establish. All European governments have shown active diligence in organizing the plan of protective measures and preparing the working of those sanitary arrangements suggested by the members of the Conference, that is, the quarantine service. It would be too soon to decide in a positive way as to the efficiency of quarantines; but it is as well to say that quite a number of competent physicians absolutely deny it, and that such an opinion is unfortunately too well supported by facts.

Proust, who has examined carefully the boundary between Russia and Persia on which Russia has established quarantines and stations of Cossacks, believes that an active enough watchfulness to defeat the entrance of cholera on that side may be exerted over that region. Yet he confesses that it is not easy to interfere with the movements of smugglers at several points. As concerns its introduction through the Caspian Sea, the question is less simple. All vessels sailing from the Persian shore of that great lake take for their point of arrival on the Russian side a certain number of ports, the chief of which are Bakou, Derbent, and Astrakhan. Some of these ports have lazarettos; others, as Astrakhan, have no sanitary establishments. The number of officials seems to be too small also; nowhere are the examination and questioning of passengers rigorously attended to. At least, this is what Proust observed. This physician was urgent with the governments of Russia and the Caucasus to obtain more rigorous and efficient oversight. He demanded especially the establishment of vigilance stations along the coast so as to prevent, in case of need, the landing of vessels intending to break the prescribed regulations. Nothing could be easier, since there are none but Russian ships on the Caspian Sea. Proust's observations, moreover, came the more seasonably, because the quarantine establishments, erected at an earlier period for protection against the plague, are in process of alteration. He engaged the attention of several high Russian functionaries in these important interests; he expressed his ideas at length on these subjects before the Medical Society at Tiflis, and came away with the conviction that if the plans suggested by him are carried out carefully, as he hopes, upon the shores of the Caspian Sea, any new introduction of disease from Persia into Russia will become very difficult; but that remains to be seen in the future.

Let us now pass over to the boundaries of Persia and of Turkey in Asia. Along the whole extent of the frontier between Persia and Turkey, from Mount Ararat to the Persian Gulf, the Ottoman Government keeps up vigilance stations, which it turns into quarantines at need. Now these posts, costly to the treasury, harassing to the inhabitants, especially to the Persians, have hitherto been powerless to keep the Ottoman territory safe from invasions of cholera. This results from the fact that there is a great number of nomad tribes on this frontier—Koords, Bactrians, and others—who in summer drive their flocks to pasture on the high table-lands of Persia, and in winter come down toward the plains of Asia Minor. There is thus kept up on this line a constant movement of migration which there is no possibility of subjecting to quarantine regulations. Tholozan believes, with reason, that in this quarter the measures proposed by the International Conference could not be put in force.

A more useful quarantine system is that which prevented the spread in Egypt of that epidemic which raged in 1871 on the west coast of the Red Sea. A part of this country, that in which Medina and Mecca are situated, was swept by the cholera about the end of 1871. In view of the danger threatening Egypt the moment the pilgrims should return, the sanitary administration of that country resolved at once that if necessary all intercourse by sea between Hedjaz and Egypt should be stopped; but, not finding the danger urgent, it afterward modified this determination, and ordered that all pilgrims returning from Mecca by Egypt should first go and perform quarantine at El-Wedj, a small port on the coast of Arabia, situated three hundred and fifty miles from Suez, after which they might cross the isthmus by canal without going into Egypt, or else undergo another inspection at the station established for that purpose at the Springs of Moses. A lazaretto under canvas was then arranged at El-Wedj, under the direction of two physicians. A special commission was stationed at Suez, to examine all arrivals, and the physicians appointed for the supervision of Hedjaz were requested to transmit to Egypt reports on the sanitary state of the pilgrims. The prescribed rules were observed, without any appearance made by cholera as usual, and it was supposed for a time that leave might be given to the vessels with their freight of pilgrims to go directly to Suez. The first one was on the point of sailing, when the epidemic broke out at Mecca. A carrier promptly brought orders to Djeddah to deliver foul bills to the vessels, and dispatch the pilgrims to El-Wedj. The disappointment of the captains and ships' agents may be imagined. Several of them even declared that they would sail straight for Suez in spite of the order. The firmness of the physicians prevented them, though with great difficulty. At the same time this revival of the cholera at Mecca created so great a panic among the pilgrims that they deserted the city with all speed, so as to put any gradual succession of departures out of the question. Hard as it was, the lazaretto at El-Wedj discharged its duty sufficiently, thanks to the sagacity and devotedness of the medical men, and the cholera did not make its way into Egypt.

If the system of sea quarantines is efficient in some cases, it does not for the most part give governments the means of intercepting the cholera with certainty. We give another instance of the most instructive kind, which will close our remarks upon international preventive measures against the Asiatic plague.

Until the month of May, in 1856, quarantine was compulsory and general for persons arriving in Russia by sea. All travelers, without exception, were placed under sanitary inspection and seclusion for from ten to twenty days. A French cultivator of the vine settled in the Crimea lately told De Valcourt that on his arrival at Odessa, in 1848, he with his family and the other passengers were made to land on the quay at ten o'clock in the morning, and the landing-plank was withdrawn. The passengers, guarded by the quarantine soldiers, were obliged to remain, without food or drink, in the hot sun till four in the afternoon. At last, surrounded by lines of functionaries, they were led to the inspection-room. There a physician questioned them and made them undress completely. A coarse shirt and Russian soldier's coat were then given them. Their clothes were not given back until twenty-four hours later, after fumigating. Their seclusion lasted fifteen days, though there was no epidemic either in Russia or in any of the ports at which the vessel had touched. In 1856 these severities were put an end to. They were again put in force, though a little moderated. At present, the cholera prevailing in Odessa, quarantine is in operation, and employs a large force of men. Now De Valcourt, on his return from Russia, asserts that thirty travelers a day, on an average, land at Odessa and perform quarantine there, while four hundred travelers arrive by rail, and pass freely into the town. On the side of Turkey it is quite as easy to elude quarantine regulations. This year, the Ottoman Government, to protect the country against the cholera prevailing in Russia, has established a quarantine of ten full days at Sulina for ships going to the Danube, on the Bosporus for those bound to Constantinople, and at Batoum for those coming from the ports of the Caucasus. Besides, it has discontinued steam service between Galatz and Odessa. What is the result? It is this, that travelers leave Russia by the Wolociska Railway to the frontier between Austria and Russia, and reach Constantinople by Vienna and Burrach, as the Russian embassador near the Sublime Porte has just done. The railway joining Kichenev to Jassy will soon be finished and the passage will be very much more shortened. Quarantine, therefore, is futile.

It must be admitted that the system of quarantines offers

complications and difficulties which make it in many instances inefficient and impracticable. Not only is it difficult to find sufficiently vigilant officials, but it is often impossible to block the transfers and the movements of travelers which are agents in spreading the epidemic.

III.

If it is out of the question to destroy the cholera at its source, if it is very difficult to prevent its making its way to us, does not science at least possess an antidote to meet it with, a remedy to fight with against it when it has succeeded in making a lodgment among us? Just as in speaking of the nature of the evil the physician must own the almost entire uncertainty of knowledge, so, in view of the victims of the cholera's attacks, he must confess the impotence of art, almost always beyond remedy. The prescriptions suggested for the cure of cholera are as numerous as the suppositions framed for its explanation. On either hand the illusion is the same. Those who regard the cholera as a disease caused by parasites,[1] naturally look for the methods of destroying these parasites. Doctors who look on it as an affection by virus, occasioning a kind of molecular change in the whole mass of the humors, and especially of the albuminoid matters, are persuaded that acids might be of healing effect in these cases. Others, supposing that the most important point of all is to restore the liquidity of blood coagulated in the veins, resort to alkalies. Salts of copper have also been employed, regarded by some physicians as genuine specifics, as also alkaloids, such as caféine, etc. Those physiologists who fix the seat of the disease in the nervous structure of the great sympathetic are

---

[1] Among the supporters of this notion must be cited a German doctor, Hallier, who thinks it is proved that the cholera is caused by *micrococcus*. And Hallier explains all diseases by micrococcus, or by infinitely little beings of the same order.

induced to preach up antispasmodic drugs. In a word, remedies have almost all seemed to fail of useful effect, and the most sensible treatment is still the same as that of cholera in the early days, the treatment of symptoms. It consists, not in prostrating the disease solidly by making one single heroic attack on it, but in fighting it through successive skirmishes by attacking the various symptoms of the evil, one after the other. Cholera-patients have cramps—we endeavor to check them. They suffer cold—we warm them by frictions and drinks. Their circulation becomes slow and languid—we try to restore its regular conditions by stimulating the flow of the blood. The secretions diminish—we provoke them by suitable means. Thus, and without attacking the evil at its root, we often reach fortunate results. The great obstacle to the action of remedies on cholera-patients is the fact that they can absorb nothing. Some doctors have had the idea of injecting medicinal principles directly, either beneath the skin, or into the veins. Some attempts of this kind have succeeded, and this method is the right one. Only we need to continue our advances in it with persistent and systematic boldness, if we would secure certain advance in the treatment of cholera and other diseases. Instead of feeling the way blindly and timidly in experiments on the living subject, there is need of force and directness in proceeding. It is the only way to have at some future day strong and tempered weapons for our contests with disease.

It is perhaps proper in connection with this to point out to the attention of physicians the remarkable properties of the alkaline borates and silicates recently disclosed by Dumas. These salts, which exert no very striking poisonous influence upon superior organisms, are on the contrary fatal to the microscopic beings and the subtile agents, organized or formless, which take an undeniable part in infectious diseases. Experiments made quite lately have proved that at least such substances check the development of every kind of fermentation, delay putrid decomposition, and impede the decay of organic matter. It is allowable to suppose that these qualities, distinctly noted in chemists' laboratories, will be effectual in the laboratory of the animal system.

Apart from the remedies used against decided cholera, there are preventives which may be prudently and seasonably employed: these are disinfecting and antiseptic substances, as phenic acid, coal-tar, chloride of lime. The corrosive nature of these substances prevents their internal administration, and the test of their therapeutic effect; but it is positive that they exert a destructive influence over all organic corpuscles, and usually annul their injurious properties. On this account it is wise to employ them in cleansing and sweetening the atmosphere, particularly the confined air of rooms and hospitals, while epidemics are prevalent. It is the duty of government to take prompt steps and give plain instructions to insure the use of these substances everywhere at periods when they are required.

From the point of view of individual hygiene, the only prescription is to live regularly and temperately. Excesses, always dangerous, are more than ever so during an epidemic. It is a matter of course that extreme cleanliness is not less imperative; what, perhaps, is yet more so is calmness and mental cheerfulness. Moral force is here no less important than physical health. While cholera prevails, disorders of the bowels are very common, and in the very great majority of cases the disease does not come as a sudden attack, but as the result of diarrhœa, more or less protracted. Experience has shown that the breaking out of cholera is often prevented by attacking this first threatening symptom with opiates and the subnitrate of bismuth. When the cholera prevails in England, the government organizes visits to every house, to ascertain and

GREAT EPIDEMICS—ASIATIC CHOLERA.

treat, if there be occasion, such forerunners of the pestilence.

We find that there is as yet no specific against cholera. Can therapeutics indulge the hope of hereafter discovering one? We have no reason to doubt it. An heroic remedy for intermittent fevers has been discovered, quinine, though we have no knowledge whatever of the first cause of that disease, nor the least notion of what the miasma of marshes is. Perhaps in the same way we shall learn how to destroy the miasma of cholera before penetrating its inner nature. Meanwhile, it is allowable to rely on this, that the cholera, subject in that respect to that mysterious law which governs the secular evolution of epidemics, will lose its intensity in proportion to its remoteness from its origin. Those morbid germs, those forms of virus, seem not to be gifted with the power of indefinite reproduction. They exhaust themselves by their own activity. The death they sow at last overtakes themselves some day. Is it the influence of civilization which thus sets a limit to their deadly work, or is that end assigned to their career the fulfillment of a fixed decree? In any case the cholera must die some day. Till then the best way of working for its annihilation is to pursue the study of it scientifically.

We must see, therefore, what science and its teachings suggest for the future in the nature of labors that may serve to elucidate the serious problem of the character of cholera, and of infectious diseases generally. Researches in physics and chemistry grow daily easier, so simple are their phenomena, so sure their formulas, their theories so interdependent, and their processes so exact. The share given in them to discovery and origination becomes ever smaller; that taken by measurement and calculation grows constantly in proportion. The masters have enounced the grand laws and fundamental methods; the scholars do little else than determine special cases. This is less true of the science of life and diseases. This is a mine in which priceless and unexplored veins are yet abundant. Great triumphs are in store for those who shall have skill to extract that metal and bring it into circulation; but such labor demands bold enterprise no less than sagacious diligence.

There are diseases which have their seat in some one of the viscera, and at first oppress it alone with suffering. Thus the lungs, the liver, the stomach, the brain, may be differently affected. Others extend to a whole organic system, as the nervous or muscular system, that of the joints or the skin, etc. Others, again, seize on the whole vital frame, and to these is given the name of general disorders. It is as to these that we have least acquaintance with the outward causes and the internal derangements, because both have hitherto remained beyond the reach of medical research. Yet we may affirm that the blood, which bathes the whole organism and maintains the connection between the parts in it, must be in such cases the chief seat of morbid change. Without here going into the details of the distinctions set up by pathologists between disorders of this nature, it will suffice to say that they have classed cholera among the infectious diseases, that is, among diseases occasioned by poisons that have their origin in the atmosphere, as the yellow fever, the plague, typhus, varioloid, typhoid fever, etc.

Whatever hypothesis we may form as to the atmospheric origin of which we have just spoken, it is clear that these diseases affect the blood. In them the nourishing fluid experiences a transformation, not merely in the order and proportion, but also in the nature, of its components, particularly the most important of all, the albuminoid matter. The latter, which is the essential and nutritive part of the blood, the plastic part, to which the exhausted tissues owe their body and spring, then undergoes a deep change in the inmost parts of its molecular composition.

It not only suffers a marked change in its physical appearance, but it loses its original organic properties. It becomes impotent to perform the part of restorer which is imposed on it. Of what nature is this corruption of the albumen? We cannot say, so long as we remain ignorant of the nature of that very albumen in its normal state. In other words, there will be no chance to begin the study of corruptions of the blood until the blood of man in sound health shall be sufficiently understood, that is, until we shall have established the nature of the albuminoid substances with definite chemical exactness. That, for the moment, is the grand desideratum of biology. Chemistry is much advanced, physiology is developing; that which remains stationary is the region of questions making the transition between those two sciences, and the answers to which, perhaps of little importance to the former, would be the source of most desirable illumination for the latter. Nutrition will never be explained until we shall have established exactly the formula for those transformations through which food passes from the moment it is dissolved in the stomach until the moment it is thrown off by the various emunctories under the form of products of disassimilation. Such an explanation would not only give the key to those difficulties in physiology which still hold *savants* in check, but would also be of very great service in the knowledge of diseases, and, to return to our direct subject, in that of infectious diseases. It is therefore to the study of the albuminoid substances, and of the complex, rapid, and infinite changes which they undergo in the blood, that capable examiners should now direct their attention. Those who undertake it will not deserve the censure of setting out on a beaten path, for they will have every thing to create, beginning with the methods. At the present time we have never yet compared, and we have not even the means of comparing, in respect to the molecular elaboration that has taken place in them, two specimens of blood taken at two different points in the body. When we shall have mastered the composition of albumen, and when we shall have it in our power to make the comparison just alluded to, the problem of infectious diseases will not be long in coming into full light, and the cholera will be no more a dismal mystery.

THE PHYSIOLOGY OF DEATH.

Of old, the spoils of death fell to the anatomist's share, while the physiologist took for his part the phenomena of life. Now we submit the corpse to the same experiments as the living organism, and pry into the relics of death for the secrets of life. Instead of seeing in the lifeless body mere forms ready to dissolve and vanish, we detect in it forces and persisting activities full of deep instructiveness in their mode of working. As theologians and moralists exhort us to study the spectre of death face to face at times, and strengthen our souls by courageous meditation on our last hour, so medicine regards it as essential to direct our attention toward all the details of that mournful drama, and thus to lead us, through gloom and shadows, to a clearer knowledge of life. But it is only with respect to medicine in the most modern days that this is true.

Leibnitz, who held profound and admirable theories of life, had one of death also, which he has unfolded in a famous letter to Arnauld. He believes that generation is only the development and evolution of an animal already existing in form, and that corruption or death is only the reënvelopment or involution of the same animal, which does not cease to subsist and continue living. The sum of vital energies, consubstantial with monads, does not vary in the world; generation and death are but changes in the order and adjustment of the principles of vitality, simple transformations from small to great, and *vice versa*. In other words, Leibnitz sees everywhere eternal and incorruptible germs of life, which neither perish at all nor begin. What does begin and perish is the organic machine of which these germs compose the original activity: the elementary gearing of the machine is broken apart, but not destroyed. This is the first view held by Leibnitz. He has another, too, conceiving of generation as a progress of life through degrees; he can conceive of death also as a gradual regress of the same principle, that is to say, that in death life withdraws little by little, just as it came forward little by little in generation. Death is no sudden phenomenon, nor instantaneous evanishing—it is a slow operation, a " retrogradation," as the Hanoverian philosopher phrases it. When death shows to us, it has been a long time wearing away the organism, though we have not perceived it, because " dissolution at first attacks parts invisibly small." Yes, death, before it betrays itself to the eye by livid pallor, to the touch by marble coldness, before chaining the movements and stiffening the blood of the dying person, creeps with insidious secrecy into the smallest and most hidden points of his organs and his humors. Here it begins to corrupt the fluids, to disorganize the tissues, to destroy the equipoise and endanger the harmony. This process is more or less lingering and deceitful, and, when we note the manifest signs of death, we may be sure that the work lacked no deliberate preparation.

These ideas of Leibnitz, like most of the conceptions of genius, waited long after the time of their appearance for confirmation by demonstrative experiment. Before his day, bodies were dissected only for the sake of studying in them the conformation and normal arrangement of the organs. When this study was once completed, science took up the methodical inquiry into the changes produced in the different parts of the body by diseases. Not until the end of the eighteenth century did death in action become the subject of investigation by Bichat.

Bichat is the greatest of the physiological historians of death. The famous work he has left on this subject, his "Physiological Researches upon Life and Death," is as noteworthy for the grandeur of its general ideas, and its beauty of style, as for its precision of facts and nicety of experiment. To this day it remains the richest mine of recorded truths as to the physiology of death. Having determined the fact that life is seriously endangered only by alterations in one of the three essential organs, the brain, the heart, and the lungs, a group forming the vital tripod, Bichat examines how the death of one of these three organs assures that of the others, and in succession the gradual stoppage of all the functions. In our day, the advance of experimental physiology in the path so successfully traversed by Bichat, has brought to light in their minutest details the various mechanical processes of death, and, what is of far greater consequence, has disclosed an entire order of activities heretofore only suspected to be at work in the corpse. The theory of death has been built up by slow degrees along with that of life, and several practical questions that had remained in a state of uncertainty, such as that of the signs of real death, have received the most decisive answer in the course of these researches.

I.

Bichat pointed out that the complete life of animals is made up of two orders of phenomena, those of circulation and nutrition, and those that fix the relations of the living being with its environment. He distinguishes organic life from animal life, properly so called. Vegetables have only the former; animals possess both, intimately blended. Now, on the occurrence of death, these two sorts of life do not disappear at one and the same moment. It is the ani-

14

mal life that suffers the first stroke; the most manifest activities of the nervous system are those which come to a halt before all the rest. How is this stoppage brought about? We must consider separately the order of occurrences in death from old age, in that occasioned by disease, and in sudden death.

The man who expires at the close of a long decline in years, dies in detail. All his senses in succession are sealed. Sight becomes dim and unsteady, and at last loses the picture of objects. Hearing grows gradually insensible to sounds; touch is blunted into dullness; odors produce but a weak impression; only taste lingers a little. At the same time that the organs of sensation waste and lose their excitability, the functions of the brain fade out little by little. Imagination becomes unfixed, memory nearly fails, judgment wavers. Further, motions are slow and difficult on account of stiffness in the muscles; the voice breaks; in short, all the functions of outward life lose their spring. Each of the bonds attaching the old man to existence parts by slow degrees. Yet the internal life persists. Nutrition still takes place, but very soon the forces desert the most essential organs. Digestion languishes, the secretions dry up, capillary circulation is clogged, that of the large vessels in their turn is checked, and, at last, the heart's contractions cease. This is the instant of death. The heart is the last thing to die. Such is the series of slow and partial deaths which, with the old man spared by disease, result in the last end of all. The individual who falls into the sleep of eternity in these conditions, dies like the vegetable which, having no consciousness of life, can have no consciousness of death. He passes insensibly from one to the other, and to die thus is to know no pain. The thought of the last hour alarms us only because it puts a sudden end to our relations with all our surroundings; but, if the feeling of these relations has long ago faded away, there can be no place for fear at the brink of the grave. The animal does not tremble in the instant before it ceases to be.

Unfortunately, death of this kind is very rare for humanity. Death from old age has become an extraordinary phenomenon. Most commonly we succumb to a disturbance in the functions of our vital system, which is sometimes sudden, sometimes gradual. In this case, as in the former one, we observe animal life disappearing first, but the modes of its conclusion are infinitely varied.[1] One of the most usual is death through the lungs; as a result of pneumonia and different forms of phthisis, the oxidation of the blood becoming impossible on account of the disorganization of the pulmonary globules, venous blood goes back to the heart without gaining revivification. In the case of serious and prolonged fevers, and of infectious diseases, whether epidemic or otherwise, which are, characteristically, blood-poisonings, death occurs through a general change in nutrition. This is still more the fact as to death consequent upon certain chronic disorders of the digestive organs. When these are affected, the secretion of those juices fitted to dissolve food dries up, and these fluids go through the intestinal canal unemployed. In this case the invalid dies of real starvation. Hæmorrhage is one of the commonest causes of death. Whenever a great artery is opened from any cause, permitting the copious outflow of blood, the skin grows pale, warmth declines, the breathing is intermittent, vertigo and dimness of sight follow, the expression of the features changes, cold and clammy sweat covers part of the face and the limbs, the pulse gets gradually weaker, and, at last, the heart stops. Virgil describes hæmorrhage with striking fidelity in the story of Dido's death.

[1] Mille modis morimur mortales, nascimur unâ. Una via est vitæ, moriendi mille figuræ.

Sudden death, unconnected with outward and accidental causes, may occur in various ways. Very violent impressions on the feelings sometimes abruptly check the movements of the heart, and produce a mortal swoon. Instances are well known of many persons dying of joy—Leo X. is one—and of persons who succumbed to fear. In *foudroyant* apoplexy, if real death is not instantaneous, there is at least the sudden occurrence of the phenomena of death. The sufferer is plunged in profound sleep, called by physicians coma, from which wakening is impossible; his breathing is difficult, his eyes set, his mouth twisted and distorted. The pulsations of the heart cease little by little, and soon life utterly vanishes. The breaking of an aneurism very often occasions sudden death. Not less often the cause of death is found in what is called embolism, that is, a check to the circulation by a clot of blood suddenly plugging up some important vessel. And there are also cases of sudden death still unaccounted for, in the sense that subsequent dissection discovers nothing that could explain the stoppage in the operations of life.

Death is usually preceded by a group of phenomena that has received the name of the death-agony. In most cases of disease the beginning of this concluding period is marked by a sudden improvement of the functions. It is the last gleam springing from the dying flame; but soon the eyes become fixed and insensible to the action of light, the nose grows pointed and cold, the mouth, wide open, seems to call for the air that fails it, the cavity within it is parched, and the lips, as if withered, cling to the curves of the teeth. The last movements of respiration are spasmodic, and a wheezing, and sometimes a marked gurgling sound, may be heard at some distance, caused by obstruction of the bronchial tubes with a quantity of mucus. The breath is cold, the temperature of the skin lowered. If the heart is examined, we note the weakening of its sounds and pulsations. The hand, placed in its neighborhood, feels no throb. Such is the physiognomy of a person in the last moments of death in the greater number of cases, that is, when death follows upon a period of illness of some duration. The death-struggle is seldom painful, and almost always the patient feels nothing of it. He is plunged into a comatose stupor, so that he is no longer conscious of his situation or his sufferings, and he passes insensibly from life to death, in a manner that renders it sometimes difficult to fix the exact instant at which a dying person expires. This is true, at least, in chronic maladies, and especially in those that consume the human body slowly and silently. Yet, when the hour of death comes for ardent organizations—for great artists, for instance, and they usually die young—there is a quick and sublime new burst of life in the creative genius. There is no better example of this than the angelic end of Beethoven, who, before he breathed out his soul, that tuneful monad, regained his lost speech and hearing, and spent them in repeating for the last time some of those sweet harmonies which he called his "Prayers to God." Some diseases, moreover, are most peculiarly marked by the gentleness of the dying agony. Of all the ills that cheat us while killing by pin-pricks, consumption is that which longest wears for us the illusive look of health, and best conceals the misery of living and the horror of dying. Nothing can be compared with that hallucination of the senses and that liveliness of hope which mark the last days of the consumptive. He takes the burning of his destroying fever for a healthful symptom, he forms his plans, and smiles calmly and cheerfully on his friends, and suddenly, some morrow of a quiet night, he falls into the sleep that never wakes.

If life is everywhere, and if, consequently, death occurs everywhere, in all the elements of the system, what must be thought of that point in the spinal marrow which a famous physiologist styled the vital knot, and in which he professed to lodge the principle of life itself? The point which Flourens regarded as this vital knot is situated nearly at the middle of the prolonged spinal cord—that is, the middle of that portion of the nerve-substance which connects the brain with the spinal marrow. This region, in fact, has a fine and dangerous excitability. A prick, or the penetration of a needle into it, is enough to cause the instant death of any animal whatever. It is the very means used in physiological laboratories to destroy life swiftly and surely in dogs. That susceptibility is explained in the most natural way. This spot is the starting-point of the nerves that go to the lungs; the moment that the slightest injury is produced in it, there follows a check on the movements of respiration, and ensuing death. This vital knot of Flourens enjoys no sort of special prerogative. Life is not more concentrated nor more essential in it than elsewhere; it simply coincides with the initial point of the nerves animating one of the organs indispensable to vitality, the organ of sanguification; and in living organisms any alteration of the nerves controlling a function brings a serious risk as to its complete performance. There is, therefore, no such thing as a vital knot, a central fire of life, in animals. They are collections of an infinity of infinitely small living creatures, and each one of these microscopic living points is its own life-centre for itself. Each on its own account grows, produces heat, and displays those characteristic activities which depend upon its structure. Each one, by virtue of a preëstablished harmony, meets all the rest in the ways that they require; but, just as each lives on its own account, so on its account each dies. And the proof that this is so is found in the fact that certain parts taken from a dead body can be transferred to a living one without suffering any interruption in their physiological activity, and in the fact that many organs which seem dead can be excited anew, awakened out of their torpor, and animated to extremely remarkable vital manifestations. This subject we now proceed to consider.

II.

Death seems to be absolute from the instant that the pulsations of the heart are stopped without renewal, because, the circulation of the blood no longer proceeding, the nutrition of the organs becomes impossible, and nutrition is demanded for the maintenance of physiological harmony; but, as we have said above, there are a thousand little springs in the organism which keep up a certain degree of activity after the great main-spring has ceased to act. There is an infinite number of partial energies that outlive the destruction of the principal energy, and withdraw only by slow degrees. In cases of sudden death especially the tissues keep their peculiar vitality a very long time. In the first place, the heat declines only quite slowly, and the more so in proportion as death has been quick. For several hours after death the hair of the head and body, and the nails, continue to grow, nor does absorption either stop at once. Even digestion, too, keeps on. The experiment performed by Spallanzani to test this is very curious. He conceived the idea of making a crow eat a certain quantity of food, and killing it immediately after the meal. Then he put it in a place kept at the same temperature as that of a live bird, and opened it six hours later. The food was thoroughly digested.

Besides these general manifestations, the dead body is capable, during some continued time, of different kinds of activity. It is not easy to study these on the bodies of persons dying of sickness, because they are not permitted to be made the subject of anatomical examinations until twenty-four hours after death; but the bodies of beheaded criminals, which are given up to *savants* a few moments after their execution, can be of use in the investigation of what takes place immediately after the stopping of the living machine. If the heart is uncovered a few minutes after execution, pulsations are remarked which continue during an hour or longer, at the rate of forty to forty-five a minute, even after the removal of the liver, the stomach, and the intestines. For several hours the muscles retain their excitability, and undergo reflex contractions from the effect of pinching. Robin noted the following phenomenon in the case of a criminal an hour after his execution: "The right arm," to quote his description, "being placed obliquely extended at the side of the trunk, with the hand about ten inches away from the hip, I scratched the skin of the chest, at about the height of the nipple, with the point of a scalpel, over a space of nearly four inches, without making any pressure on the muscles lying beneath. We immediately saw the great pectoral muscle, then the biceps, then the anterior brachial, successively and quickly contract. The result was a movement of approach of the whole arm toward the trunk, with rotation inward of the limb, and half flexion of the forearm upon the arm, a true defensive movement, which threw the hand forward toward the chest as far as the pit of the stomach."

These spontaneous exhibitions of life in a corpse are trifles compared with those excited by means of certain stimulants, particularly of electricity. Aldini, in 1802, subjected two criminals, beheaded at Bologna, to the action of a powerful battery. Influenced by the current, the facial muscles contracted, producing the effect of horrid grimaces. All the limbs were seized with convulsive movements; the bodies seemed to feel the stir of resurrection, and to make efforts to rise. The springs of the system retained the power of answering the electric stimulus for several hours after beheading. A few years later, at Glasgow, Ure made some equally noted experiments on the body of a criminal that had remained more than an hour hanging on the gallows. One of the poles of a battery of seven hundred pairs having been connected with the spinal marrow below the nape of the neck, and the other brought in contact with the heel, the leg, before bent back on itself, was thrust violently forward, almost throwing down one of the assistants, who had hard work to keep it in place. When one of the poles was placed on the seventh rib, and the other on one of the nerves of the neck, the chest rose and fell, and the abdomen repeated the like movement, as takes place in respiration. On touching a nerve of the eyebrow at the same time with the head, the facial muscles contracted. "Wrath, terror, despair, anguish, and frightful grins, blended in horrible expression on the assassin's countenance."

The most remarkable instance of a momentary reappearance of vital properties, not in the whole organism, but in the head alone, is the famous experiment suggested by Legallois, and carried out for the first time in 1858 by Brown-Séquard. This skillful physiologist beheads a dog, taking pains to make the section below the point at which the vertebral arteries enter their bony sheath. Ten minutes afterward he sends the galvanic current into the different parts of the head thus severed from its body, without producing any result of movement. He then fits to the four arteries, the extremities of which appear in the cutting of the neck, little pipes connected by tubes with a reservoir full of fresh oxygenated blood, and guides the injection of this blood into the vessels of the brain. Immediately irregular motions of the eyes and the facial muscles occur, succeeded by the appearance of regular harmonious contractions, seeming to be prompted by the will. The head has regained life. The motions continue to be performed during a quarter of an hour, while the injection of blood into the cerebral arteries lasts. On stopping the injection, the motions cease, and give place to the spasms of agony, and then to death.

Physiologists asked whether such a momentary resurrection of the functions of life might not be brought about in the human subject—that is, whether movement might not be excited and expression reanimated by injecting fresh blood into a head just severed from a man's body, as in Brown-Séquard's experiment. It was suggested to try it on the heads of decapitated criminals, but anatomical observations, particularly those of Charles Robin, showed that the arteries of the neck are cut by the guillotine in such a way that air penetrates and fills them. It follows that it is impracticable to inject them with blood that can produce the effects noted by Brown-Séquard. Indeed, we know that blood circulating in the vessels becomes frothy on contact with air, and loses fitness for its functions. Robin supposes that the experiment in question could be successful only if made upon the head of a man killed by a ball that should strike below the neck; in that case it would be possible to effect such a section of the arteries that no entrance of air would occur, and, if the head were separated at the place pointed out by Brown-Séquard, those manifestations of function remarked in the dog's head would probably be obtained by the injection of oxygenated blood. Brown-Séquard is convinced that they might be obtained, if certain precautions were observed, even with the head of a decapitated criminal; and so strong is his conviction that, when it was proposed to him to try the experiment—that is, to perform the injection of blood into the head of a person executed—he refused to do so, not choosing, as he said, to witness the tortures of this fragment of a being recalled for an instant to sensibility and life. We understand Brown-Séquard's scruples, but it is allowable to doubt whether he would have inflicted great suffering on the head of the subject; at most, he would only have aroused in it a degree of very dim and uncertain sensibility. This is easily explained. In life, the slightest perturbation in the cerebral circulation is enough to prevent thought and sensation utterly. Now, if a few drops of blood too much or too little in the brain of an animal in full health suffice to alter the regularity of its psychical manifestations, much more certainly will the completeness of the brain's action be deranged if it is awakened by an injection of foreign blood, a forcible ingress too, which, of necessity, cannot cause the blood to circulate with suitable pressure and equipoise.

Corpse-like rigidity is one of the most characteristic phenomena of death. This is a general hardening of the muscles, so great that they lose the property of extension till even the joints cannot be bent; this phenomenon begins some hours after death. The muscles of the lower jaw are the first to stiffen; then rigidity invades in succession the abdominal muscles, those of the neck, and at last the thoracic ones. This hardening takes place through the coagulation of the half-fluid albuminoid matter which composes the muscular fibres, as the solidification of the blood results from coagulation of its fibrine. After a few hours the coagulated musculine grows fluid again, rigidity passes away, and the muscles relax. Something not dissimilar takes place also in the blood. The globules change, lose shape, and suffer the beginning of dissociation. The agents of putrefaction, vibrios and bacteria, thus enter upon their great work by insidiously breaking up the least seen parts.

At last, when partial revivals are no longer possible, when the last flicker of life has gone out and corpse-like rigidity has ceased, a new work begins. The living germs that had collected on the surface of the body and in the digestive canal develop, multiply, pierce into all the points of the organism, and produce in it a complete separation of the tissues and humors; this is putrefaction. The moment of its appearance varies with the causes of death and the degree of outward temperature. When death is the result of a putrid malady, putrefaction begins almost immediately when the body has grown cold. It is the same when the atmosphere is warm.[1] In general, in our climates, the work of decomposition becomes evident after from thirty-eight to forty hours. Its first effects are noticeable on the skin of the stomach; this takes on a greenish discoloration, which soon spreads and covers successively the whole surface of the body. At the same time the moist parts, the eye, the inside of the mouth, soften and decay; then the cadaverous odor is gradually developed, at first faint and slightly fetid, a mouldy smell, then a pungent and ammoniacal stench. Little by little the flesh sinks in·and grows watery; the organs cease to be distinguishable. Every thing is seized upon by what is termed putridity. If the tissues are examined under the microscope at this moment, we no longer recognize any of the anatomical elements of which the organic fabric is made up in its normal state. "Our flesh," Bossuet exclaims in his funeral-sermon on Henrietta of England, "soon changes its nature, our body takes another name; even that of a corpse, used because it still exhibits something of the human figure, does not long remain with it. It becomes a thing without a shape, which in every language is without a name." When structure has wholly disappeared, nothing more remains but a mixture of saline, fat, and proteic matters, which are either dissolved and carried away by water, or slowly burned up by the air's oxygen, and transmuted into new products, and the whole substance of the body, except the skeleton, returns piecemeal to the earth whence it came forth. Thus the ingredients of our organs, the

---

[1] Yet a very high temperature acts as cold does in delaying the moment of putrefaction by so coagulating the albuminoid matters as to make them less liable to decay.

chemical elements of our bodies, turn to mud and dust again. From this mud and this dust issue unceasingly new life and energetic activity; but a clay fit for the commonest uses may also be got from it, and, in the words of Shakespeare's *Hamlet*, the dust of Alexander or Cæsar may plug the vent of a beer-cask, or "stop a hole to keep the wind away." These "base uses," of which the Prince of Denmark speaks to *Horatio*, mark the extreme limits of the transformation of matter. In any case, the beings of lowest order that toil and engender in the bosom of putrefaction are really absorbing and storing away life, since without their aid the corpse could not serve as nutriment to plants, which in their turn are the necessary reservoir whence animality draws its sap and strength. It is in this sense that Buffon's doctrine of organic molecules is a true one.

Death is the necessary end of all organic existence. We may hope more or less to set at a distance its inevitable hour, but it would be madness to dream of its indefinite postponement in any species whatsoever. No doubt there is no contradiction in conceiving of a perfect equilibrium between assimilation and disassimilation, such that the system would be maintained in immortal health. In any case, no one has yet even gained a glimpse of the modes of realizing such an equilibrium, and death continues, till further orders, a fixed law of Fate. Still, though immortality for a complete organism seems chimerical, perhaps it is not the sense with the immortality of a separate organ in the sense we now explain. We have already alluded to the experiments of Paul Bert on animal-grafting. He has proved that, on the head of a rat, certain organs of the same animal—as the tail, for instance—may be grafted. And this physiologist asks himself the question, whether it would not be possible, when a rat provided with such an appendage draws near the close of his existence, to remove the appendage from him, and transplant it to a young animal, which in his turn would be deprived of the ornament in the same way in his old age in favor of some specimen of a new generation, and so on in succession. This tail, transplanted in regular course to young animals, and imbibing at each transference blood full of vitality, perpetually renewed, yet ever remaining the same, would thus escape death. The experiment, delicate and difficult, as we well see, was yet undertaken by Bert, but circumstances did not allow it to be prolonged for any considerable time, and the fact of the perpetuity of an organ, periodically rejuvenated, remains to be demonstrated.

III.

Real death, then, is characterized by the positive ceasing of vital properties and functions both in the organic or vegetative life, and in the animal life, properly so termed. When animal life disappears without any interruption occurring in organic life, the system is in a state of seeming death. In this state the body is possessed by profound sleep quite similar to that of hibernating animals; all the usual expressions and all signs of internal activity have disappeared, and give place to invincible torpor. The most powerful chemical stimulants exert no control over the organs, the walls of the chest are motionless; in short, seeing the body presenting this appearance, it is impossible not to think of it as dead. There are quite numerous states of the organism which may thus imitate death more or less closely; the commonest one is that of fainting. In this case neither sensation nor movements of circulation or respiration are any longer perceptible; the warmth is lowered, the skin pallid and colorless. Instances of hysteria are cited in which the attack has been prolonged for several days, attended with fainting. In this strange condition all physiological manifestations remain suspended; yet they are not, as it was long supposed, 'suspended absolutely. Bouchut has proved that, in the gravest cases of fainting, the pulsations of the heart continue, weaker and rarer, and harder to be heard than in normal life, but clearly distinguishable when the ear is laid on the precordial region. On the other hand, the muscles retain their suppleness and the limbs their pliability.

Asphyxia, which properly is suspension of breathing, and consequently of the blood's revivification, sometimes passes into a serious fainting condition followed by seeming death, from which the sufferer recovers after a period of varying length. This state may be induced either by drowning or by inhaling gas unfit for respiration, such as carbonic acid in deep wells, emanations from latrines, or the choke-damp of mines, or by suffocation. In 1650 a woman named Ann Green was hanged at Oxford. She had been hanging for half an hour, and several people, to shorten her sufferings, had pulled her by the feet with all their strength. After she was placed in her coffin it was observed that she still breathed. The executioner's assistants attempted to end her existence, but, thanks to the help of physicians, she came back to life, and continued to live some time afterward. Drowning occasions an equally deep insensibility, during which, very singularly, the psychical faculties retain some degree of activity. Sailors, after timely resuscitation from drowning, declare that, while under water, they had returned in thought to their families, and sadly fancied the grief about to be caused by their death. After a few minutes of physical rest, they suffered violent *colic* of the heart, which seemed to twist itself about in their chests; afterward this anguish was followed by utter annihilation of consciousness. It is very difficult, moreover, to determine how long apparent death may be protracted in an organism under water. It varies greatly with temperaments.

In the islands of the Greek archipelago, where the business of gathering sponges from the bottom of the sea is pursued, children are not allowed to drink wine until, by practice, they have grown accustomed to remain a certain time under water. Old divers of the archipelago say that the time to return and take breath at the surface is indicated to them by painful convulsions of the limbs, and very severe contractions in the region of the heart. This power of enduring asphyxia for some time, and resisting by force of will the movements of respiration, has been remarked under other circumstances. The case of a Hindoo is mentioned, who used to creep into the palisaded inclosures used for bathing, in the Ganges, by the ladies of Calcutta, seize one of them by the legs, drown her, and rob her of her rings. It was supposed that a crocodile carried her off. One of his intended victims succeeding in escaping, the assassin was seized and executed in 1817. He confessed that he had practised the horrible business for seven years. Another instance is that of a spy, who, seeing preparations making for his execution, endeavored to escape it by feigning death. He held his breath, and suspended all voluntary motions for twelve hours, and endured all the tests applied to him to put the reality of his death beyond doubt. Anæsthetics, too, like chloroform and ether, sometimes produce stronger effects than the surgeons using them desire, and occasion a state of seeming death instead of temporary insensibility.

It is easy to recall persons to life who are in a state of seeming death; it is only needful to stimulate powerfully the two mechanical systems that are more or less completely suspended in action, namely, those of respiration and circulation. Such movements are communicated to the frame of the chest, that the lungs are alternately compressed and dilated. A sort of shampooing is applied over the whole body, which restores the capillary circulation;

chemical stimulants, such as ammonia or acetic acid, are brought under the patient's nostrils. This is the mode of treatment for drowned persons, whose condition is brought on by ceasing to breathe the air, not by taking in too much water. A very effective method in cases of apparent death, caused by inhaling a poisonous gas, such as carbonic acid or sulphuretted hydrogen, consists in making the patient draw in large quantities of pure oxygen. And, again, it has very lately been proposed, as Hallé suggested without success early in this century, to adopt the use of strong electric currents for stimulating movement in persons who are in a state of syncope.

In all the cases of seeming death we have just mentioned, one mark of vitality persistently remains, that is, pulsation of the heart. Its throbs are less strong and frequent, but they continue perceptible on auscultation. They are regularly discernible in the deepest fainting-fits, in the various kinds of asphyxia, in poisonings by the most violent narcotics, in hysteria, in the torpor of epilepsy, in short, in the most diverse and protracted states of lethargy and seeming death.

Yet, this result, now a practical certainty, was unknown to physicians of old, and it cannot be denied that, in former times, seeming death was quite often mistaken for true death. The annals of science have recorded a certain number of errors of this kind, many of which have resulted in the interment of unfortunate wretches who were not dead. And for one of these mistakes that chance has brought to light either too late, or in time for the rescue, even then, of the victim, how many are there, particularly in times of ignorance and carelessness, that no one has ever known! How many live men have only given up their last breath after a vain struggle to break out of their coffin! The facts collected by Bruhier and Lallemand in two works that have become classic compose a most mournful and dramatic history. These are some of its episodes, marked by the strange part that chance plays in them. A rural guard, having no family, dies in a little village of Lower Charente. Hardly grown cold, his body is taken out of bed, and laid on a straw ticking covered with a coarse cloth. An old hired woman is charged with the watch over the bed of death. At the foot of the corpse were a branch of box, put into a vessel filled with holy water, and a lighted taper. Toward midnight the old watcher, yielding to the invincible need of sleep, fell into a deep slumber. Two hours later she awoke surrounded by flames from a fire that had caught her clothes. She rushed out, crying with all her might for help, and the neighbors, running together at her screams, saw in a moment a naked spectre issue from the hut, limping and hobbling on limbs covered with burns. While the old woman slept, a spark had probably dropped on the straw bed, and the fire it kindled had aroused both the watcher from her sleep and the guard from his seeming death. With timely assistance he recovered from his burns, and grew sound and well again.

On the 15th of October, 1842, a farmer in the neighborhood of Neufchâtel, in the Lower Seine, climbed into a loft over his barn to sleep, as he usually did, among the hay. Early the next day, his customary hour of rising being past, his wife, wishing to know the cause of his delay, went to look for him, and found him dead. At the time of interment, more than twenty-four hours after, the bearers placed the body in a coffin, which was closed, and carried it slowly down the ladder by which they had gained the loft. Suddenly one of the rounds of the ladder snapped, and the bearers fell together with the coffin, which burst open with the shock. The accident, which might have been fatal to a live man, was very serviceable to the dead one, who was roused from his lethargy by the concussion, returned to life, and hastened to get out of his shroud. with the assistance of those of the by-standers who had not been frightened away by his sudden resurrection. An hour later he could recognize his friends, and felt no uneasiness except a slight confusion in his head, and the next day was able to go to work again. At about the same time a resident of Nantes gave up life after a long illness. His heirs made arrangements for a grand funeral, and, while the performance of a requiem was going on, the dead man returned to life and stirred in the coffin, that stood in the middle of the church. When carried home, he soon regained his health. Some time afterward, the *curé*, not caring to be at the trouble of the burial ceremonies for nothing, sent a bill to the ex-corpse, who declined to pay it, and referred the *curé* to the heirs who had given orders for the funeral. A lawsuit followed, with which the papers of the day kept the public greatly amused. A few years ago Cardinal Donnet, in the Senate, told his own story of the circumstances under which he narrowly escaped being buried alive.

Besides these instances of premature burial in which the victim escaped the fearful consequences of the mistake made, others may be cited in which the blunder was discovered only too late. Quite a number of such cases are known, some of which are told with details too romantic to entitle them to implicit belief, while, however, many of them show unquestionable signs of authenticity. There long prevailed a tradition, not easily traceable to any source, which attributed the death of the Abbé Prévost to a mistake of this kind. All his biographers relate that the famous author of "Manon Lescaut," falling senseless from the effect of a rush of blood, in the depths of the forest of Chantilly, was supposed to be dead; that then the surgeon of the village having made an incision into his stomach, by direction of the magistrate, to ascertain the cause of death, Prévost uttered a cry, and did then die in earnest. But it has since been proved that the story is imaginary, and that it was made up after Prévost's death; nor do any of the necrological accounts published at the time refer it to the consequences of a premature autopsy. Though the account of Prévost dissected alive seems doubtful, that is not the case with the story told with regard to an operation by the famous accoucheur, Philip Small. A woman, about to be confined, fell into a state of seeming death. Small relates that when he was summoned to perform the Cesarean operation, the by-standers, convinced that the woman was dead, urged him to proceed with it. "I supposed so, too," he says, "for I felt no pulse in the region of the heart, and a glass held over her face showed no sign of respiration." Then he plunged his knife into the body, and was cutting among the bleeding tissues, when the subject awoke from her lethargy.

We cite some still more startling instances. Thirty years ago, a resident of the village of Eymes, in Dordogne, had been suffering for a long time from a chronic disorder of little consequence in itself, but marked by the distressing symptom of constant wakefulness, which forbade the patient any kind of rest. Worn out with this condition, he consulted a doctor, who prescribed opium, advising great caution in its use. The invalid, possessed with that common-enough notion that the efficacy of a drug is proportioned to its quantity, took at one time a dose sufficient for several days. He soon fell into a deep sleep, which continued unbroken for more than twenty-four hours. The village doctor, being summoned, finds the body without warmth, the pulse extinct, and, on opening the veins of both arms in succession, obtains but a few drops of thick blood. The day after, they prepared for his burial. But, a few days later, closer inquiry revealed the imprudence the poor wretch had committed in taking an excessive quantity of the prescribed narcotic. The report spreading among the villagers, they insist on his disinterment, which is allowed. Gathering in a crowd at the cemetery, they take up the coffin, open it, and are met by a horrible sight. The miserable man had turned over in his coffin, the blood gushing from the two opened veins had soaked the shroud; his features were frightfully contorted, and his convulsed limbs bore witness to the cruel anguish that had preceded death. Most of the facts of this kind are of rather remote date. The latest instances have happened in the country, among an ignorant population, usually in neighborhoods where no physician was called on to ascertain the decease, that is, to distinguish the cases of seeming death from those of true death.

How, then, can we certainly know apparent from real death? There is a certain number of positive signs of death; that is to say, signs which, when absolutely discerned, leave no room for mistake. Yet some physicians, and many people who know nothing of science, are still so doubtful about the certainty of these signs as to wish that physiology could detect others of a more positive character. A zealous philanthropist quite lately gave a sum for a prize of twenty thousand francs to the discoverer of an infallible sign of death. Doubtless the intention is excellent, but we are safe henceforward in regarding the sexton's work without alarm; the signs already known are clear enough to prevent any mistake, and to make the fatal risk of premature burial impossible.

We must point out, in the first place, the immediate signs of death. The first and the most decisive is the absolute stoppage of the heart's pulsations, noted for a duration of at least five minutes, not by the touch, but by the ear. "Death is certain," says the reporter of the commission named in 1848 by the Academy of Sciences to award the prize of competition as to the signs of true death, "when positive cessation of pulsations of the heart in the subject has been ascertained, which is immediately followed, if it has not been preceded, by cessation of respiration and of the functions of sensation and motion." The remote signs equally deserve attention. Of these, three are recognized: corpse-like rigidity, resistance to the action of galvanic currents, and putrefaction. As we have already seen, rigidity does not begin till several hours after death, while general and complete disappearance of muscular contractility, under the stimulus of currents, and, last of all, putrefaction, are only manifest at a still later period. These remote signs, particularly the last, have this advantage, that they may be ascertained by those unacquainted with medicine, and it is very well to pay some attention to them in countries where physicians are not charged with the verification of the disease, but they are of no importance wherever there are doctors to examine the heart with instruments, and to decide promptly and surely upon the death, from the complete stoppage of pulsation in that organ. At the beginning of the century, Hufeland and several other physicians, convinced that all the signs of death then known were uncertain, except putrefaction, proposed and obtained in Germany the establishment of a certain number of mortuary houses, intended to receive and keep for some time the bodies of deceased persons. During the whole existence of these establishments, not one of the bodies transported into those asylums has been known to return to life, as the authentic declarations of the attendant doctors agree. The usefulness of such mortuary houses is still more questionable in our time, when we have a positive and certain means of recognizing real death. Those police regulations that forbid autopsies and interments until the full term of delay for twenty-four hours, measured from the declaration of death, still remain prudent precautions, but they do not lessen at all the certainty of that evidence furnished by the stopping of the heart. When the heart has definitely ceased to beat, then resurrection is no longer possible, and the life which deserts it is preparing to enter upon a new cycle.

Hamlet, in his famous soliloquy, speaks of "that undiscovered country from whose bourn no traveler returns," and mournfully asks what must be the dreams of the man to whom death has opened the portals of those gloomy regions. We can give no clearer answer in the name of physiology than Shakespeare's prince gives. Physiology is dumb as to the destiny of the soul after death; of that it teaches, and it can teach us, nothing. It is plain, and it would be childish to deny it, that any psychical or sentient manifestation and any concrete representation of the personality are impossible after death. The dissolution of the organism annihilates surely, and of necessity, the functions of sensation, motion, and will, which are inseparable from a certain combination of material conditions. We can feel, move, and will, only so far as we have organs for reception, transmission, and execution. These assurances of science are above discussion, and should be accepted without reserve. Do they tell us any thing of the destiny of the psychical principles themselves? Again we say, No, and for the very simple reason that science does not attain to those principles; but metaphysics, which does attain to them, authorizes us, nay, further, compels us, to believe that they are immortal. They are immortal, as the principles of motion, the principles of perception, all the active unities of the world, are immortal. What is the general characteristic of those unities? It is that of being simple, which means being indestructible, which means being in harmonious mutual connection, after such a manner that each one of them perceives the infinite order of the other. If this connection did not exist, there would be no world. What is the characteristic of the psychical unities more especially? It is that of having, moreover, the consciousness of such perception, the feeling also of the relations that bind the whole together, and those faculties, more or less developed, which that consciousness and that perception imply. But why should these unities be any more perishable than the others? Why, if all these forces, all these activities, are eternal, should those alone not possess eternity which have this high privilege, that of knowing the infinite relations which the others sustain without knowing that they do so?

To form a conception of the immortality of the soul, then, we must place ourselves at that point of view to which men rarely and hardly rise, of the simplicity and the indefectibility of all those principles of force that fill the universe. We must train ourselves to understand that what we see is nothing in comparison with what we do not see. The whole force, the whole spring, of the most complex movements, the most magnificent phenomena of Nature and the most subtile operations of life, thought included, proceed from the infinite commingling of an infinity of series of invisible and unextended principles, whose activities ascend in the scale of perfection from simple power of movement up to supreme reason. Human personality, such as we see and know it, is only a coarse and complex result from those of these primitive activities which are the best and deepest thing in us. It is not that personality which is immortal—that is no more immortal than the motive force of a steam-engine is, or the electricity of a voltaic battery, although movement and electricity are of themselves indestructible. It is not that personality which can aspire to a home in the bosom of God. Our true personality, our real *I*, that which may without illusion count on a future life, is unity released from every material bond, and all concrete alloy; it is that force, necessarily pure, which has a more or less clear consciousness of its own relations with the infinity of like unities, and which more or less draws near to them by thought and by love. It is beyond our power to conceive what will become of that unity when, quitting its prison of flesh, and soaring into the ideal ether, it will no longer have organs with which to act; but what we can affirm is that, precisely by reason of this freedom, it will rise to a clearer knowledge of all that it had only known obscurely, and to a purer love of what it had adored only through the veil of sense. And this certainty, which is the ennobling and elevating force of life, is also the consolation for death.

HEREDITY IN PHYSIOLOGY, IN MEDICINE, AND IN PSYCHOLOGY.

THERE are many grounds of pride and satisfaction for the mind in the sciences known to man, but reasons for humility and bitter regret are also supplied by them to the full. Spite of the persistent strivings and labored meditations of the legions of investigators who have gone before us, Nature still has her deep and dark abysses, at whose blank look all insight turns to blindness, all boldness dies in fear, and all confidence becomes despair. When we attempt to throw a little light upon the heart of these mysterious chasms, that light merely reflects to our view the ghosts of our own ignorance, and we gain from the futile effort only a fresh conviction of our own impotence and poverty. It would be wise to gain from it something more ; I mean, a lesson to benefit us. Indeed, nothing should so chide us back to humility and patience, so cool our presuming eagerness and daunt our daring arrogance, as the study of those phenomena which Providence seems to have ordained purposely to baffle human inquisitiveness. Yet many men affect to be unconscious of the astounding and intricate operations which are taking place in regions that sight and sense never sound, and stubbornly dispute the existence of unseen activities and unfelt powers. This is the deadly, doubting temper that the evidence of those sphinxes of which we are now treating must be brought to attack. The lesson is all the more eloquent because, by strange contrast, those questions that defy every kind of theoretical exposition and of pictured conception are precisely the ones best understood on their practical side. Familiarity with effects seems in these cases unavailing to gain any understanding of causes.

These reflections have a particular application to heredity. The fact exists that the ovule contains in its substance, seemingly homogeneous, not simply the anatomical organism of the individual about to issue from it, but, moreover, his temperament, character, capacities, his thoughts, and his feelings. The parents lodge in that molecule the future of an existence almost always identical with their own from the physiological point of view, often so in respect to the pathological one, and wholly so in many instances when psychologically regarded. We propose to bring to our readers' knowledge the results of the latest researches on the subject of that amazing work of vital economy.[1]

I.

Heredity is that biological law in virtue of which living beings incline to transmit to their progeny a certain portion of the traits which characterize themselves. It is a very delicate problem to decide whether we are to attribute to heredity the handing down of the anatomical forms and the physiological functions of that species which is represented in the particular system. At all events, in this respect it is plain that the reproduction of parents in their children is thorough and absolute; otherwise there would be no such thing as species; there would be mere successions of beings, with no other relations to each other than that of generation. Within our experience, as limited by history, the constant new production of specific characteristics, always identical, in other words, the permanent integrity of species, is a fact almost beyond dispute. Such

[1] *See* particularly Th. Ribot, "Heredity, its Phenomena, its Laws," etc. Paris, 8vo, 1873.

characteristics as mark the differences between races and varieties are transmitted with less certainty and uniformity, and the fact of the various transformations which these may undergo from generation to generation is precisely the one upon which a famous school of naturalists insists, in its attempt to demonstrate, within certain limits, as to extent, the utter change of organisms in the lapse of ages. Still less fixed and amenable to rule is the reproduction of those characteristics, not so general as those of race and species, which may be looked on as peculiar to the individual. Thus, as characteristics increase in peculiarity and specialty, escaping the law of heredity, the chances increase that children will differ from their parents. Yet observation—and that as ancient as man himself is—fixes the truth that these completely personal characteristics may be transmitted by generation. Within what limits, and under what conditions? This is the point that we must examine with the wariest caution, for a question does not exist about which there is a greater risk of slipping in perilous downward paths.

Heredity is peculiarly manifest in continuous existence of pathological and physiological conditions. It is especially betrayed in the expression and features of the face. The ancients took note of this; hence, among the Romans, the *nasones, labeones, buccones, capitones,* etc. The nose is perhaps that one of all the features which heredity most persistently maintains; the Bourbon nose is famous. Heredity shows itself also in fecundity and longevity. In the old French nobility many families possessed immense vigor in propagation. Anne de Montmorency, who, when past seventy-five, was still strong enough to smash with his sword the teeth of the Scotch soldier who gave him his death-blow in the battle of Saint-Denis, was the father of twelve children. Three of his ancestors, Matthew (1st), Matthew (2d), and Matthew (3d), had among them eighteen children, fifteen of whom were boys. The son and the grandson of the great Condé counted nineteen children in their two families, and their great-grandfather, killed at Jarnac, had ten. The first four Guises counted together forty-three children, thirty of them boys. Achille de Harlay, father of the first President de Harlay, had nine children, his father ten, his great-grandfather eighteen. In some families this fertility persisted for five or six generations. The mean length of human life depends on localities, food, state of civilization, but individual longevity seems to be wholly independent of these conditions. It is remarked among those who lead lives of the hardest toil, as well as among those who take the greatest care of their health, and it seems to depend upon some inward potency of vitality received by individuals from their ancestors. This is so well understood that, in England, life-insurance companies require from their agents full reports as to the longevity of the ancestors of applicants. In the family of Turgot the age of fifty-nine years was seldom outlived, and the man who has given lustre to its name, on the day he reached his fiftieth year, felt a presentiment that the end of his life was not far off. Notwithstanding his appearance of perfectly good health, and his extremely vigorous constitution, from that time he held himself in readiness for death, and he did in fact die at the age of fifty-three.

Heredity often transmits muscular strength, and various other motive energies. Antiquity had its families of athletes. The English have their families of boxers. The late inquiries of Mr. Galton on the subject of wrestlers and racing-crews, prove that the victors in the contests in which these men take part usually belong to a small number of families in which skill and agility come by descent. Suppleness and grace in dancing movements are transmitted, too, as the famous family of the Vestris witnesses. It is the same with different peculiarities of the voice, stammering, nasal speaking, slurring the *r*, etc. Families of singers are numerous. Most children born of talkative people chatter from their cradle. Dr. Lucas mentions an instance of a servant of boundless loquacity. She talked people utterly out of breath; she would chatter to animals, to things; she gabbled aloud to herself. Her master was obliged to dismiss her. "But," she said, "it is not my fault, it comes from my father; it was so strong in him that it drove my mother wild, and he had a father exactly like me in that."

Heredity in anomalies of the organization has been noticed in a great number of cases. One of the strangest is that of Edward Lambert, whose body, excepting his face, the palms of his hands, and the soles of his feet, was covered with a sort of armor of horny excrescences. He had six children, all of whom, from six weeks of age, showed the same singularity. The only one that survived transmitted it, like his father, to all his sons, and this transmission, passing from male to male, continued for five generations. The Colburn family is mentioned also, in which the parents transmitted to the children, during four generations, what is called sexdigitism, that is, six fingers on each hand, and feet with six toes each. In the same way albinism, lameness, hare-lip, and other anomalies, are reproduced in the progeny. It has been observed that entirely individual peculiarities may be subject to a like tendency to reappearance. Giron de Buzareingues says that he knew a man who had the habit, when in bed, of lying on his back and crossing the right leg over the left one. One of his daughters was born with the same habit; she regularly took that position in the cradle, in spite of the impediment of her baby-dress. The same author declares that he has often remarked children who had inherited habits equally singular, which could be accounted for neither by imitation nor by education. Darwin mentions another instance of the kind: A child had the odd trick of moving his fingers rapidly about when pleased. When greatly excited he would raise both hands on either side of the face, as high as the eyes, still shaking his fingers. After reaching old age, he still found it troublesome to refrain from making those gestures. He had eight children, one of them a little girl, who from the age of four years had her father's trick of shaking her fingers and lifting her hands. So, too, heredity in handwriting has been noticed. There are families in which left-handedness is hereditary. Various peculiarities in the state of the organs of sense are transmitted in like manner. Almost all the members of the Montmorency family were affected with a slight squint, which was called the Montmorency look. Inability to distinguish between different colors is well known to run in families; the famous English chemist Dalton, and two of his brothers, were thus affected; and hence the name of daltonism is given to that peculiarity. Deafness and blindness are sometimes hereditary, though rarely so; the condition of deaf-muteness still more rarely. Many strange instances of the transmission of certain perversities of the sense of taste are cited. Lucas relates, Zimmermann says, the following fact: In Scotland a man was haunted by an unconquerable longing to eat human flesh. He had a daughter. Though separated from her father and mother, who were sentenced to burning before she was a year old, and though brought up among people in a good station of life, this young girl gave way, like her father, to the incredible craving for cannibalism. This instance clearly borders on insanity.

Insanity is assuredly transmitted by heredity. Esquirol found among thirteen hundred and seventy-five cases of madness three hundred and thirty-seven in which it was inherited. Guislain and other physicians calculate in a general way that the number of cases of hereditary mental alienation represents a quarter of all those who are thus diseased. Moreau (of Tours) and others state that the proportion is even greater. Heredity in madness does not merely comprise direct transmission of insanity properly so called; hysteria, epilepsy, chorea, idiocy, hypochondria, may proceed from madness, and it may in turn reproduce them. In their passage from one generation to another, these various diseases of the nerves become in a manner mutually transformed.[1] Herpin, the Genevese, noted, among the ancestors of two hundred and forty-three epileptic subjects, seven epileptics, twenty-one insane, and twenty-four persons affected with cerebro-spinal diseases. Georget draws the conclusion, from numerous observations made at la Salpêtrière, that hysterical women almost always had among their near relatives those who were hysteric, epileptic, hypochondriac, or insane. Moreau dwells on the very frequent occurrence of morbid nervous conditions among the ancestors of the idiotic and imbecile. A single fact will suffice to convey some conception of the various and strange complications following on the transmission by descent of nervous disorders. Dr. Morel attended four brothers of the same family. The grandfather of these children died insane; their father was quite incapable of fixing his mind on any thing; their uncle, a distinguished physician, marked by high intellectual power, was noted for his eccentricities. Now, these four children, sprung from the same stock, exhibited very differing forms of psychical disorders: one was a madman, subject to periodi-

---

[1] Mere alcoholic intoxication may be transformed into serious nervous diseases. Children conceived in an acute attack of drunkenness are often epileptic, insane, idiotic, etc. These facts have been remarked since very ancient days. A law of Carthage forbade any other beverage but water on the day of marital cohabitation, and Amyot says, " Drunkenness begets nothing of any worth." Late and accurate researches prove that a child begotten even in a mere passing fit of intoxication always bears ineffaceable marks of more or less grave degeneracy.

cal and furious fits; the second, a hypochondriac, was reduced by brooding inaction to the state of a mere automaton; the third was peculiar from his excessive irascibility, and his disposition to suicide; the fourth was distinguished by great capabilities for the arts, but was timid and suspicious by nature.

Scrofula, cancer, tubercles, syphilis, gout, arthritis, tetter, and generally those chronic constitutional complaints which take the name of *diatheses* and *cachexies*, very often descend from parents to children. The heredity of these diseased states is almost as common and positive as that of nervous affections. It may also be asserted, though the case is much more unusual, that disorders of the skin, especially psoriasis, may be transmitted.

Nothing can be more dramatically interesting than the evolution of these hereditary maladies, which, lodged in the system of children in the form of germs, of mere predispositions, sometimes are destroyed utterly by a combination of fortunate conditions and precautions, sometimes begin at once their destined destructive work, sometimes lurk in secret for years, and are aroused some day, pitiless and terrible, under the goad of various stimulations. Thus age, sex, temperament, practices, habits, conditions of health, the surrounding medium, all take part in the development of diseased action, coming from heredity. Insanity is rare in childhood; epilepsy most commonly breaks out in early youth. Hysteria, scrofula, rachitis, and tubercles, make their appearance in childhood and youth; gout, gravel, calculi, baldness, cancer, are hereditary conditions manifest in the adult. Women are more liable to insanity, epilepsy, and hysteria, than men. The latter, to balance the scale, are much oftener attacked by gout, gravel, and stone. The nervous temperament facilitates the appearance of neuroses, the lymphatic-sanguine temperament that of arthritis and tetter, the lymphatic that of scrofula. The changes that occur in the physiological balance of the individual act decidedly upon the progress and the appearance of constitutional disorders. Thus insanity very often makes itself known just after menstruation, pregnancy, or childbirth; epilepsy and hysteria in like manner become active at the time when the signs of puberty first appear. Education and manners have a similar influence. Cruel treatment and extreme severity, as also utter want of discipline and of watchful care, often produce lamentable effects on the brain of young children. Alcoholic indulgences and high living are fatal to persons born of parents afflicted with gout and gravel; while poverty and unwholesomeness in their surroundings decimate those who bear the seeds of consumption within them.

At any rate, the destructiveness of hereditary diseases is a sad and striking fact, known in all its mournfulness only to those who are called every day to observe its consequences. One needs to see the premature infirmities, the wasting sufferings, the irredeemable misfortunes, the keen and lingering anguish to which parents often doom their children while they believe they are transmitting to them the blessing of life, if one would judge of the might of that fell spirit of disease lurking in the inmost depths of their being. One must read the authors who have written on these subjects, and especially our learned French specialists in insanity, to gain acquaintance with that mysterious and maleficent potency which that frail and innocent being, the object, for one fleeting moment of illusions, of every joy, and blessing, and smiling hope, so often brings as its companion when it opens its eyes to the light of day.

As a general statement, it may be said that hereditary transmission, either of personal peculiarities in anatomical structure and in temperament, or of aptitudes to take on one or another morbid state, which also depends on certain bodily dispositions, is a very common though not a uniform phenomenon among animals and in man.

Transmission by descent of individual peculiarities in the order of intellect or the affections, and heredity in predisposition to some one or other moral or speculative activity, are also phenomena sometimes remarked, but not so commonly as the foregoing ones. When we review the series of instances and proofs collected and appealed to by some authors, we are struck, it is true, by the seeming strength of these arguments, and we are ready to concede to heredity a very large share in the development of the intellect and character in the genesis of the thinking individual. We fail to see, or we forget, the prodigious number of facts that bear witness the contrary way. The illusions of that mirage have not been without their use, in the sense that they have induced very interesting researches, but they would be a source of danger did they lead the public to put faith in the conclusions drawn by some authors from these investigations. We will briefly point out the real advantage to be gained from these researches, and will attempt to disprove the inferences.

According to Galton, the faculty of memory in the family of Richard Porson, the famous Greek scholar, was so wonderful that it had passed into a byword—"the Porson memory." Lady Esther Stanhope, who led so adventurous a life, notes, among many points of likeness between herself and her grandfather, that of the memory. "I have my grandfather's gray eyes and his memory for places," she says. "If he saw a stone on the road, he recollected it, and I do the same; his eyes, dull and without expression at ordinary times, blazed with a startling light as mine do when sudden emotion seized him." The creative and imaginative faculties, which take a dominant part in poetry and the arts, sometimes pass down from father to son.

Galton, in the work published by him four years ago,[1] and Th. Ribot, in his very late book, give long lists of painters, poets, and musicians, designed to prove the part which heredity takes in the production of these artists' talents. In these lists many instances appear in which that influence cannot be called in question, but there are very many more in which it is extremely disputable. Thus these authors discover the influence of heredity in the poetic genius of Byron, Goethe, and Schiller, because they find in their ancestors certain passions, certain vices or qualities, as if such peculiarities of character could have any thing to do with determining poetic genius. In fact, their catalogues do not name one great poet who inherited his powers from his parents. We do learn from them that a great poet sometimes becomes the father of tolerably good poets, which is by no means the same thing. Hereditary predisposition for painting is more real; in a list of forty-two famous Italian, Spanish, or Flemish painters, Galton cites twenty-one who had famous parents. The names of Bellini, Caracci, Teniers, Van Ostade, Mieris, Van der Velde, Vernet, are proof enough of the existence of families of painters. In Titian's family nine meritorious painters are met with. The history of musicians presents more striking instances. The family of Bach begins in 1550 and ends in 1800; its founder was Veit Bach, a baker at Presburg, who sought recreation from his work in music and singing. He had two sons, who began that unbroken succession of musicians of the same name which filled Thuringia, Saxony, and Franconia, for nearly two centuries. They were all organists, or parish singers, or town musicians, as they are styled in Germany. When the members of this family had scattered, becoming too numerous to live in the same neighborhood, they agreed to come together on a fixed day once a year, in order to keep up a sort of patri-

[1] "Hereditary Genius," London, 1869.

archal bond among them. This custom was observed till toward the middle of the eighteenth century, and as many as a hundred and twenty persons, men, women, and children, of the name of Bach, were often seen together. In that family are enumerated twenty-nine eminent musicians, and twenty-eight of inferior repute. The father of Mozart was second chapel-master to the Prince-bishop of Salzburg. Beethoven's was a tenor in the chapel of the Elector of Cologne. His grandfather had been a singer in the same chapel, and afterward chapel-master. The parents of Rossini used to perform music at fairs.

We find that heredity intervenes almost as powerfully and constantly in the transmission of those passions and feelings, of a wholly different order, which produce vicious inclinations. The taste for alcohol, the habit of debauchery, the passion for gaming, gain a control over some persons from their ancestors. "A lady among my intimates, possessing a large fortune," says Gama Machado, "had a passion for play, and passed her nights at the gaming-table; she died while young, of a pulmonary complaint. Her eldest son, who was like her in every respect, was equally mad for gambling; he, too, died of consumption, like his mother, and at nearly the same age. His daughter, who resembled him, inherited the same tastes, and died young." Heredity in a disposition to theft, to rape, to assassination, to suicide, has been noted in very many cases.

In the degree in which we rise from purely physiological or pathological regions to those in which mental activity is more clearly present, heredity is observed to lose its force and its uniformity. There have been families of *savants*, as those of Cassini, Jussieu, Bernouilli, Darwin, Saussure, Geoffroy, Pictet. In learning and literature we may mention those of Estienne, Grotius, and a few others. The Mortemart family were famous for their wit. A genius for statesmanship, or for war, has sometimes been traced continuously for several generations in some families. Taken all together, these facts of transmission of the psychic faculties are not numerous. If they are so carefully noted, and put forward so prominently, it seems to be because they are not common, even apart from the remark that there are several of them with which perhaps education has had as much to do as ancestral influence.

Several years ago there appeared a book under the title "Phrenyogeny," in which is to be found, together with many visionary or paradoxical propositions, one idea that deserves attention, the more so because it points at a peculiarity about which physiologists hitherto seem not to have concerned themselves. The author of this book, Bernard Moulin, attempts to prove in it that children are living photographs of their parents as these are at the very instant of conception: in his view parents transmit to children those tastes and predispositions which were at that instant exerting their most powerful effect, whether spontaneously or of intention. The positive conclusions drawn by Moulin, from his researches as to the art of procreating children of the best kind, sometimes cause a smile, but the facts adduced in support of them are curious. We mention some of them. Nine months before the birth of Napoleon I., Corsica was in a state of confusion. The famous Paoli, at the head of an army of citizens formed by his exertions, was striving to quench civil war and prevent a foreign invasion. Charles Buonaparte, his aide-de-camp and secretary, exhibited admirable courage by his side. The young officer had his wife with him, Letitia Ramolino, Roman in her beauty, and of vigorous and masculine character. Napoleon was conceived under canvas, on the eve of a battle, two paces from the guns trained on the enemy. Robespierre had his origin in the year 1758, that year which saw the regicide Damiens broken on the wheel and quartered in the Place de Grève, a year of war, famine, and disquiet.

His father was a lawyer, and an insatiate reader of the "Contrat social." Peter the Cruel, King of Castile, was the son of Alphonso XI., who lived on bad terms with his wife. Scandalous scenes of anger, jealousy, and violence, continually disturbed the royal household, and the issue of the intercourse of the married pair was Peter the Cruel, a monster of physical and moral ugliness. History shows us Raphael's parents, both devoted to the art of painting. The wife, a real Madonna, delighted in pious and graceful subjects. The father, a vigorous dauber, preferred energy for his share.

Ribot, in the remarkable work which he has just devoted to heredity, examines the laws of that mysterious influence which he judges to be a kind of habit, or perpetual memory. These laws are little else than the ascertainment of the usual directions in which the hereditary impulse acts. Sometimes transmission passes from the father to the daughter, from the mother to the son; sometimes the child takes from both its parents. Again, it often occurs that the child, instead of being like its immediate parents, resembles one of its grandparents or some yet more remote ancestor, or some distant member of a collateral branch of the family. This is what is called atavism, or reversed heredity.[1] The latter fact was well known to the ancients. Montaigne expresses his wonder at it. "What a prodigy is it," he says, "that the drop of seed from which we spring bears in itself not

[1] The singular phenomenon of alternating generations has been compared with atavism. In 1818, Chamisso, in studying the *biphora* or *salpas*, discovered that these creatures are alternately single or grouped. In the first generation the biphora are found as *chains*, produced by gemmation; in the second they are single, produced by spores; in the third we find chains of biphora again, so that the son is never like its father, and always like its grandfather. The researches of Saars and Steenstrup have brought the fact to light that in some other creatures the cycle goes through three generations, and that the likeness, instead of being one between the grandfather and grandson, is one between the great-grandfather and the great-grandson.

merely the impress of the corporeal form of our fathers, but their thoughts and dispositions too! That drop of fluid, where does it find room for that infinite multitude of forms? and how does it carry those resemblances in so strange and irregular a course that the great-grandson will answer to the great-grandfather, the nephew to the uncle?" Montaigne's amazement is reasonable, nor do we understand any better now than they did in the sixteenth century the causes of these singular transmissions.

Such are the facts. We should in vain attempt to get rid of their character by multiplying their number, or by reasoning upon them. In the region of psychology, the instances of heredity will never be any thing but exceptions, compared with those that stand for the opposite. Now, if they are exceptions, by what right can heredity be set up as the general law of development of intellectual action? By what right is it asserted that in this matter heredity is the rule, and non-heredity the exception? Ribot piles up the most ingenious arguments to prop up that singular proposition, but he wastes his time and ability in it. Any fashion of explaining how the heredity of intellectual aptitudes is almost uniformly overcome by opposing or disturbing causes, does not make it out as overcoming them. Whatever ingenious reasons may be found for consolation because the fancied sovereignty of heredity is seen to be brought down in the nature of things to a very limited control, they do not enlarge that control. In a word, if in fact non-heredity does have a far greater power and sway than heredity, the question is, Why does Ribot adopt a formula that implies the reverse?

Moreover, does not the spectacle of the development of civilization by itself alone clearly prove the dominant efficacy, in man's bosom, of a permanent tendency toward transformation, innovation, change? Unalterableness in thoughts and permanence in habits were the law of primitive races, it is true, and they still are the law of savage tribes; but nothing, to begin with, proves that heredity is the cause of this. Such a reappearance, during a longer or shorter tract of time, of societies exactly alike, seems to be much more properly attributable to the potent and irresistible instinct of imitation, and to positive respect for rites and customs commanded by religion. With these tribes, the future is like the present, and the present repeats the past only because the same unbending rule, the same authority and the same tyrannical superstition, press on all alike. Nothing has any strength or respect among such people, except through tradition, and tradition among them is merely the honored memory of a will once of old expressed by mysterious powers. When the English desire to interest the Hindoos in the works of communication and of hygiene that they are effecting in India, they are even at this day forced to convince them first that the usefulness of such works was well understood by the Brahmans in the remotest times, so difficult is it for that ancient race to believe that a rule can be obligatory unless it is traditional.

At all events, and whatever part heredity may be allowed in this matter, it is certain that its part is not great, because that strange homogeneity of primitive races, instead of maintaining and strengthening itself, yields sooner or later to diversity. Every people in turn is invaded by a force as powerful for action counter to that of hereditary influences as it is in striking off the iron yoke of primal customs. It was in Greece, nearly three thousand years ago, that the first throe of that force shaped and worked what Goethe calls "the liberation of humanity." Since then, the crossings of distinct races, new needs and the diversified inventions which they have suggested without end, the ideas awakened in man by the ever-growing closeness of his contact with Nature, have brought into the place of primitive simplicity a manifold and resistless variability, of which the present condition of the world is the convincing proof.

II.

What precedes is but an historic refutation. A more direct and scientific refutation will, at the same time, be more positive and more instructive. After proving that heredity has not exerted exclusive and unbroken influence, we must state the causes which act together with and in opposition to it. We must point out the continuous and potent activity of those forces which tend, as we have said, to modify, to alter, and complicate thought, feeling, passion, manners, and customs.

The special object of education is to transmit to the child the sum of those habits to which he will need to conform in practical life, and the sum of those acquirements which will be essential to him for pursuing his calling; but it must begin by unfolding in him those powers which will enable him to become master of such habits and of such acquisitions. It teaches the child to speak, to move, to see, to feel, to hear, to understand, to judge, to love. Now the influence of education, counter to that of heredity, is so great that the former of itself, in most cases, has the power of effecting a real moral and psychological likeness between parents and children. If heredity positively and irresistibly brought about in descendants the reproduction of all the characteristics constituting the personality of their ancestors, education would be of no use. Since education, and that a protracted, watchful, and toilsome education, is indispensable to bring out the appearance and produce the development of the child's aptitudes and mental qualities, we must needs conclude that heredity takes merely a secondary part in this wonderful genesis of the moral person. This argument is unanswerable. It would be highly unscientific to deny that hereditary influences are manifest in predispositions and fixed tendencies; but it would be quite as inexact to maintain that these implicitly contain the future conditions and control the evolution of the psychical being.

There is nothing more complicated than education. We cannot here undertake to go to the depths of its general management, which has been the subject of so many volumes. The importance everywhere attributed to works on the training of children is in itself alone a protest against the abuse of theories on heredity. A few novel details as to one of the main instruments of education, the instinct of imitation, and as to the share it has in the development of individuals and races, will suffice to teach an estimate of the power of those influences alien to heredity.

A learned English historian, Bagehot, has lately written some admirable pages to prove how strong an influence the unconscious imitation of a popular character or type, and the general favor shown to this character or this type, the traits of which are instinctively copied by the public, exerts over the formation of customs and of tastes, while at the same time giving the key to periodical revolutions in such tastes and customs. In his view, national character is nothing else than local character which has made its way upward, precisely as the national tongue is merely the lasting extension of a local dialect. Nothing is more real than the force of that tendency to imitation, in consequence of which, in industry, the arts, literature, and manners, certain ways of doing, devised under very special conditions, gain general prevalence, and very soon impress themselves, at first on the unreflecting and obedient multitude, and then upon those who have most ability to test and resist them. This leads to the remark that the chosen few are almost always forced to follow the tastes and demands of the many, under pain of being neglected or despised. A writer conceives a style which the public enthusiastically welcomes. He strikes a vein. He breaks in the readers of his books, the hearers of his plays, to this style, be it good or bad; and we see for a time all authors sentenced, if they would succeed, to imitate the lucky inventor. Thus, even if there were no natural or instinctive imitation, there would be interested or compulsory imitation. The founder of the *Times* was asked one day how it happened that all the articles in that paper seemed to come from the same hand. "Oh," he answered, "there is always one editor superior to the rest, and all the others imitate him."

The whole history of religions is full of instances proving to what extent men are led, not by reasonings, but by examples, and what a disposition they have to repeat what they have seen or heard, to govern their lives in accordance with the striking or successful models they have in view. Many a winning cause, famous for the persuasive genius of its advocates, owes its triumph rather to that hidden impulse which urges us irresistibly to imitation of others. Is not this potency of surroundings in producing by degrees radical changes in habits, opinions, and even in creeds, manifest also in the scene of political society? Is there any thing easier than for a man, who has gained control over the multitude, to bring it round to his feelings, his thoughts, his visions? Is not this as strikingly and as distinctly taught by the daily experience in the education of children? We often remark in a school that the outward characteristics, the tone, the ways, the amusements, change from year to year. It is because some leading spirits, two or three children who had an ascendency, have gone. Others have come, and every thing is altered. As the models change, the copies change too. New things are praised, and different things are ridiculed. The instinct of imitation is specially developed among men who are wanting in education or civilization. Savages copy quicker and better than Europeans. Like children, they are natural mimics, and cannot refrain from aping what is done in their presence. Their mind supplies nothing that can resist that inclination to imitate. Every enlightened man has within himself a large reserve of ideas toward which he can turn his mind; that resource does not exist for the savage and the child. The occurrences that take place before them are their peculiar life. They live upon what they see and hear. They are the sport of external things. In civilized nations, uncultivated people are in the same condition. Send a chambermaid and a philosopher to a country of the language of which both are ignorant, it is likely that the girl will learn it before the philosopher does. He has something else to do. He can live with his thoughts, but she, unless she is talking, is lost. The instinct of imitation is in inverse ratio to the power of mental abstraction.

We learn from these details that the potent and instinctive force of doing as others do, which plays so great a part in the education of persons and of races, differs wholly from heredity. It may act, and it does act, concurrently with hereditary impulses, but it works much oftener in an independent and even a contrary fashion. This is quite as true of another force, a bolder rival and stronger opponent of heredity, the work of which is next to be studied: we mean personality.

Eminently the instrument of free invention, the unfailing spring of the voluntary action that makes things new, the individual personality of the soul, may be designated, in opposition to the term heredity, by the name *innateness*. To give an idea of the power of innateness as compared with that of heredity, lists might be drawn up, containing the instances in which the manifestation of various passions or various talents does not proceed from ancestors, in which the individual is born distinct from those who went before him, or has made himself distinct from them by the reaction of his own will. Such lists would be endless, because, contrary to the opinion of those who advocate absolute heredity, it is innateness, it is personal activity, which is the general rule in the unfolding of mind. On the whole (and this is an essential point), heredity has its root in innateness; for, after all those aptitudes and those qualities which ancestors transmit, beginning at a certain fixed time and for a longer or shorter continuance, to their descendants, these very aptitudes and qualities necessarily come to birth at such time through the spontaneous effort of a more or less independent will. On the one hand, we are bid to notice hysterical, epileptic, and insane people; and, on the other, painters, musicians, and poets, who evidently get from their parents the activity, in doing well or ill, which characterizes them. True, doubtless, but the point is now to learn whence the parents themselves in their turn got it, and whether we must not rest in our retrospective examination of ancestry at some point at which innateness was sovereign. This supremacy is the less disputable, inasmuch as it soon reappears too in the descendants. The effects of heredity come to an end, just as they once made a beginning. At the outset they prevail over innateness, whose influence they suspend; then they run out, and the latter regains its rights. Thus innateness is the enduring and continuous force, while heredity is the intermittent and perishing force. Human nature, studied in its course through ages, is a succession of free souls, the more free in the degree that they have less need, for will and action, of aid from mechanical or organic powers. When they do need any such aid, they resign a part of their innate liberty to the sway of the blind influences of heredity. Yet, even with respect to the origin of æsthetic aptitudes, innateness keeps its predominance.

In the study of the history of famous men, how numberless are the instances we find of marvelous memories, glowing imaginations, extraordinary capacities for the arts, for poetry, for composition, which are not in the slightest degree derived from transmission! We need not look very far for proofs. Lamartine, Alfred de Musset, Meyerbeer, Ingres, Delacroix, Mérimée, Henry Regnault,[1] not to instance the living, exhibited talents for which they are not in the least indebted to their forefathers. The history of *savants*, properly so called, shows us the share of heredity still further reduced. Families of *savants* are cited. How many of them are there? A dozen at most. On the other hand, how many famous *savants* are there among whose forefathers we find either mere commonplace people, or else people noted for talents very different from those that distinguish the *savant!* Where are the ancestral influences that have formed a Cuvier, a Biot, a Fresnel, a Magendie, an Ampère, a Blainville, a Gay-Lussac? It is plain that in this matter innateness and education have taken the chief part. Neither is the life of literary men at all more accordant with the claims of the thorough partisans of heredity.

[1] "I believe that the sun which shines on you is not the same as ours," he wrote from Tangiers, "and I am terrified on seeing afar the moment when I must once again in Europe look on the mournful aspect of houses and crowds; but before returning thither I intend to make the real Moors live once again—then Tunis, Egypt, India. I shall soar from enthusiasm to enthusiasm, I shall be intoxicated with wonders, until, transported and ecstatic, I shall be able to fall back again into our dull and commonplace world, without fearing lest my eyes lose the light they will have drunk in for two or three years. Whenever, once more in Paris, I shall long for clear vision, I shall need only to close my eyes, and then Moriscos, Fellahs, Hindoos, granite colossi, white-marble elephants, fairy palaces, plains of gold and lakes of azure, and diamond cities, the whole East will pass again in procession before me. Oh, what an intoxication is light!"—"Correspondence of Henry Regnault," collected by M. Arthur Duparc, 1872.

Assuredly these thoughts and emotions were not hereditary in Henry Regnault.

The case in which innateness seems especially triumphant is that of the philosophers. The authors give no lists of philosophers who inherited from their forefathers aptitudes for speculation. There is here a series of expressly negative facts which they pass over in silence, and to which sufficient attention is not usually paid. Metaphysicians, precisely because the spiritual element alone works in them, are freed from all influences of hereditary predestination. That loses its energy just in proportion as there is occasion for transmitting such qualities as are less physiological and more psychological. Now, what can be more psychological, what more free from elements mixed with sense, and factors that work mechanically, than the mind of a speculative philosopher? In truth, great metaphysicians had no ancestors, and have left no posterity. The philosophic genius has always appeared completely individual, inalienable, and untransmissible. There is not a single renowned thinker in whose ascending or descending line can be found the warning forerunner or the reminder of the eminent capabilities that made his fame. Descartes and Newton, Leibnitz and Spinoza, Diderot and Hume, Kant and Maine du Biran, Cousin and Jouffroy, have neither ancestors nor posterity.

Such is innateness. To estimate exactly its function, we should need to ascertain in a general way and in its relations with the temperament, the training, the cosmic and social medium, etc., the production and development of those capacities by which some man of a high order is clearly differenced from his ancestors; and we should need to bring into one view, and as far as possible to coördinate, those characteristic elements which make up the very essence of personality and of individuality, those elements of bold departure from the beaten track, of plenary self-dependence, so mighty and so amazing, by which genius asserts itself. We should then see how, in almost all instances, eminent capacities are so inmost to those who display them, so deep and instinct with life, that training and discipline, instead of aiding them, impede their improvement. We should discover in the man of genius a self-reliant precocity, an adventurous ardor, a powerful conviction of his mission, a pride lifting him above prejudices of sect and party ambitions, and attaching him solely to the object of his thoughts, which alone gives life a charm for him. Even though his daily needs compel him to intercourse with men, the world is for him only a peopled desert in which his soul dwells apart.

A part of the materials for such a study exists; it may be sought in the biographies prepared by the secretaries of the great academies during the last two hundred years, and in the autobiographical memoirs left by many famous men. A learned and ingenious Russian writer, Wechniakof, has lately published several papers, in which he investigates from this point of view the anthropological and sociological peculiarities that have affected the individual development of original geniuses. These little works, unfortunately, do not form a complete whole; yet nothing could be more curious and useful than a treatise on innateness.

The group of all the causes of diversity, heterogeneity, and innovation, which are working upon the human race in opposition to the principles of simplicity, homogeneity, and conservation, may be described in a single word, that of evolution or progress. Regarded within the limits of our actual observation, blind Nature remains identically ever the same. It is to-day, in its totality, what it was in Homer's time, and what it will assuredly be many ages hence. The same skies exist, the same oceans, the same mountains, forests, and flowers. Man, on the contrary, is ceaselessly changing. Generations follow and do not resemble each other. They are, in relation to their beliefs, their arts, their wants, in a state of rapid and constant transformation. Nations, like individuals, have their times of greatness and of decay. Looking on the face of Nature in Greece, Childe Harold exclaims:

> "Yet are thy skies as blue, thy crags as wild;
> Sweet are thy groves, and verdant are thy fields;
> Thine olive ripe as when Minerva smiled,
> And still his honeyed wealth Hymettus yields;
> There the blithe bee his fragrant fortress builds,
> The free-born wanderer of thy mountain air;
> Apollo still thy long, long summer gilds,
> Still in his beam Mendeli's marbles glare;
> Art, glory, freedom fail, but Nature still is fair."

We might multiply endlessly these historic contrasts between the unchangeableness of that general determinism that rules in Nature and the ceaseless movement of human freedom and inventiveness, the eternal struggle of the soul to wrench itself from the grip of fatality. History is merely the story of what that movement and struggle have brought forth in the ages. It is a lengthened drama, through which the good genius of freedom strives for victory with the evil genius of brute force, in which, under the divine eye and with divine aid, through lingering and suffering, triumph is won for the spirit which seeks, discovers, invents, creates, loves, and worships.

III.

In the first part of this essay, we proved the existence of the facts of heredity, and pointed out the part they take in the indefinite reproduction of physiological and psychological characteristics in man. In the second, we noted and examined the causes that work in opposition to the more or less imperious impulses of Nature and to the restraints of mechanical structure. It is well now to state some practical conclusions as to the use that may be made of these kinds of knowledge for the improvement of the race.

Homer's valiant warriors invoked the name of their fathers and forefathers and the noble blood they inherited. It was a high instinct, and men who have good claims to boast of their ancestors will always have the better chance to deserve the gratitude of their posterity too. In fact, the phenomena of heredity justify the belief that parents, endowed with bodily and mental excellence, are in the best conditions for procreating descendants who shall be like them.

What measures, then, should be resorted to to make sure of fortunate alliances able to originate children distinguished in physical and moral respects? The delicacy of this question may be readily seen, and we can answer it here only in a very general way, relying particularly on an original essay, yet unpublished, by our distinguished surgeon, Sédillot, who devotes the leisure of his honored retirement to studies on the means of improving the race. Sédillot begins with the suggestion that very good information as to an individual's quality may be gained by consulting his genealogy—the history of his forefathers for four or five generations, examined from the point of view of intelligence, morality, vigor, health, longevity, social position, contains potentially a part of his own history. An examination of the head may also give hints of the greatest value. It was settled long before Gall's time, and it continues settled, apart from Gall's exaggerations, that the shape of the head betrays to some extent the degree of mental worth in the man. From the remotest antiquity popular good sense had noticed the relation existing between a very large head and eminent abilities, and language is full of expressions witnessing to the reality of that relation. Pericles of old excited the wonder of the Athenians on account of the extraordinary size of his head. Cromwell, Descartes, Leibnitz, Voltaire, Byron, Goethe, Talleyrand, Napoleon, Cuvier, etc., had very large heads. We know that Cuvier's brain weighed 1,829 grammes (64 + oz.), while the mean weight of the brain among Europeans, as Broca states, is from 1,350 to 1,400 grammes (48 + to 50 oz.). Sédillot regrets that we do not have, and wishes that pains were taken to obtain, the measure of the different dimensions of the skull among men conspicuous for marked capacities, in order to study the very noteworthy relations existing between those dimensions and such capacities. At least we know, in a general way, what characteristics and what proportions in the skull correspond with the various degrees of cerebral activity. Almost all anthropologists are aware that the man whose head does not measure fifty centimetres (19.68 inches) in horizontal circumference is almost doomed to mediocrity, and that one in whom that measurement equals or exceeds fifty-eight centimetres (22.83 inches) has many chances to become quite eminent. It is true, some instances of distinguished men with small heads are mentioned, but, then, the case is that of men eminent in some very narrow specialty. These dimensions, however, form only one of the external signs by which the intellectual quality of the individual may be determined with some accuracy. We must study besides these the general shape and the relative proportions of the different regions of the cranium, that is to say, the harmony which is called beauty. An easy way, Sédillot thinks, to judge of the conformation of the head, is to look at it from the side or in profile, and slightly back from the front of it. This strikingly brings out the relations of the height and breadth of the forehead and temples with the face, and shows clearly the relative proportions between the anterior or frontal contour of the head and the occipital or posterior one. Any one who has the eyebrow arches prominent, the temples open, straight or almost vertical, and high, whose forehead is broad and high, and his expression of countenance neither wandering nor sleepy, may be regarded in general as presenting a really human type, as the mask of a soul capable of doing honor to his species. The story is told of an Englishman, a friend of Shakespeare, who once sent a groom into an inn to look for him. "How shall I know him?" the servant said. "Nothing is easier," was the answer. "Every face looks something like some animal's; but, when you see Shakespeare, you will say, 'There is the *man*.'" Yes, man imagined in the fullness of his harmonious beauty; that is the ideal toward the realization of which the efforts of our present imperfect humanity should strive, and it is full time that we should neglect no means for bringing ourselves, by the skillful management of heredity, that is, by propagation in a sound and wise way, nearer to a human race from which the last traces of animalism shall have vanished, and among whom *man* shall be less rare.

What constitutes the superiority of the English aristocracy? It is the constant interest they are animated by to endow their descendants with the best bodily, mental, and moral qualities. An Englishman does not marry from fancy or passion; he marries under the conditions fittest to insure his children's happiness, for he knows that his own and the honor of his name depend on this. The respect with which young English women are surrounded, the honorable freedom they enjoy, the little consequence that is attached to their fortune, and the esteem in which their personal merit is held, are all so many causes for the increase among that people of happy marriages, and consequently for the growing vigor of their population. This is one of the grand secrets of improvement through heredity. Men, instead of requiring wealth with their brides, must ask for beauty, character, and virtue. So long as they have no fear of intermarrying with women who are feeble, or wanting in solid qualities, the race will decline and grow worthless, and the like deplorable result follows from the marriage of women of distinction and high natural qualities with men more or less degraded. Happily, the tact and dignity instinctive in women, the natural sympathy they feel for superior natures, very often prevent them from stooping to humiliating or unsafe marriages, and almost always protect them from ill-assorted ones. "Instead of yielding to passionate attractions," says Sédillot, "which easily disturb the judgment, let one ask, on seeing an agreeable person, whether one would wish to have sons and daughters like her, and the frequency of negative answers would be surprising. Certainly it would hardly be reasonable to give up the advantages of the present for those of an uncertain futurity, but wisdom bids us reconcile them both, remembering the swiftness with which time flies, and the little worth of the passing hour, compared with the hopes and enjoyments of the future." Sédillot adds that, in ordinary times, hygienic care and the moral evidence of the advantages of health and intelligence will suffice for the regeneration of a people. Unfortunately, France needs a more powerful and effectual source of elasticity, if she would rise again. She must bathe in the very spring of restoration and of life. She must plan the readiest means for preparing a future of energy and virtue for the generations that are coming forward. At another time it would have perhaps seemed difficult or unwise to introduce into discussions relating to human reproduction such calculations and such valuations as resemble those of zootechny, the art that has so long made practical use of *selection*. At this day such refined scruples must vanish before the warnings of necessity, telling us with its most solemn and earnest voice that not one blunder more must be committed.[1]

---

[1] With respect to the outward indications that may give some idea of capacities, the remarkable researches of Quetelet deserve to be consulted, condensed in the late work published by him under the title of "Anthropometry."

Upon this point the means should be indicated for checking and diminishing as much as possible that persistent morbid heredity which is so formidable an impediment to improvement. The preventive or *prophylactic* measures that may properly be used in staying the evolution of the germs of disease must, of course, depend on the nature of those germs. A mother suffering from phthisis, or predisposed to tubercles, should not suckle her child, but trust it to a good nurse. To persons born of consumptive parents, a highly-animalized *régime* is unsuitable; white meats and food without fat are better adapted for them. As regards a pursuit, such persons must carefully avoid those that would expose them to inhaling dust, to sudden changes of heat and cold, or to the constant exercise of the voice. Residence at places on the southern seaboard, and in regions where phthisis is uncommon, is the best preventive of that formidable disease. The essential things for persons predisposed to scrofula are pure air, substantial tonic nourishment, and the maritime atmosphere of the northwest of Europe. Those who are threatened with gout or gravel must restrict themselves to rigid temperance, and take much exercise. Regularity and uniformity of living are the rule for those with a tendency to cancer. Persons who count epileptics among their ancestors require the most watchful attention. Quiet in all their ways of life must be assured them, all excess be forbidden, all fatigue shunned, all emotions kept at a distance; in a word, every thing that can excite must be put out of their way. Those who are disposed to insanity should be treated in a similar way, that is, with great gentleness. Their passions must be lulled to sleep. The existence most suitable for them is one requiring them to put forth no strong mental action, and free from exciting hopes of fortune or fame. To check or to destroy the development of morbid germs in the constitution of such persons themselves, is but the secondary point in these cases; the main one is to prevent the transmission of these germs to new generations. To be certain of this result, it is important not only to make those marriages conformed to the laws of health and of morality easier and more common, but, still further, to thwart such unions as can only produce children wretched in body and mind. Physicians should use all their influence to forbid marriage between two persons both with strong constitutional tendencies toward the various nerve-disorders, toward tubercles, scrofula, etc. When one of two such persons has morbid hereditary antecedents, the physician should at least urge the necessity of union between the unsound person and a husband or wife in a perfect state of health, of superior strength and sexuality, and, above all, different in temperament. In this way we should at least lessen those chances of hereditary contamination to which it would be far better not to expose one's offspring at all. This is too delicate a subject to be urged here. Yet something should be said of marriages between blood relations, which have occasioned warm controversies of late years. Some physicians and anthropologists, Broca and Bertillon among the rest, maintain that the purest and least mixed races resist causes of degeneracy better than crossed races. In their view, the bad results attributed to consanguinity depend on agencies altogether foreign to it, mainly upon ancestral hereditary disorders. Trousseau and Boudin, on their side, maintain that unions between persons of the same family often produce unsound offspring, insane, and idiotic. The discussion seems at the present time to be settled in favor of the partisans of the former opinion. Quite lately, again, Auguste Voisin decided, after inquiring among the connections of more than fifteen hundred patients at Bicêtre and la Salpêtrière, that the condition of none of those sufferers could be charged upon the effect of consanguinity.

If that were so decisive a cause of degeneracy, its influence must have been seen among that multitude of the insane and idiotic.

At any rate, whatever exaggeration there may be among those who theorize on heredity, it has an indisputable share in the production of temperament and character, and the reality of that fact justifies every practice of a kind calculated to aid the transmission of the best tendencies. At Rome, the most distinguished and respected women sometimes, with their husbands' consent, contributed to some other family the superior qualities of their blood. Quintus Hortensius, Cato's friend and admirer, not succeeding in gaining his daughter Pereia, asked for his wife, Marcia, and Cato gave her up to him. The coarseness of such usages shocks our sense of delicacy, but it is easily explained by the desire always felt by the head of a Roman family to make sure in his descendants of the most manly vigor and the highest virtues. In our old French society, the continuance of masterships, of offices and professions in the same families in which they were handed down from father to son, originated in and was founded on the unconscious remarking of hereditary transmission of aptitudes; and Sédillot regrets that the overturnings in modern societies have banished that wholesome tradition which held the son morally bound, in all degrees of the social scale, to take the father's place. This is another recollection which should not be left out of view by races desirous of their own improvement.

Something which should be equally kept in view, and which is yet more easy of appreciation, is the system of precepts of a watchful and intelligent education. In this respect those men who are most concerned for the future of France have now but one opinion: the new generations must be built up by giving more room for bodily exercises, and by loading children less with labors ruinous to their health. It is not a question about disturbing classical studies or the humanities, which will continue to be the chief element of moral culture; it is a question merely of finding out whether children might not gain an acquaintance with the treasures of Latin and Greek learning a little more quickly and more thoroughly, and at the same time live in a little closer intercourse with modern interests. Many of those things are never taught them, though they are such as might be taught them with great advantage to their mental development. This is not the place to dwell upon the subject; but it does seem, and nobody doubts it, that by a vigorous training, one that aims boldly at renovation, it might be possible, if not, as Leibnitz asserted, to change the nature of a people, at least to destroy most of those causes of decline to which a people surrenders itself when uncorrected by suitable discipline.

The conviction that it is possible actively to countervail the dangerous tendencies of heredity, and to triumph over its ruinous domination, at least in the region of morals, is, moreover, one of the most wholesome that could gain currency and credit in the world. To will strongly, is of itself the power to do. Even though it were not so easy as it really is to quell those blind forces by the mere ascendency of a firm and enlightened will, there still would be reasons for persuading men that they are their own masters as to modifying and correcting themselves; that they are not the playthings of an unbending fate, and that they have no right to give way to their evil instincts without resistance and without remorse. Let us have faith in the might of heredity in so far as it can become a means of melioration and free improvement. Let us have no faith in it if it is averred to exert so absolute a tyranny that it would be folly to refuse submission. Education should not only take the improvement of men for its aim, it should also assume the task of animating them with a passion for improvement by convincing them that they can be made better. United with judicious cultivation of heredity when working for good, education thus conquers heredity in its evil working, and gives new life to the generations.

Yet we must not concede to education an exaggerated influence, nor assume that it can by itself alone produce superior characters of great eminence. It has, like heredity itself, but a limited power. Genius eludes the one, as it does the other. Genius, the most whole and perfect expression of the mind regarded as a free creative force, combines in one immortal consolation with eternal despair for our nature. It is a solace, because it is the fountain of all light and all rapture; it bids us despair precisely because it is singular, exceptional, capricious, strange, disdainful of the meddling touch of those who strive to pierce its mysterious secret, stubbornly defiant of the efforts of those who strive to subdue it, in a word, absolutely beyond the ken of the logic and discipline of the common run of men. It is a mighty tree, bearing fruit of food for the ages, and growing under conditions that forbid us to hope either to incite or foretell its production, or to rule its existence or calculate its fertility. We must wait humbly and patiently till it pleases Providence to bestow on us its blessing and glory. Happily, men of genius are not indispensable to humanity. The more the general level of a nation is lifted, the less essential do they become. Now that level rises irresistibly, whenever the will and the ready force of all citizens know but one sincere desire, that of self-improvement. The culture of heredity by relentlessly eradicating all causes that tend to degeneracy, and fostering causes that work improvement, may be commended with all assurance to nations ambitious of winning by its means the foremost rank in the world.

THE END.

International Scientific Series.

D. APPLETON & Co. have the pleasure of announcing that they have made arrangements for publishing, and have recently commenced the issue of, a SERIES OF POPULAR MONOGRAPHS, or small works, under the above title, which will embody the results of recent inquiry in the most interesting departments of advancing science.

The character and scope of this series will be best indicated by a reference to the names and subjects included in the subjoined list, from which it will be seen that the coöperation of the most distinguished professors in England, Germany, France, and the United States, has been secured, and negotiations are pending for contributions from other eminent scientific writers.

The works will be issued in New York, London, Paris, Leipsic, Milan, and St. Petersburg.

The INTERNATIONAL SCIENTIFIC SERIES is entirely an American project, and was originated and organized by Dr. E. L. Youmans, who spent the greater part of a year in Europe, arranging with authors and publishers. The forthcoming volumes are as follows:

Prof. LOMMEL (University of Erlangen), *Optics.* (In press.)

Rev. M. J. BERKELEY, M. A., F. L. S., and M. COOKE, M. A., LL. D., *Fungi; their Nature, Influences, and Uses.* (In press.)

Prof. W. KINGDON CLIFFORD, M. A., *The First Principles of the Exact Sciences explained to the non-mathematical.*

Prof. T. H. HUXLEY, LL. D., F. R. S., *Bodily Motion and Consciousness.*

Dr. W. B. CARPENTER, LL. D., F. R. S., *The Physical Geography of the Sea.*

Prof. WILLIAM ODLONG, F. R. S., *The Old Chemistry viewed from the New Standpoint.*

W. LAUDER LINDSAY, M. D., F. R. S. E., *Mind in the Lower Animals.*

Sir JOHN LUBBOCK, Bart., F. R. S., *The Antiquity of Man.*

Prof. W. T. THISELTON DYER, B. A., B. Sc., *Form and Habit in Flowering Plants.*

Mr. J. N. LOCKYER, F. R. S., *Spectrum Analysis.*

Prof. MICHAEL FOSTER, M. D., *Protoplasm and the Cell Theory.*

Prof. W. STANLEY JEVONS, *Money: and the Mechanism of Exchange.*

H. CHARLTON BASTIAN, M. D., F. R. S., *The Brain as an Organ of Mind.*

Prof. A. C. RAMSAY, LL. D., F. R. S., *Earth Sculpture: Hills, Valleys, Mountains, Plains, Rivers, Lakes; how they were produced, and how they have been destroyed.*

Prof. RUDOLPH VIRCHOW (Berlin University), *Morbid Physiological Action.*

Prof. CLAUDE BERNARD, *Physical and Metaphysical Phenomena of Life.*

Prof. H. SAINTE-CLAIRE DEVILLE, *An Introduction to General Chemistry.*

Prof. WURTZ, *Atoms and the Atomic Theory.*

Prof. DE QUATREFAGES, *The Negro Races.*

Prof. LACAZE-DUTHIERS, *Zoology since Cuvier.*

Prof. BERTHELOT, *Chemical Synthesis.*

Prof. J. ROSENTHAL, *General Physiology of Muscles and Nerves.*

Prof. JAMES D. DANA, M. A., LL. D., *On Cephalization; or, Head-Characters in the Gradation and Progress of Life.*

Prof. S. W. JOHNSON, M. A., *On the Nutrition of Plants.*

Prof. AUSTIN FLINT, Jr., M. D., *The Nervous System and its Relation to the Bodily Functions.*

Prof. W. D. WHITNEY, *Modern Linguistic Science.*

Prof. C. A. YOUNG, Ph. D. (of Dartmouth College), *The Sun.*

Prof. BERNSTEIN (University of Halle), *Physiology of the Senses.*

Prof. FERDINAND COHN (Breslau University), *Thallophytes (Algæ, Lichens, Fungi).*

Prof. HERMANN (University of Zurich), *Respiration.*

Prof. LEUCKART (University of Leipsic), *Outlines of Animal Organization.*

Prof. LIEBREICH (University of Berlin), *Outlines of Toxicology.*

Prof. KUNDT (University of Strasburg), *On Sound.*

Prof. REES (University of Erlangen), *On Parasitic Plants.*

Prof. STEINTHAL (University of Berlin), *Outlines of the Science of Language.*

E. ALGLAVE (Professor of Constitutional and Administrative Law at Douai, and of Political Economy at Lille), *The Primitive Elements of Political Constitutions.*

P. LORAIN (Professor of Medicine, Paris), *Modern Epidemics.*

Prof. SCHÜTZENBERGER (Director of the Chemical Laboratory at the Sorbonne), *On Fermentations.*

Mons. DEBRAY, *Precious Metals.*

Opinions of the Press on the "International Scientific Series."

I.
Tyndall's Forms of Water.

1 vol., 12mo.   Cloth.   Illustrated. . . . .   Price, $1.50.

"In the volume now published, Professor Tyndall has presented a noble illustration of the acuteness and subtlety of his intellectual powers, the scope and insight of his scientific vision, his singular command of the appropriate language of exposition, and the peculiar vivacity and grace with which he unfolds the results of intricate scientific research."—*N. Y. Tribune.*

"The 'Forms of Water,' by Professor Tyndall, is an interesting and instructive little volume, admirably printed and illustrated. Prepared expressly for this series, it is in some measure a guarantee of the excellence of the volumes that will follow, and an indication that the publishers will spare no pains to include in the series the freshest investigations of the best scientific minds."—*Boston Journal.*

"This series is admirably commenced by this little volume from the pen of Prof. Tyndall. A perfect master of his subject, he presents in a style easy and attractive his methods of investigation, and the results obtained, and gives to the reader a clear conception of all the wondrous transformations to which water is subjected."—*Churchman.*

II.
Bagehot's Physics and Politics.

1 vol., 12mo.   Price, $1.50.

"If the 'International Scientific Series' proceeds as it has begun, it will more than fulfil the promise given to the reading public in its prospectus. The first volume, by Professor Tyndall, was a model of lucid and attractive scientific exposition; and now we have a second, by Mr. Walter Bagehot, which is not only very lucid and charming, but also original and suggestive in the highest degree. Nowhere since the publication of Sir Henry Maine's 'Ancient Law,' have we seen so many fruitful thoughts suggested in the course of a couple of hundred pages. . . . To do justice to Mr. Bagehot's fertile book, would require a long article. With the best of intentions, we are conscious of having given but a sorry account of it in these brief paragraphs. But we hope we have said enough to commend it to the attention of the thoughtful reader."—Prof. JOHN FISKE, in the *Atlantic Monthly.*

"Mr. Bagehot's style is clear and vigorous. We refrain from giving a fuller account of these suggestive essays, only because we are sure that our readers will find it worth their while to peruse the book for themselves; and we sincerely hope that the forthcoming parts of the 'International Scientific Series' will be as interesting."—*Athenæum.*

"Mr. Bagehot discusses an immense variety of topics connected with the progress of societies and nations, and the development of their distinctive peculiarities; and his book shows an abundance of ingenious and original thought."—ALFRED RUSSELL WALLACE, in *Nature.*

D. APPLETON & CO., Publishers, 549 & 551 Broadway, N. Y.

Opinions of the Press on the "International Scientific Series."

III.
Foods.
By Dr. EDWARD SMITH.

1 vol., 12mo.   Cloth.   Illustrated.   . . . .   Price, $1.75.

In making up THE INTERNATIONAL SCIENTIFIC SERIES, Dr. Edward Smith was selected as the ablest man in England to treat the important subject of Foods. His services were secured for the undertaking, and the little treatise he has produced shows that the choice of a writer on this subject was most fortunate, as the book is unquestionably the clearest and best-digested compend of the Science of Foods that has appeared in our language.

"The book contains a series of diagrams, displaying the effects of sleep and meals on pulsation and respiration, and of various kinds of food on respiration, which, as the results of Dr. Smith's own experiments, possess a very high value. We have not far to go in this work for occasions of favorable criticism; they occur throughout, but are perhaps most apparent in those parts of the subject with which Dr. Smith's name is especially linked."—*London Examiner.*

"The union of scientific and popular treatment in the composition of this work will afford an attraction to many readers who would have been indifferent to purely theoretical details. . . . Still his work abounds in information, much of which is of great value, and a part of which could not easily be obtained from other sources. Its interest is decidedly enhanced for students who demand both clearness and exactness of statement, by the profusion of well-executed woodcuts, diagrams, and tables, which accompany the volume. . . . The suggestions of the author on the use of tea and coffee, and of the various forms of alcohol, although perhaps not strictly of a novel character, are highly instructive, and form an interesting portion of the volume."—*N. Y. Tribune.*

IV.
Body and Mind.
THE THEORIES OF THEIR RELATION.
By ALEXANDER BAIN, LL. D.

1 vol., 12mo.   Cloth.   . . . .   Price, $1.50.

PROFESSOR BAIN is the author of two well-known standard works upon the Science of Mind—"The Senses and the Intellect," and "The Emotions and the Will." He is one of the highest living authorities in the school which holds that there can be no sound or valid psychology unless the mind and the body are studied, as they exist, together.

"It contains a forcible statement of the connection between mind and body, studying their subtle interworkings by the light of the most recent physiological investigations. The summary in Chapter V., of the investigations of Dr. Lionel Beale of the embodiment of the intellectual functions in the cerebral system, will be found the freshest and most interesting part of his book. Prof. Bain's own theory of the connection between the mental and the bodily part in man is stated by himself to be as follows: There is 'one substance, with two sets of properties, two sides, the physical and the mental—a *double-faced unity.*' While, in the strongest manner, asserting the union of mind with brain, he yet denies 'the association of union *in place*,' but asserts the union of close succession in time,' holding that 'the same being is, by alternate fits, under extended and under unextended consciousness."'—*Christian Register.*

D. APPLETON & CO., Publishers, 549 & 551 Broadway, N. Y.

Opinions of the Press on the "International Scientific Series."

V.
The Study of Sociology.
By HERBERT SPENCER.

1 vol., 12mo. Cloth. . . . . Price, $1.50.

"The philosopher whose distinguished name gives weight and influence to this volume, has given in its pages some of the finest specimens of reasoning in all its forms and departments. There is a fascination in his array of facts, incidents, and opinions, which draws on the reader to ascertain his conclusions. The coolness and calmness of his treatment of acknowledged difficulties and grave objections to his theories win for him a close attention and sustained effort, on the part of the reader, to comprehend, follow, grasp, and appropriate his principles. This book, independently of its bearing upon sociology, is valuable as lucidly showing what those essential characteristics are which entitle any arrangement and connection of facts and deductions to be called a science."—*Episcopalian.*

"This work compels admiration by the evidence which it gives of immense research, study, and observation, and is, withal, written in a popular and very pleasing style. It is a fascinating work, as well as one of deep practical thought."—*Bost. Post.*

"Herbert Spencer is unquestionably the foremost living thinker in the psychological and sociological fields, and this volume is an important contribution to the science of which it treats. . . . It will prove more popular than any of its author's other creations, for it is more plainly addressed to the people and has a more practical and less speculative cast. It will require thought, but it is well worth thinking about."—*Albany Evening Journal.*

VI.
The New Chemistry.
By JOSIAH P. COOKE, Jr.,
Erving Professor of Chemistry and Mineralogy in Harvard University.

1 vol., 12mo. Cloth. . . . . Price, $2.00.

"The book of Prof. Cooke is a model of the modern popular science work. It has just the due proportion of fact, philosophy, and true romance, to make it a fascinating companion, either for the voyage or the study."—*Daily Graphic.*

"This admirable monograph, by the distinguished Erving Professor of Chemistry in Harvard University, is the first American contribution to 'The International Scientific Series,' and a more attractive piece of work in the way of popular exposition upon a difficult subject has not appeared in a long time. It not only well sustains the character of the volumes with which it is associated, but its reproduction in European countries will be an honor to American science."—*New York Tribune.*

"All the chemists in the country will enjoy its perusal, and many will seize upon it as a thing longed for. For, to those advanced students who have kept well abreast of the chemical tide, it offers a calm philosophy. To those others, youngest of the class, who have emerged from the schools since new methods have prevailed, it presents a generalization, drawing to its use all the data, the relations of which the newly-fledged fact-seeker may but dimly perceive without its aid. . . . To the old chemists, Prof. Cooke's treatise is like a message from beyond the mountain. They have heard of changes in the science; the clash of the battle of old and new theories has stirred them from afar. The tidings, too, had come that the old had given way; and little more than this they knew. . . . Prof. Cooke's 'New Chemistry' must do wide service in bringing to close sight the little known and the longed for. . . . As a philosophy it is elementary, but, as a book of science, ordinary readers will find it sufficiently advanced."—*Utica Morning Herald.*

D. APPLETON & CO., Publishers, 549 & 551 Broadway, N. Y.

Opinions of the Press on the "International Scientific Series."

VII.

The Conservation of Energy.

By BALFOUR STEWART, LL. D., F. R. S.

With an Appendix treating of the Vital and Mental Applications of the Doctrine.

1 vol., 12mo. Cloth. Price, $1.50.

"The author has succeeded in presenting the facts in a clear and satisfactory manner, using simple language and copious illustration in the presentation of facts and principles, confining himself, however, to the physical aspect of the subject. In the Appendix the operation of the principles in the spheres of life and mind is supplied by the essays of Professors Le Conte and Bain."—*Ohio Farmer.*

"Prof. Stewart is one of the best known teachers in Owens College in Manchester. The volume of THE INTERNATIONAL SCIENTIFIC SERIES now before us is an excellent illustration of the true method of teaching, and will well compare with Prof. Tyndall's charming little book in the same series on 'Forms of Water,' with illustrations enough to make clear, but not to conceal his thoughts, in a style simple and brief."—*Christian Register, Boston.*

"The writer has wonderful ability to compress much information into a few words. It is a rich treat to read such a book as this, when there is so much beauty and force combined with such simplicity.—*Eastern Press.*

VIII.

Animal Locomotion;

Or, WALKING, SWIMMING, AND FLYING.

With a Dissertation on Aëronautics.

By J. BELL PETTIGREW, M. D., F. R. S., F. R. S. E., F. R. C. P. E.

1 vol., 12mo. . . . . . Price, $1.75.

"This work is more than a contribution to the stock of entertaining knowledge, though, if it only pleased, that would be sufficient excuse for its publication. But Dr. Pettigrew has given his time to these investigations with the ultimate purpose of solving the difficult problem of Aëronautics. To this he devotes the last fifty pages of his book. Dr. Pettigrew is confident that man will yet conquer the domain of the air."—*N. Y. Journal of Commerce.*

"Most persons claim to know how to walk, but few could explain the mechanical principles involved in this most ordinary transaction, and will be surprised that the movements of bipeds and quadrupeds, the darting and rushing motion of fish, and the erratic flight of the denizens of the air, are not only analogous, but can be reduced to similar formula. The work is profusely illustrated, and, without reference to the theory it is designed to expound, will be regarded as a valuable addition to natural history."—*Omaha Republic.*

D. APPLETON & CO., PUBLISHERS, 549 & 551 Broadway, N. Y.

Opinions of the Press on the "International Scientific Series."

IX.
Responsibility in Mental Disease.
By HENRY MAUDSLEY, M. D.,
Fellow of the Royal College of Physicians; Professor of Medical Jurisprudence in University College, London.

1 vol., 12mo. Cloth. . . Price, $1.50.

"Having lectured in a medical college on Mental Disease, this book has been a feast to us. It handles a great subject in a masterly manner, and, in our judgment, the positions taken by the author are correct and well sustained."—*Pastor and People.*

"The author is at home in his subject, and presents his views in an almost singularly clear and satisfactory manner. . . . The volume is a valuable contribution to one of the most difficult, and at the same time one of the most important subjects of investigation at the present day."—*N. Y. Observer.*

"It is a work profound and searching, and abounds in wisdom."—*Pittsburg Commercial.*

"Handles the important topic with masterly power, and its suggestions are practical and of great value."—*Providence Press.*

X.
The Science of Law.
By SHELDON AMOS, M. A.,
Professor of Jurisprudence in University College, London; author of "A Systematic View of the Science of Jurisprudence," "An English Code, its Difficulties and the Modes of overcoming them," etc., etc.

1 vol., 12mo. Cloth. . . . . Price, $1.75.

"The valuable series of 'International Scientific' works, prepared by eminent specialists, with the intention of popularizing information in their several branches of knowledge, has received a good accession in this compact and thoughtful volume. It is a difficult task to give the outlines of a complete theory of law in a portable volume, which he who runs may read, and probably Professor Amos himself would be the last to claim that he has perfectly succeeded in doing this. But he has certainly done much to clear the science of law from the technical obscurities which darken it to minds which have had no legal training, and to make clear to his 'lay' readers in how true and high a sense it can assert its right to be considered a science, and not a mere practice."—*The Christian Register.*

"The works of Bentham and Austin are abstruse and philosophical, and Maine's require hard study and a certain amount of special training. The writers also pursue different lines of investigation, and can only be regarded as comprehensive in the departments they confined themselves to. It was left to Amos to gather up the result and present the science in its fullness. The unquestionable merits of this, his last book, are, that it contains a complete treatment of a subject which has hitherto been handled by specialists, and it opens up that subject to every inquiring mind. . . . To do justice to 'The Science of Law' would require a longer review than we have space for. We have read no more interesting and instructive book for some time. Its themes concern every one who renders obedience to laws, and who would have those laws the best possible. The tide of legal reform which set in fifty years ago has to sweep yet higher if the flaws in our jurisprudence are to be removed. The process of change cannot be better guided than by a well-informed public mind, and Prof. Amos has done great service in materially helping to promote this end."—*Buffalo Courier.*

D. APPLETON & CO., PUBLISHERS, 549 & 551 Broadway, N. Y.

Opinions of the Press on the "International Scientific Series."

XI.

Animal Mechanism,

A Treatise on Terrestrial and Aërial Locomotion.

By E. J. MAREY,

Professor at the College of France, and Member of the Academy of Medicine.

With 117 Illustrations, drawn and engraved under the direction of the author.

1 vol., 12mo. Cloth. . . . . Price, $1.75

"We hope that, in the short glance which we have taken of some of the most important points discussed in the work before us, we have succeeded in interesting our readers sufficiently in its contents to make them curious to learn more of its subject-matter. We cordially recommend it to their attention.

"The author of the present work, it is well known, stands at the head of those physiologists who have investigated the mechanism of animal dynamics—indeed, we may almost say that he has made the subject his own. By the originality of his conceptions, the ingenuity of his constructions, the skill of his analysis, and the perseverance of his investigations, he has surpassed all others in the power of unveiling the complex and intricate movements of animated beings."—*Popular Science Monthly.*

XII.

History of the Conflict between Religion and Science.

By JOHN WILLIAM DRAPER, M. D., LL. D.,

Author of "The Intellectual Development of Europe."

1 vol., 12mo. . . . . Price, $1.75.

"This little 'History' would have been a valuable contribution to literature at any time, and is, in fact, an admirable text-book upon a subject that is at present engrossing the attention of a large number of the most serious-minded people, and it is no small compliment to the sagacity of its distinguished author that he has so well gauged the requirements of the times, and so adequately met them by the preparation of this volume. It remains to be added that, while the writer has flinched from no responsibility in his statements, and has written with entire fidelity to the demands of truth and justice, there is not a word in his book that can give offense to candid and fair-minded readers."—*N. Y. Evening Post.*

"The key-note to this volume is found in the antagonism between the progressive tendencies of the human mind and the pretensions of ecclesiastical authority, as developed in the history of modern science. No previous writer has treated the subject from this point of view, and the present monograph will be found to possess no less originality of conception than vigor of reasoning and wealth of erudition. . . . The method of Dr. Draper, in his treatment of the various questions that come up for discussion, is marked by singular impartiality as well as consummate ability. Throughout his work he maintains the position of an historian, not of an advocate. His tone is tranquil and serene, as becomes the search after truth, with no trace of the impassioned ardor of controversy. He endeavors so far to identify himself with the contending parties as to gain a clear comprehension of their motives, but, at the same time, he submits their actions to the tests of a cool and impartial examination."—*N. Y. Tribune.*

D. APPLETON & CO., PUBLISHERS, 549 & 551 Broadway, N. Y.

THE GREVILLE MEMOIRS.

COMPLETE IN TWO VOLS.

A JOURNAL OF THE REIGNS OF
King George IV. & King William IV.

By the Late CHAS. C. F. GREVILLE, Esq.,
Clerk of the Council to those Sovereigns.

Edited by HENRY REEVE, Registrar of the Privy Council.

12mo. PRICE, $4.00.

This edition contains the complete text as published in the three volumes of the English edition.

"The sensation created by these Memoirs, on their first appearance, was not out of proportion to their real interest. They relate to a period of our history second only in importance to the Revolution of 1688; they portray manners which have now disappeared from society, yet have disappeared so recently that middle-aged men can recollect them; and they concern the conduct of very eminent persons, of whom some are still living, while of others the memory is so fresh that they still seem almost to be contemporaneous."—*The Academy.*

"Such Memoirs as these are the most interesting contributions to history that can be made, and the most valuable as well. The man deserves gratitude from his posterity who, being placed in the midst of events that have any importance, and of people who bear any considerable part in them, sits down day by day and makes a record of his observations."—*Buffalo Courier.*

"The Greville Memoirs, already in a third edition in London, in little more than two months, have been republished by D. Appleton & Co., New York. The three loosely-printed English volumes are here given in two, without the slightest abridgment, and the price, which is nine dollars across the water, here is only four. It is not too much to say that this work, though not so ambitious in its style as Horace Walpole's well-known 'Correspondence,' is much more interesting. In a word, these Greville Memoirs supply valuable materials not alone for political, but also for social history during the time they cover. They are additionally attractive from the large quantity of racy anecdotes which they contain."—*Philadelphia Press.*

"These are a few among many illustrations of the pleasant, gossipy information conveyed in these Memoirs, whose great charm is the free and straightforward manner in which the writer chronicles his impressions of men and events."—*Boston Daily Globe.*

"As will be seen, these volumes are of remarkable interest, and fully justify the encomiums that heralded their appearance in this country. They will attract a large circle of readers here, who will find in their gossipy pages an almost inexhaustible fund of instruction and amusement."—*Boston Saturday Evening Gazette.*

"Since the publication of Horace Walpole's Letters, no book of greater historical interest has seen the light than the Greville Memoirs. It throws a curious, and, we may almost say, a terrible light on the conduct and character of the public men in England under the reigns of George IV. and William IV. Its descriptions of those kings and their kinsfolk are never likely to be forgotten."—*N. Y. Times.*

D. APPLETON & CO., PUBLISHERS, 549 & 551 Broadway, N. Y.

THE LIFE OF
HIS ROYAL HIGHNESS
THE PRINCE CONSORT.
By THEODORE MARTIN.

With Portraits and Views. Volume the First. 12mo. Cloth. Price, $2.00.

"The book, indeed, is more comprehensive than its title implies. Purporting to tell the life of the Prince Consort, it includes a scarcely less minute biography—which may be regarded as almost an autobiography—of the Queen herself; and, when it is complete, it will probably present a more minute history of the domestic life of a queen and her 'master' (the term is Her Majesty's) than has ever before appeared."—*From the Athenæum.*

"Mr. Martin has accomplished his task with a success which could scarcely have been anticipated. His biography of Prince Albert would be valuable and instructive even if it were addressed to remote and indifferent readers who had no special interest in the English court or in the royal family. Prince Albert's actual celebrity is inseparably associated with the high position which he occupied, but his claim to permanent reputation depends on the moral and intellectual qualities which were singularly adapted to the circumstances of his career. In any rank of life he would probably have attained distinction; but his prudence, his self-denial, and his aptitude for acquiring practical knowledge, could scarcely have found a more suitable field of exercise than in his peculiar situation as the acknowledged head of a constitutional monarchy."—*From the Saturday Review.*

"The author writes with dignity and grace, he values his subject, and treats him with a certain courtly reverence, yet never once sinks into the panegyrist, and while apparently most frank—so frank, that the reticent English people may feel the intimacy of his domestic narratives almost painful—he is never once betrayed into a momentary indiscretion. The almost idyllic beauty of the relation between the Prince Consort and the Queen comes out as fully as in all previous histories of that relation—and we have now had three—as does also a good deal of evidence as to the Queen's own character, hitherto always kept down, and, as it were, self effaced in publications written or sanctioned by herself."—*From the London Spectator.*

"Of the abilities which have been claimed for the Prince Consort, this work affords us small means of judging. But of his wisdom, strong sense of duty, and great dignity and purity of character, the volume furnishes ample evidence. In this way it will be of service to any one who reads it."—*From the New York Evening Post.*

"There is a striking contrast between this volume and the Greville Memoirs, which relate to a period in English history immediately preceding Prince Albert's marriage with Queen Victoria. Radical changes were effected in court-life by Victoria's accession to the throne. . . . In the work before us, which is the unfolding of a model home-life, a life in fact unrivaled in the abodes of modern royalty, there is nothing but what the purest mind can read with real pleasure and profit.

"Mr. Martin draws a most exquisite portraiture of the married life of the royal pair, which seems to have been as nearly perfect as any thing human can be. The volume closes shortly after the Revolution of 1848, at Paris, when Louis Philippe and his hapless queen were fleeing to England in search of an asylum from the fearful forebodings which overhung their pathway. It was a trying time for England, but, says Mr. Martin with true dramatic effect in the closing passages of his book: 'When the storm burst, it found him prepared. In rising to meet the difficulties of the hour, the prince found the best support in the cheerful courage of the queen,' who on the 4th of April of that same year wrote to King Leopold: 'I never was calmer and quieter or less nervous. Great events make me calm; it is only trifles that irritate my nerves.' Thus ends the first volume of one of the most important biographies of the present time. The second volume will follow as soon as its preparation can be effected."—*From the Hartford Evening Post.*

D. APPLETON & CO., PUBLISHERS, 549 & 551 Broadway, N. Y.

RECENT PUBLICATIONS.

THE NATIVE RACES OF THE PACIFIC STATES.

By HERBERT H. BANCROFT. To be completed in 5 vols. Vol. I. now ready. Containing Wild Tribes: their Manners and Customs. 1 vol., 8vo. Cloth, $6; sheep, $7.

"We can only say that if the remaining volumes are executed in the same spirit of candid and careful investigation, the same untiring industry, and intelligent good sense, which mark the volume before us, Mr. Bancroft's 'Native Races of the Pacific States' will form, as regards aboriginal America, an encyclopædia of knowledge not only un equalled but unapproached. A literary enterprise more deserving of a generous sympathy and support has never been undertaken on this side of the Atlantic."—FRANCIS PARKMAN, in the *North American Review*.

"The industry, sound judgment, and the excellent literary style displayed in this work, cannot be too highly praised."—*Boston Post*.

A BRIEF HISTORY OF CULTURE.

By JOHN S. HITTELL. 1 vol., 12mo. Price, $1.50.

"He writes in a popular style for popular use. He takes ground which has never been fully occupied before, although the general subject has been treated more or less distinctly by several writers. . . . Mr. Hittell's method is compact, embracing a wide field in a few words, often presenting a mere hint, when a fuller treatment is craved by the reader; but, although his book cannot be commended as a model of literary art, it may be consulted to great advantage by every lover of free thought and novel suggestions."—*N. Y. Tribune*.

THE HISTORY OF THE CONFLICT BETWEEN RELIGION AND SCIENCE.

By JOHN W. DRAPER, M. D., author of "The Intellectual Development of Europe." 1 vol., 12mo. Cloth. Price, $1.75.

"The conflict of which he treats has been a mighty tragedy of humanity that has dragged nations into its vortex and involved the fate of empires. The work, though small, is full of instruction regarding the rise of the great ideas of science and philosophy; and he describes in an impressive manner and with dramatic effect the way religious authority has employed the secular power to obstruct the progress of knowledge and crush out the spirit of investigation. While there is not in his book a word of disrespect for things sacred, he writes with a directness of speech, and a vividness of characterization and an unflinching fidelity to the facts, which show him to be in thorough earnest with his work. The 'History of the Conflict between Religion and Science' is a fitting sequel to the 'History of the Intellectual Development of Europe,' and will add to its author's already high reputation as a philosophic historian."—*N. Y. Tribune*.

THEOLOGY IN THE ENGLISH POETS.

COWPER, COLERIDGE, WORDSWORTH, and BURNS. By Rev. STOPFORD BROOKE. 1 vol., 12mo. Price, $2.

"Apart from its literary merits, the book may be said to possess an independent value, as tending to familiarize a certain section of the English public with more enlightened views of theology."—*London Athenæum*.

BLOOMER'S COMMERCIAL CRYPTOGRAPH.

A Telegraph Code and Double Index—Holocryptic Cipher. By J. G. BLOOMER. 1 vol., 8vo. Price, $5.

By the use of this work, business communications of whatever nature may be telegraphed with secrecy and economy.

D. APPLETON & CO., Publishers, New York.

RECENT PUBLICATIONS.—SCIENTIFIC.

THE PRINCIPLES OF MENTAL PHYSIOLOGY. With their Applications to the Training and Discipline of the Mind, and the Study of its Morbid Conditions. By W. B. CARPENTER, F. R. S., etc. Illustrated. 12mo. 737 pages. Price, $3.00.

"The work is probably the ablest exposition of the subject which has been given to the world, and goes far to establish a new system of Mental Philosophy, upon a much broader and more substantial basis than it has heretofore stood."—*St. Louis Democrat.*

"Let us add that nothing we have said, or in any limited space could say, would give an adequate conception of the valuable and curious collection of facts bearing on morbid mental conditions, the learned physiological exposition, and the treasure-house of useful hints for mental training, which make this large and yet very amusing, as well as instructive book, an encyclopædia of well-classified and often very startling psychological experiences."—*London Spectator.*

THE EXPANSE OF HEAVEN. A Series of Essays on the Wonders of the Firmament. By R. A. PROCTOR, B. A.

"A very charming work; cannot fail to lift the reader's mind up 'through Nature's work to Nature's God.'"—*London Standard.*

"Prof. R. A. Proctor is one of the very few rhetorical scientists who have the art of making science popular without making it or themselves contemptible. It will be hard to find anywhere else so much skill in effective expression, combined with so much genuine astronomical learning, as is to be seen in his new volume."—*Christian Union.*

PHYSIOLOGY FOR PRACTICAL USE. By various Writers. Edited by JAMES HINTON. With 50 Illustrations. 1 vol., 12mo. Price, $2.25.

"This book is one of rare value, and will prove useful to a large class in the community. Its chief recommendation is in its applying the laws of the science of physiology to cases of the deranged or diseased operations of the organs or processes of the human system. It is as thoroughly practical as is a book of formulas of medicine, and the style in which the information is given is so entirely devoid of the mystification of technical or scientific terms that the most simple can easily comprehend it."—*Boston Gazette.*

"Of all the works upon health of a popular character which we have met with for some time, and we are glad to think that this most important branch of knowledge is becoming more enlarged every day, the work before us appears to be the simplest, the soundest, and the best."—*Chicago Inter-Ocean.*

THE GREAT ICE AGE, and its Relations to the Antiquity of Man. By JAMES GEIKIE, F. R. S. E. With Maps, Charts, and numerous Illustrations. 1 vol., thick 12mo. Price, $2.50.

"'The Great Ice Age' is a work of extraordinary interest and value. The subject is peculiarly attractive in the immensity of its scope, and exercises a fascination over the imagination so absorbing that it can scarcely find expression in words. It has all the charms of wonder-tales, and excites scientific and unscientific minds alike."—*Boston Gazette.*

"Every step in the process is traced with admirable perspicuity and fullness by Mr. Geikie."—*London Saturday Review.*

"'The Great Ice Age,' by James Geikie, is a book that unites the popular and abstruse elements of scientific research to a remarkable degree. The author recounts a story that is more romantic than nine novels out of ten, and we have read the book from first to last with unflagging interest."—*Boston Commercial Bulletin.*

ADDRESS DELIVERED BEFORE THE BRITISH ASSOCIATION, assembled at Belfast. By JOHN TYNDALL, F. R. S., President. Revised, with additions, by the author, since the delivery. 12mo. 120 pages. Paper. Price, 50 cents.

This edition of this now famous address is the only one authorized by the author, and contains additions and corrections not in the newspaper reports.

THE PHYSIOLOGY OF MAN. Designed to represent the Existing State of Physiological Science as applied to the Functions of the Human Body. By AUSTIN FLINT, Jr., M. D. Complete in Five Volumes, octavo, of about 500 pages each, with 105 Illustrations. Cloth, $22.00; sheep, $27.00. Each volume sold separately. Price, cloth, $4.50; sheep, $5.50. The fifth and last volume has just been issued.

The above is by far the most complete work on human physiology in the English language. It treats of the functions of the human body from a practical point of view, and is enriched by many original experiments and observations by the author. Considerable space is given to physiological anatomy, particularly the structure of glandular organs, the digestive system, nervous system, blood-vessels, organs of special sense, and organs of generation. It not only considers the various functions of the body, from an experimental stand-point, but is peculiarly rich in citations of the literature of physiology. It is therefore invaluable as a work of reference for those who wish to study the subject of physiology exhaustively. As a complete treatise on a subject of such interest, it should be in the libraries of literary and scientific men, as well as in the hands of practitioners and students of medicine. Illustrations are introduced wherever they are necessary for the elucidation of the text.

D. APPLETON & CO., PUBLISHERS, 549 & 551 Broadway, N. Y.

A New Magazine for Students and Cultivated Readers.

THE POPULAR SCIENCE MONTHLY,

CONDUCTED BY
Professor E. L. YOUMANS.

THE growing importance of scientific knowledge to all classes of the community calls for more efficient means of diffusing it. THE POPULAR SCIENCE MONTHLY has been started to promote this object, and supplies a want met by no other periodical in the United States.

It contains instructive and attractive articles, and abstracts of articles, original, selected, and illustrated, from the leading scientific men of different countries, giving the latest interpretations of natural phenomena, explaining the applications of science to the practical arts, and to the operations of domestic life.

It is designed to give especial prominence to those branches of science which help to a better understanding of the nature of man; to present the claims of scientific education; and the bearings of science upon questions of society and government. How the various subjects of current opinion are affected by the advance of scientific inquiry will also be considered.

In its literary character, this periodical aims to be popular, without being superficial, and appeals to the intelligent reading-classes of the community. It seeks to procure authentic statements from men who know their subjects, and who will address the non-scientific public for purposes of exposition and explanation.

It will have contributions from HERBERT SPENCER, Professor HUXLEY, Professor TYNDALL, Mr. DARWIN, and other writers identified with speculative thought and scientific investigation.

THE POPULAR SCIENCE MONTHLY is published in a large octavo, handsomely printed on clear type. Terms, Five Dollars per annum, or Fifty Cents per copy.

OPINIONS OF THE PRESS.

"Just the publication needed at the present day."—*Montreal Gazette.*
"It is, beyond comparison, the best attempt at journalism of the kind ever made in this country."—*Home Journal.*
"The initial number is admirably constituted."—*Evening Mail.*
"In our opinion, the right idea has been happily hit in the plan of this new monthly."—*Buffalo Courier.*
"A journal which promises to be of eminent value to the cause of popular education in this country."—*N. Y. Tribune.*

IMPORTANT TO CLUBS.

THE POPULAR SCIENCE MONTHLY will be supplied at reduced rates with any periodical published in this country.

Any person remitting Twenty Dollars for four yearly subscriptions will receive an extra copy gratis, or five yearly subscriptions for $20.

THE POPULAR SCIENCE MONTHLY and APPLETONS' JOURNAL (weekly), per annum, $8.00

☞ *Payment, in all cases, must be in advance.*

Remittances should be made by postal money-order or check to the Publishers,

D. APPLETON & CO., 549 & 551 Broadway, New York.

www.ingramcontent.com/pod-product-compliance
Lightning Source LLC
Chambersburg PA
CBHW030346230426
43664CB00007BB/549